ASHLAND COMMUNITY & TECHNICAL COLLEGE

3 3631 1136403 9

HQ 1034 .U5 W46 2012

Whitehead, Jaye Cee.

The nuptial deal WITHDRAWN

W9-ASD-772

MonTReaL

INSIGHT *City* GUIDES

Edited by Stephen Scharper and Hilary Cunningham
Principal Photography: Carl and Ann Purcell
Editorial Director: Brian Bell

A P A
PUBLICATIONS

NO part of this book may be reproduced, stored in a retrieval system or transmitted in any form or means electronic, mechanical, photocopying, recording or otherwise, without prior written permission of Apa Publications. Brief text quotations with use of photographs are exempted for book review purposes only.

As every effort is made to provide accurate information in this publication, we would appreciate it if readers would call our attention to any errors that may occur by communicating with Höfer Media (Pte) Ltd., Orchard Point Post Office Box 219, Singapore 9123. Information has been obtained from sources believed to be reliable, but its accuracy and completeness, and the opinions based thereon, are not guaranteed.

MonTReal

First Edition
© 1991 APA PUBLICATIONS (HK) LTD
All Rights Reserved
Printed in Singapore by Höfer Press Pte. Ltd

ABOUT THIS BOOK

In 1913 the English poet Rupert Brooke formed "a vague general impression that Montreal consists of banks and churches." In 1979 a leading British journalist, Cal McCrystal, formed the impression that "Montreal now surpasses San Francisco as the most interesting North American city." In the 1990s the newspaper-reading world formed the impression that linguistic warfare, particularly between Montreal's francophones and anglophones, could be almost as devastating as armed combat.

Such a fascinating city was bound to attract the attention of Apa Publications, whose Insight Guides and City Guides cover more than 130 countries, regions and cities. The guides' reputation lies with their blend of frank reporting and bold photojournalism – a formula which especially suited the controversial, visually arresting capital of Quebec.

Anthropological approach

As project editors for the book, Apa appointed a husband-and-wife team, **Stephen Scharper** and **Hilary Cunningham**. Scharper, at the time an editor of Orbis Books and Twenty-Third Publications, has contributed articles to numerous religious and secular publications. He has since abandoned a comfortable home and job to accompany his wife on her field research in Arizona, Mexico, and Guatemala, and has followed that experience with a doctoral program in religious studies at McGill University in Montreal. Cunningham, project editor for *Insight Guide: Canada*, brings her training as an urban anthropologist to travel writing. She served as Apa's consulting editor for North America, all the while pursuing her PhD in cultural anthropology at Yale University.

The couple soon assembled a team of writers and photographers who set about capturing "the two solitudes" of this bilingual city.

Lysiane Gagnon, who wrote the introductory chapter, is a native of Montreal and a journalist with more than 20 years' experience. She has long been a political columnist for *La Presse*, Canada's major French-speaking daily and is a frequent contributor to magazines, radio, and television. She has won two National Newspaper Awards and is the author of several books, including *Chroniques Politiques* (Boreal, 1985), a collection of columns on national politics.

Mark Kingwell, a distinguished journalist whose contributions range from history to ice hockey, is a former member of the Rusty Staub *"Grande Orange"* fan club of the Montreal Expos. He holds degrees from the Universities of Toronto and Edinburgh, and has taken a doctorate in political philosophy at Yale University. He continues to hold in creative tension his enthusiasm for sports and his academic career and, ever since Rusty Staub's departure from Montreal, has remained a steadfast Toronto Blue Jays fan.

Charles Foran and **Mary Ladky**, another married team, were major contributors, writing several of the Places chapters as well as features. Foran, a widely-published fiction writer, holds a BA degree from the University of Toronto, and both he and Ladky hold masters degrees in literature from University College, Dublin. Foran's colorful reviews and incisive commentaries inform the pages of the *Montreal Gazette, Canadian Forum,* the *Globe and Mail, Saturday Night,* and *Insight Guide: Canada.* Ladky, who has taken a degree in education at McGill, has taught in

Scharper *Cunningham* *Gagnon* *Foran* *Ladky*

the US, and, with Foran, in China. Their latest collaborative effort is especially notable: a baby girl, Anna Eileen.

Matthew Parfitt, a Montreal aficionado with a moderate interest in baseball, writes authoritatively about gardens, parks, stadiums and bohemian mores in his home town. His vibrant writing appears in *Insight Guide: Canada*, as well as numerous periodicals and journals. A graduate of the University of Toronto, he has been taking a doctorate in English literature at Boston College. Though too modest to admit it, Parfitt is known internationally as a friend to refugee felines and as a master muffin maker.

Emil Sher writes with insight and first-hand experience of Jewish life in his native Montreal. His essays have been published in the *Globe and Mail*, *Compass* and numerous other journals, and his work has been broadcast nationally on the Canadian Broadcasting Company. He is currently completing his first novel and is seeking to establish a dairy farm in downtown Toronto.

Nancy Lyon, some of whose photography enlivens this volume, also plied her literary skills in the Day Trips chapter. A Montreal resident, Lyon has met with considerable success in her vibrant career as a travel writer. As a travel columnist for the *Montreal Gazette*, she has rafted "frantically" down the turgid rapids of the Rouge and Batiscan Rivers, biked through the rolling mountains of Estrie, Quebec, and explored the culturally rich streets of Quebec City. She describes herself as "an American, born in Nashville, raised in Indianapolis, schooled in Virginia, but an exile at heart."

Louise Legault, another Montreal resident and distinguished travel writer, channels her self-described "fanaticism" for Mon-

treal into her article on festivals and her piece on shopping in the Travel Tips section. A translator and former editor of a Montreal travel magazine, Legault is co-author of *Montreal, the International City*, and has been working on a tour guide to Quebec.

Katherine Snyder, the diligent compiler of the fact-packed Travel Tips section, has a remarkable talent for being "imaginatively efficient." An expert on café culture and avant-garde films, she has put together a comprehensive guide to Montreal's best offerings. A diehard vegetarian, she hopes some day to found a sanctuary for pigs, her favorites of the animal kingdom.

Visual Excitement

Like all Insight City Guides, this book owes much to its superb photography. The images here are mostly the work of **Carl** and **Ann Purcell**, an internationally known photographic and writing team based in the Washington DC area. They have written and illustrated two books, *The Traveling Photographer* (Amphoto) and *A Guide to Travel Writing and Photography* (Writer's Digest Books), and have also photographed *Insight Guide: Bermuda*. They fell in love with the diverse visual excitement of Montreal and delighted in discovering "the hidden nooks and crannies in a truly multicultural city."

The editors would like to give special thanks to **Archives Canada**, to the **Canadian Hockey Hall of Fame**, to **Gilles Bengel** of the Montreal Chamber of Commerce and to **Diane Di Tomasso** of the Quebec Government Office in London. They also wish to thank the people of Montreal, whose convivial spirit shines through in this book.

Parfitt   *Sher*   *Lyon*   *Legault*   *C. Purcell*   *A. Purcell*

History

23 **Montreal: A Tale of Two Solitudes**
—by Lysiane Gagnon

32 **Historical Overview**
—by Hilary Cunningham

35 **Beginnings: The River and the Mountain**
—by Mark Kingwell

44 *Religious Roots*
—by Hilary Cunningham

49 **The Coming of the British**
—by Mark Kingwell

52 *A Woman's Lot*
—by Hilary Cunningham

56 *The Habitants*
—by Hilary Cunningham

60 **Conflict and Confederation**
—by Mark Kingwell

67 *Games for Idle Hours*
—by Hilary Cunningham

71 **Modern Montreal:
A Tarnished Golden Age**
—by Mark Kingwell

76 *The Quiet Revolution*
—by Mark Kingwell

Features

81 The Montrealer
—by Charles Foran

87 The Jews of Montreal
—by Emil Sher

95 Politics, Language and Identity
—by Charles Foran

101 *Intellectuals versus Streetfighters*
—by Mark Kingwell

102 *The Life and Times of Pierre Trudeau*
—by Mark Kingwell

107 Why Ice Hockey Matters
—by Mark Kingwell

Places

121 Introduction
—by Stephen Scharper

125 Old Montreal
—by Charles Foran

132 *A Living Language*
—by Charles Foran

147 *Festival City*
—by Louise Legault

151 Downtown
—by Mary Ladky

156 *The Grande Dame of Sherbrooke Street*
—by Mary Ladky

173 Bohemian Montreal
—by Matthew Parfitt

179 *The Jazz Scene*
—by Matthew Parfitt

183 Westmount and Outremont
—by Mary Ladky

186 *Park Mount Royal*
—by Hilary Cunningham

191 *Outremont Cafés*
—by Mary Ladky

194 *St Joseph's Oratory*
—by Hilary Cunningham

199 Stadiums and Gardens
—by Matthew Parfitt

209 Day Trips
—by Nancy Lyon

Maps

122 Montreal
126 Old Montreal
152 Downtown
200 Olympic Park and Botanical Garden

TRAVEL TIPS

Getting There

226   By Air
226   By Rail
226   By Land

Travel Essentials

226   Visas & Passports
226   Money Matters
227   Health
227   What to Wear
227   Animal Quarantine
227   Customs
227   Extension of Stay

Getting Acquainted

227   Government & Economy
228   Geography & Population
228   Time Zones
228   Climate
228   Etiquette
228   Language
229   Business Hours
229   Holidays
229   Festivals & Events

Communications

230   Postal Services
230   Telegram & Fax
230   Telephone
231   News Media

Emergencies

231   Security & Crime
231   Medical Services
232   Pharmacies
232   Other Services

Getting Around

232   Maps
232   From the Airport
232   Public Transport
232   Taxis
232   Private Transport
233   By Foot
233   Bicycle Rental

Where to Stay

233   Hotels
236   Bed & Breakfasts

Food Digest

237   Where to Eat
242   Drinking Notes

Things to Do

242   City
244   Tours & Attractions

Culture Plus

245   Museums
246   Art Galleries
246   Concerts & Operas
247   Ballet & Theaters
247   Public Libraries

Nightlife

248   Cabarets & Dinner Theater
248   Jazz & Dancing

Shopping

250   What to Buy
251   Department Stores

Sports

251   Participant
253   Spectator

Special Information

253   Children
254   Disabled

Further Reading

255   Booklist

Useful Addresses

255   Tourist Information
255   Embassies & Consulates

Viewed from the south, Montreal reads like an open book. The left-hand page, spreading to the west, is in English. The right-hand page, opening to the east, is in French. But ethnic groups from all over the world populate the twin pages. Close the book, and the cover is in French. Yet the text is bilingual, with strong cosmopolitan accents.

Simple? Not really. Montreal is a city of obvious charm. It offers a gentle way of life exceptional in North America, and is one of those rare cities that can boast of having preserved a lively downtown where you can still take an evening walk in perfect safety. But Montreal is nonetheless a city of tensions – not racial tensions, but linguistic ones. They are resolved, day after day, in a lifestyle developed over the years by a population that has long since mastered the art of compromise.

Montreal is the second largest French city in the world (after Paris), where the sidewalk cafés and the breakfast croissants are not considered at all exotic. It was built by Scottish merchants, whose Victorian homes remind you of London and Edinburgh. It is the city where, with French the official language, you can pass your whole life speaking nothing but English.

Montreal is also an Italian, Greek, Vietnamese, Haitian, or Lebanese city, a city of the Ashkenazi Jews and the Sephardic Jews. You never have far to walk to find "lemon grass" and grape leaves, falafels or sea-urchins, kiwis and raw-milk paste, fresh pasta and Paris-style baguettes – not to mention the world's best bagels. (No, not in Manhattan, not even in Brooklyn, will you find bagels more golden on the outside and more tender on the inside than the ones you buy in Montreal, fresh out of the old wood-stoked ovens of Fairmount and St-Viateur streets, whose recipe emanates from the *stetls* of Romania.)

In Montreal you can see French and European films while they're playing in Paris, and American films while they're playing in New York. This is a city where the newsstands bend under their stacks of dailies in French and English – from Montreal, from Paris, the *Times* of New York and the *Times* of London – and where the TV offers two

public channels in French and two in English, two commercial channels in French and one in English (plus the big US networks and a channel that rebroadcasts the best TV programs of France, Belgium and Switzerland.

Beginnings: The origins of Montreal lie in the St Lawrence River, from whose waters, in 1642, appeared the founders of the humble little French town christened Ville-Marie. The vestiges of Ville-Marie are still to be seen, not far from the docks, in the beautiful stone buildings, humble chapels, and narrow paving-stone streets of "Old Montreal."

French Canadians are not a "minority"

Preceding pages: the Ministry of Culture's public face; Jacques Cartier Bridge; Raymond Mason's "Illuminated Crowd" sculpture on McGill College Avenue; flags; view from the port; tourist carriages; sleighing to the ski slopes. <u>Left</u>, café society. <u>Above</u>, boy at a Christ Church wedding.

here as are the Puerto Ricans of New York, the Cubans of Miami, or the Asians of Los Angeles. The forebears of the *Montréalais* were the first settlers of European stock in North America. Beginning in 1534, they founded a sedentary society organized on a Western model. Nor are French Canadians French Europeans in exile: from as early as the 17th century, they established a society that was distinct from that of their European ancestors.

The city of Quebec, the only city in America to be surrounded by ramparts like the fortified cities of Europe, was founded in 1608, at a moment when North America was

still a continent unknown except to the Amerindians and Inuits. It is this little cluster of colonists, trappers, and adventurers that dispatched the great *voyageurs* who discovered the Mississippi and the Rocky Mountains to the west, and who founded the first colonies from which would issue the great cities of the northeastern United States.

In the United States, only Louisiana has retained some of the traits of the far-off days of French rule, through the Cajun culture and a Civil Code inherited from the Napoleonic era. In Canada, meanwhile, the descendants of the first French colonists have multiplied

to form a mighty minority who live, learn, and work in French – 6 million people (nearly a quarter of the population of Canada), of whom 5 million are concentrated in the province of Quebec.

Unique status: With its 6½ million inhabitants, Quebec is the second largest province in Canada (after Ontario, which numbers 9½ million). Canada is a federation, dividing its political power between the central government and the 10 provinces. Each province has its own parliament and relatively extensive powers, especially in the areas of education, health, and social affairs, as well as a goodly share of the economic ones.

Because the province of Quebec is the main home of the French Canadians and the only territory where they comprise the majority of the electorate, its successive governments have gradually acquired additional special powers, following upon accords with the federal government. Quebec is the only province that collects its own taxes, for example, and it maintains a network of delegations abroad functioning somewhat after the fashion of consulates.

Quebec is likewise the only province whose official language is French, although the considerable English-speaking minority reaps the ongoing benefits of a complete network of schools, universities, and hospitals, entirely at public expense, and functioning in English. It is in the Montreal vicinity that immigrants make their homes – turning this region into a cosmopolitan, bilingual islet.

In 1760 the British conquest changed the face of the continent. French Canadians, suddenly deprived of their elite, who returned to France, turned inward upon their own little community, under the protective wing of the only institution left to them, the Catholic church, whose precepts they observed by reproducing at a rate historians find nowhere outside of China.

Long undereducated, and thought of only as cheap labor, the French-speaking Québécois today make up one of the most sophisticated populations of the continent. In just a few years, beginning with the close of the 1950s, the Québécois decided to make up for lost time. They modernized their educational system, took on more public responsibility, and shook off the tutelage of the church. Once the "City of a Hundred Belfreys," Montreal now became the cutting edge of this "quiet revolution" – appropriately named, since it was accomplished without civil violence. Today the city's monasteries, convents, and seminaries are condominiums, and its churches serve as recreation centers.

This period of intense intellectual and cultural ferment inevitably engendered a strong independence movement. In 1980, a popular referendum came out 60 percent against a secessionist project proposed by the pro-

played second fiddle to the city of Quebec. It was only with the English conquest and the arrival of the Scottish merchants that Montreal "took off" to become the great metropolis of Canada – a position it retained until the 1950s, when Toronto supplanted it as Canada's center of commerce and finance.

The proud memory of this period remains incrusted in the beautiful Victorian buildings of the Golden Square Mile, that 19th-century fief of the first great Canadian businesses, and in the campus of McGill, the first university of Canada, on Sherbrooke Street. A great part of the architectural legacy of Montreal is of British inspiration. Indeed,

sovereignty government of René Lévesque. However, aspirations for autonomy, always within the limits of a parliamentary democracy, remain lively. Many francophones are still haunted by the fear of assimilation, all the more so now that demography is no longer on their side. (The pendulum has swung, and the Québécois birth rate is the lowest in the world after the Federal Republic of Germany).

Under the French regime, Montreal

Left, Christ Church's reflected glory. **Above**, Montreal Trust Building.

Montrealers visiting London experience a sense of having been there before: a thousand-and-one details – in the architecture, the street map, and the statuary – remind them of their own city.

Anglophones and francophones: In Montreal, the two great founding peoples of Canada live their lives side by side. Of the 2 million inhabitants of the metropolitan area, some 60 percent are French-speaking, one-fourth use English as their native tongue, and the remainder are more or less recent immigrants who, with the passing of the years, have been integrated into either of the two great linguistic groups – often to the anglophone, so potent is the natural attraction of the English language.

Coexistence has almost always been peaceful. But the francophone and anglophone communities – the "two solitudes," as Canadian novelist Hugh McLennan has described them – have developed into two parallel, homogeneous societies. They have emerged side by side without ever melding, each with its own schools, colleges and universities, hospitals, newspapers, novels, theaters, business communities, and insurance companies. Each community also has its own proletariat and bourgeoisie – the

While most Montrealers are bilingual, rarely does their network of friends and activities encompass both communities to any significant extent. Francophones and anglophones meet at work, in business and the subway, or at the Forum, where they cheer with equal enthusiasm "their" hockey team, the Montreal Canadiens. But Montreal resolutely remains the city of two solitudes. There have been a number of intermarriages over the years, but one language finally prevails in most of them and the family is acculturated to only one of the two great language groups.

This division obviously undermines Mon-

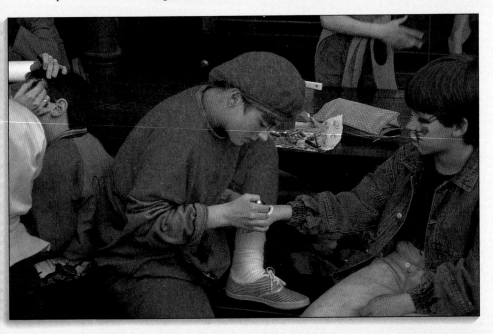

anglophone bourgeoisie is established at Westmount, on the southwest slope of Mount Royal, while the francophone bourgeoisie is located in Outremont, on the northeast side of the same mountain.

Even the night crawlers have parallel habits. The center of anglophone night life are the pubs and discos of Crescent and Bishop streets; francophone night life is in the sidewalk cafés and bistros of Rue St-Denis. But these are not ghettos, and many Montrealers like an occasional stroll on the "other side," becoming temporary tourists in their home town.

treal's cultural potential, and the misunderstandings engendered by mutual ignorance sharpen the linguistic tensions. French, long considered the tongue of "peasants," has been the dominant language since the early 1970s, even in large private business. Francophones, once relegated to second-class jobs, have vigorously asserted themselves in the business area, and now control a great proportion of Montreal's erstwhile anglophone institutions. Not all anglophones welcome this development, and not all francophones have forgotten the old vexations. And both communities battle, with the weapons of law and administrative measures, to attract new immigrants.

The basic problem is that each of the two communities perceives itself as a vulnerable minority. The anglophones, a majority in Canada but a minority in Quebec, see their numbers dwindling, and fear for the survival of their institutions. The francophones, in the majority in Quebec but in the minority in Canada, have the feeling of speaking an ever-threatened language. All of this sparks endless political battles – battles which fortunately have remained verbal.

Montreal is not Belfast. In daily living (let the politicians go on clashing) Montrealers have developed the art of good-humored coexistence. On Saint Patrick's Day, thousands of francophones don the green and descend to Ste Catherine's Street for the parade, celebrating with their anglophone fellow-citizens and cheering the floats that depict the history of the large Irish minority of Montreal, who have been a fixture here since the mid-19th century.

Québécois French: The French spoken in Montreal is shot through with English expressions, and Quebec English is laced with gallicisms. An anglophone Montrealer will speak of a "manifestation" instead of a demonstration, a "cocktail" for a cocktail party, a "convention" for a contract, and a "*dépanneur*" for a convenience store.

While Montreal has two languages, it also has a throng of ethnic and cultural communities. The two most populous – Italian and Jewish – are also the oldest. The immigration of southern Italians and European Jews goes back to the 19th century, continuing through the first decades of the 20th century. Their respective contributions have melded into the city as a whole, like a powerful, fecund graft. Italian and Yiddish are scarcely ever spoken any more, and these two communities, where the rate of French-English bilingualism is remarkably high, have long been integrated into the common life of Montreal.

Their family closeness, however, has enabled them to retain more of their own characteristics than have other European immi-

grants. Germans, Hungarians, Slavs and Scandinavians, for example, have, in fewer than two generations, melted into the anglophone community. True, the motivation for this separatism is no longer economic, but there are still Italian quarters in the northeastern corner of the isle of Montreal, where Montrealers of Sicilian origin make a living from prosperous construction businesses, and from open-air markets.

There are also municipalities with a strong Jewish majority, like Côte-St-Luc or Hampstead. The Ashkenazi community of Montreal is especially noteworthy in that, of all the Diaspora communities, it is home to the

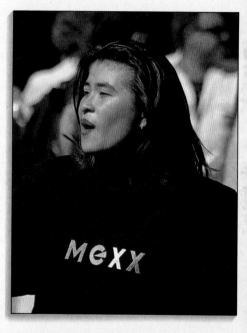

largest proportion of survivors. (This makes the community very sensitive to any manifestation of Quebec nationalism, even a peaceful one.) Characterized by an extremely high level of education, the Jewish community is distinguished in all domains, especially medicine, and has left a deep mark on the intellectual life of Montreal.

The European immigration, which formed so many successive layers in so many quarters of Montreal, has given way in recent years to mighty waves of immigrants from Asia, the Antilles, and the Near East. The presence of these new groups has trans-

Left and **above**, Montreal's love of festivals takes creativity onto the streets.

formed the face of the city. Haitians work the taxis, Chinese and Greeks the fast-food restaurants, and Moroccan Jews the garment district. Tomorrow their children will be physicians, professors, and – why not? – prime ministers.

New communities: Rue St-Laurent is the best place to find the traces of these new communities. Running from the St Lawrence River all the way to the River of the Prairies, and dividing the isle of Montreal in two – the francophone part to the east, the anglophone to the west – this street was the traditional path of the immigrants as they got off their boats and gradually made their way

Sprinkled with avant-garde fashion shops and postmodern restaurants, it is now the place to go if you want to find youth of every national extraction, in an exciting mix of colors and tongues. Moreover, every year, the city is host to an impressive series of popular festivals: a film festival, a jazz festival, a winter festival, an international theater festival, and more.

French lifestyle: The Protestant work ethic once fueled Montreal's economic expansion; but it is the French influence that has specially marked its lifestyle. When Toronto closes its bars at one in the morning and forbids liquor on Sundays, Montreal drinks

"up" to the quarters of the lower middle class in the northern end of the city. They then streamed toward the middle-class neighborhoods, eastward or westward, depending on the language of their adoption.

To the south you will still find Chinese grocery shops, little Jewish stalls, Portuguese fish stands, Greek tavernas, and creole bars, with each new layer of immigrants covering the last and pushing northward. The most recent wave has been the yuppies. The old garment factories are "lofts" now, and the old thoroughfare, St Lawrence Street, is under accelerated gentrification.

to 3 a.m., Sundays and weekdays alike!

Montreal women have the reputation of being the most elegant and stylish in all of North America. The most modest secretary will not go out without her makeup, and her skirt, shoes and blouse will be in the latest style. All the polls indicate that the Francophones – men and women – spend more on clothes, as well as on home furnishings, than any other community in the continent. (As a case in point, Montreal has as many, if not more, importers of Milanese furniture than New York.)

Montreal is the only city in America where

French cuisine is not reserved for a special outing but is part of everyday life. When Montrealers entertain, the five-course dinner will always be enhanced with wine, generally imported from France. (A Montrealer would never stoop to drinking Canadian wine!)

Cosmopolitan character: It is characteristic of small countries to be less ethnocentric, and more open to foreign contributions, than the great, self-sufficient powers. Because Canadian culture is too limited as a sole reference point, the Montreal elite, even before the appearance of Marshall McLuhan's "global village," have always been among

prose of a Mordecai Richler and the lyricism of a Réjean Ducharme, with its provocative avant-garde theater and its vibrant motion picture industry (Montrealers invariably pull down the Canadian cinema prizes), Montreal can boast that it offers the most creative and most diversified cultural life in Canada.

One of the reasons for this is that the francophones, isolated by language yet too North American to import everything from France, have been obliged to develop their own cultural products. They have also been unwilling, unlike their compatriots of the other Canadian provinces, to settle for US

the most cosmopolitan in the world. They read *Le Nouvel Observateur* and the *New Yorker*, Marguerite Yourcenar and Milan Kundera or Tom Wolfe, and explore the universe with the open mind that comes from the practice of two languages and a long habit of life in a heterogeneous milieu.

With four universities, two French and two English, three French dailies and one English, with a rich, challenging literature, serving up at one the same time the biting

Left, mural with a message. **Above**, life on St-Denis Street.

imports. And so Montreal is one of the rare cities of the world where, in the 1980s, *Dallas* was not perched near the top of the TV ratings. The most-watched "soaps" are produced in Montreal.

Welcome to Montreal, then. But be careful crossing the street: Montrealers are always a little anarchic, and a stop light doesn't mean a thing. Montrealers have raised jaywalking to a high art, and they flaunt it. Drivers participate in this artistic display by slowing down only at the last second. If you survive this first contact with Montreal's "street" scene, the rest will be easy.

1535: On his second trip to North America, the French navigator Jacques Cartier visits an Iroquois village, Hochelaga, later to become the site of Montreal. He names the mountain there *Mont Réal*.

1608: Sammuel de Champlain, the French explorer, establishes Quebec City, the first permanent settlement in Canada.

1611: Samuel de Champlain explores Montreal and builds a wall, the first European construction on the island, near the St-Pierre River.

1615: First Catholic mass in North America is celebrated on the island of Montreal.

1642: The first colonists arrive, establish a tiny colony and name it Ville-Marie.

1643: After severe flooding, the commander of Ville-Marie, Paul de Chomedy de Maisonneuve, erects a wooden cross on Mount Royal.

1648: On November 24 Barbe Meusnier is born – the first European to be born in Ville-Marie.

1658: Montreal's first teacher, Marguerite Bourgeoys, begins teaching in a stable located in Ville-Marie.

1672: The first streets are laid out and named by Dollier de Casson: among them is Notre-Dame, in honor of the Virgin Mary, the patron saint of the colony.

1716: The French decide to build a wall around Montreal to fortify it.

1734: A devastating fire destroys 46 houses, the Hotel-Dieu and the convent.

1754-63: The French Indian War (called the Seven Years' War in Canada and Europe). French and British tensions (the latter joined by the Iroquois) escalate in North America. The French build a series of new forts and refuse to withdraw as the British protest. The French beat Washington's troops at Fort Necessity in the first battle of the war.

1759: General James Wolfe attacks French forces near Quebec City and, after three months, defeats them on the Plains of Abraham. Montreal is captured by general Jeffery Amherst in 1760. The surrender of New France is signed in Montreal and British troops take over the town, which has 60,000 inhabitants.

1763: Under the Treaty of Paris, the French give most of their land in Canada to the British. They keep two tiny islands south of Newfoundland: St-Pierre and Miquelon.

1774: The Quebec Act is enacted: it extends Quebec's borders and guarantees the use of French language and freedom of religion.

1775: As the American revolution begins, United Empire Loyalists come north.

1776: Benjamin Franklin, Samuel Chase and the Jesuit, Charles Caroll, visit Montreal and try to convince French Canadians to join the American revolutionary cause. English troops arrive in June and the Americans withdraw.

1778: The first issue of *Gazette du Commerce et litéraire pour la ville et le district de Montréal* is printed. It later becomes *The Gazette*.

1783: Britain signs a peace treaty with the recently formed United States.

1792: Montreal is divided into two sections, east and west, with Saint-Laurent Street as the dividing line.

1801–20: The walls around Montreal are demolished.

1809: Canada's first steamboat, *The Accommodation*, sails the St Lawrence River from Montreal to Quebec City.

1812–14: The Americans attempt to invade Canada but are eventually repelled. The Treaty of Ghent ends the war.

1832: Montreal is incorporated as a city. From 1844 to 1849 it serves as the capital of the Province of Canada.

1833: Jacques Viger is elected the first mayor of Montreal. On July 19, the city adopts the coat of arms and the motto *Concordia Salus*.

1837–38: French Canadians lead a rebellion against the Château Clique; one leader, Louis Joseph Papineau, is exiled.

1843: The first classes are held at McGill University.

1852: The Great Fire in Montreal: 9,000 people are left homeless.

1860: The Crystal Palace, designed by J.W. Hopkins, is constructed.

1861: The first streetcars begin running.

1867: Canada and the Atlantic Provinces of Nova Scotia and New Brunswick become the Dominion of Canada.

1885: The Canadian Pacific Railway, based in Montreal, completes Canada's first continental railroad.

1886: Canada's first transcontinental railway train leaves Montreal for Vancouver.

1889: First automobile arrives in Montreal.

1906: The first fatal automobile accident is recorded in Montreal.

1914: As World War I begins, conscription for military service divides French and English Canadians.

1924: Cross on Mount Royal is illuminated.

1928: 22,000 people attend the opening of Montreal Stadium.

1929: The Stock Market crashes and the Great Depression ravages Montreal's finances. The bridge across the St Lawrence River is completed. It is named after Jacques Cartier in 1934.

1940: Montreal Mayor Camillien Houde urges French Canadians to defy a government plan for conscription during World War II. Most French Canadians oppose the military draft. Federal authorities put Houde in a prison camp until 1944.

1954: Jean Drapeau is first elected mayor of Montreal.

1959: Britain's Queen Elizabeth II and US president Dwight D. Eisenhower officially open the St Lawrence Seaway.

1962: Construction of the Métro begins.

1963: The Front de Libération de Québec (FLQ), a terrorist organization, joins the Quebec separatist movement. Between 1963 and 1968, the FLQ claims responsibility for hundreds of bombings and armed robberies in the Montreal area.

1967: Opening of the World's Fair, Expo '67, in Montreal. Over 50 million people attend the event.

1970: In October the FLQ kidnap British Trade Commissioner James R. Cross and Quebec Labor Minster Pierre Laporte. Prime Minster Pierre Trudeau sends federal troops to Montreal. Laporte is murdered. Cross is released after the government guarantees his kidnappers safe passage to Cuba.

1976: The Parti Québécois wins the provincial election; Olympic Games are held in Montreal.

1980: Voters defeat a proposal to give provincial leaders the right to negotiate Quebec's political independence from Canada.

1982: Marguerite Bourgeoys is canonized.

1985: The Liberals gain control of the provincial legislature and Robert Bourassa becomes premier of Quebec.

1987: Montreal is made an international banking center.

1988: Meech Lake Constitutional Accord acknowledges the importance of Quebec's "separate and distinct culture."

1990: Amid threats of Quebec's separation from Canada, the Meech Lake Accord fails to be ratified.

1992: The 350th anniversary of Montreal's founding is celebrated.

BEGINNINGS: THE RIVER AND THE MOUNTAIN

Each in its way symbolizes the influences which have shaped the city. The mountain, ancient symbol of man's spiritual journey, dramatizes the missionary faith which founded the first European settlement here. The river, flowing past the island on which the city stands, created the highway which made Montreal such a natural center for trade and commerce.

—Aline Gubbay, urban historian

Begin with the obvious. The fortunes of Montreal have been varied and spectacular – sketchy Indian settlement, French missionary outpost and trading center, throbbing industrial pile, tourist destination. Through all this, two facts have remained constant: the broad flow of a river and the upward thrust of a mountain.

In Montreal, understanding history begins with understanding geology. For here, in a time before history, hot lava from beneath the earth's crust forced its way to the surface and created the volcanic mountain whose burnt-out remains Jacques Cartier was to claim, millennia later, for King Francis I of France. At 760 ft (230 meters) Cartier's "Mount Royal" (Mont Réal) is hardly in the class of the Rockies, but its hardened cone of volcanic basalt nevertheless withstood the glacial ice that scoured the rest of this region more than 10,000 years ago.

Those same glaciers, receding sheets of ice two or three miles thick, forged the complex waterways and thousands of islands that mark the fertile St Lawrence River Valley. The island now known as Montreal is situated near the confluence of two powerful rivers, the St Lawrence and the Ottawa, whose waters meet in violent confrontation before heading east to the Atlantic. With its flat, fertile expanse and single conspicuous peak, the island is a peaceful contrast to the turgid rapids that surround it.

Preceding pages: Montreal's maritime past. <u>Left</u>, Lake of Two Mountains. <u>Above</u>, Samuel de Champlain, the city's first developer, in 1611.

The river and the mountain serve to frame the city's unique history. Montreal's early mixture of contradictory impulses – the first French settlers traded as assiduously for furs as they did for souls – has characterized the city through the centuries. It is a place where opposites not only attract, but marry. French and English, wealthy and destitute, radical and conservative, federalist and separatist – all have found a place, sometimes an uneasy one, in this rich human settlement.

The history of Montreal is therefore a narrative in two dimensions, a history that mirrors its fortuitous location. Horizontally, it is one of arduous co-existence, conquest, uneasy reconciliation and assimilation. That story continues today as Montrealers struggle to maintain a common life when their cultural and linguistic differences threaten to pull them apart.

Vertically, the story of Montreal is a story of individual visions – political, commercial and religious – that drive men and women to these shores to carve out ideal cities that appear in their dreams. But other dreams have always persisted and Montreal can neither boast nor mourn any single vision of itself. It is no city on a hill, no new Jerusalem. Instead it has been, and is, *many* cities, a place where successive generations of dreamers have come to try and make their dreams real.

Early Montreal: The earliest settlers of the island now known as Montreal were, of course, Indians, mainly of the Huron, Algonquin and Montagnais tribes. There is no way of telling how long these people had been residing on the island when the first European, Jacques Cartier, set foot here on October 2, 1535. His account speaks of an

island already criss-crossed with Indian trails and possessing one apparently permanent settlement, Hochelaga ("at the place of the beaver dam"). This was a circular, palisaded village inhabited by Algonquin and Hurons living in communal long houses. The site is probably close to where McGill University now stands.

Though the inhabitants appeared filthy and ignorant to Cartier, they in fact enjoyed the benefits of a disease-free, complex society. It was governed by a closely guarded oral history, sophisticated natural pantheism, and a consensual form of rule in which

senior men of the settlement would meet to agree on policy, war measures, and division of labor. The tribes existed as loose associations of many far-flung settlements and roving bands. Together, the Algonquin, Huron, Iroquois and Montagnais nations occupied most of the St Lawrence River Valley, the Great Lakes, and what is now New England.

Among the Indians, meat was not consumed every day, and, in addition to the fruits of the hunt, many Indians subsisted on a paste of cold corn-meal and animal fat later known to the French as *sagamité*. The Hurons turned their efforts to cultivating the land. Beans, squash and corn were their staples and were mashed into pastes or boiled to make soups. This semi-agricultural way of life made for settlements more permanent than those of the Algonquin or the Iroquois, and it was probably Hochelaga Hurons whom Cartier encountered in the early months of 1535.

Jacques Cartier was a professional sailor from the town of St-Malo, a proud Frenchman in an age whose most accomplished naval men were Italian and Iberian. His king, Francis I, had charged him with a simple task: "To discover islands and countries where they say there is a lot of gold." King Francis was a man of limited imagination but boundless ambition, and the voyage on which he sent Cartier was only the first of many undertaken at his behest.

In these early days of the Age of Discovery, France's influence in North America became unparalleled, driven by the cupidity and religious aspirations of French monarchs, and realized by the unusual versatility and capabilities of their subjects. Cartier was one of these men, a brilliant navigator and a surprisingly deft diplomat.

As a geographer, he was unfortunately limited by the ignorance of his times. Like everyone else, Cartier thought that North America was Asia, and that the rumored mountains of gold and unlimited supplies of spice and silk were within his grasp. He sailed his convoy of three ships, led by the flagship *Grande Hermine*, as far as he could up the St Lawrence until, near the north shore of an island, his progress was stopped by impassable rapids. It was here that the fateful encounter between European and Indian, the beginnings of Montreal, took place.

Cartier dressed himself "gorgeously" for his first formal call on Hochelaga, and upon entering the village saw the horeshoe-shaped stockade typical of a Huron village. The Hurons were friendly to Cartier, and, impressed by his "floating island" and strange dress, they took him to be a traveling minor deity. He was shown their settlement and taken to meet Agouhanna, the chief of Hochelaga.

Agouhanna, wary of the strange visitor, decided to show him the local sights; Cartier was conveyed to the summit of the island's

cheerfully supplied him with some rock samples and Cartier hurried back to his ship. After a brutal winter's sailing, he reached France to report to King Francis and have the samples of "gold" and "diamonds" analyzed. They turned out to be iron pyrite (fool's gold) and quartz crystal.

But Cartier had also brought back another gift from Agouhanna, a different kind of treasure that was to fuel much of the exploration and colonization of Montreal – and Canada. It was the pelt of the Canadian beaver, a clever herbivore native to North America and possessed of a rich warm coat.

Over the next two centuries, European

small mountain, and from this vantage could see the river winding its way east for hundreds of miles. Here was the route to the Orient! He planted a cross, claimed the site for King Francis as the Hurons looked on baffled and pronounced the site Mont Réal – a name that did not come into general usage until a century later.

He also asked Agouhanna if he knew where to find the "shining rocks" he had heard were to be found in the area. The chief

Left, an early Québécois winter. **Above**, spring cleaning, pioneer-style.

demand for the pelts, which could be made into fashionable hats and garments, would explode. During this same period, many of the Indians, who found the pelts could be traded for weapons and implements, came to view the beaver as a powerful animal deity whose merits they had failed to recognize. Their desire for the products of European technology – pots, guns, alcohol – allowed profit-driven Europeans to exploit their canoeing and trapping skills. The value of goods traded for pelts was far below the price they would bring in Europe.

Cartier revisited Montreal in 1541, but did

not linger long, and the general settlement of New France was now centered on what are now the Canadian provinces of Nova Scotia and New Brunswick. By 1604, the new French king, Henry IV, a devout Huguenot (Protestant), had granted to his Huguenot friend, the Sieur de Monte, a monopoly on all the furs in New France.

Without manpower, such a monopoly was worthless, of course, but one of Monte's closest friends was a tireless figure who possessed the drive and imagination needed to settle New France and allow the fur trade to flourish. His name was Samuel de Champlain, a man of unusual resourcefulness who

COUREUR DE BOIS.

would be known as "the Father of New France." Champlain, an accomplished soldier and scholar, made several journeys to New France in the early years of the 17th century, and he founded settlements in Acadia (part of what is now Nova Scotia) and Quebec.

In 1611 he visited the island of Montreal and found that the Hochelaga settlement mentioned in Cartier's account had disappeared. He ordered his men to clear an area by the river bank and called it "Place Royale," a name the area possesses to this day. Champlain also took a fancy to the small

island offshore from Montreal and used the dowry of his teenage wife, Hélène Boulé, to buy it. Like many Montreal place names, it was informally canonized when Champlain's wife was long dead: it is known today as Ile Ste-Hélène, and is part of the permanent park erected when the World's Fair, Expo '67, was held in Montreal.

Champlain's main settlement was at Quebec, which he founded on July 3, 1603. But he visited Montreal again in 1615, this time on the north shore of the island, and here happened to meet two priests of the Récollet (Franciscan Minor) Order, Denis Janet and Joseph le Caron, both arrived from France.

Together with Champlain's men, these two performed the first Catholic Mass in North America on June 24, 1615. The setting was not auspicious for this momentous event, nothing more than a clearing and some rough wooden tables, but Champlain knelt with the two tough little priests. Many, many more masses would be said in New France.

Champlain, known to the Indians as Agnonha, was a colonial governor who was devout and warlike by turns. He had earned the enduring enmity of the Iroquois by killing more than 300 of them at Ticonderoga, matching European technology – primitive firearms known as arquebuses – against bow and arrow. His allies, the Hurons and Algonquins, also feared and hated him. Yet they bowed to his attempts at regulating the fur trade. He was not a man lightly crossed.

While Champlain was consolidating his power at Quebec, the energetic Récollet priests were doing their best to consolidate God's power further upstream. Not surprisingly, the Indians proved unwilling converts. The continuing aggression of the Iroquois against Port Royale created many early Christian martyrs among the Récollets and the Jesuits, known to the Indians as Black Robes. The priests were sometimes befriended by the Hurons or Algonquins, but were more often despised and feared as bizarre sorcerors who refused to have sex, share their belongings, or live communally.

Conversions were recorded, especially by the resourceful Jesuits, but they were of dubious theological validity and cost a high price in French lives. Jesuit priests were cruelly tortured and then gruesomely killed by the Indians, who believed that signs of weakness in conquered enemies made the conquerors stronger.

The *Relations* of these events, which were graphic tales written and circulated by the Jesuits in France, inspired a general religious zeal. The name "Mont Réal" became synonymous with a forlorn heathen place in need of salvation. In 1627, the prime minister of France was the Machiavellian figure Armand Jean du Plessis, better known as Cardinal Richelieu, who, seeking tirelessly to make France the preeminent power in the

of the Order of St Sulpice, and Jerome de la Royer de la Dauversière, a tax collector from Anjou. Olier and Dauversière had met by chance in Paris, discovered a common missionary passion for converting "heathen" Indians, and determined to start a permanent mission at Montreal.

They could not help viewing their meeting as providential. Pooling their resources, they sent off in 1641 with a group of 50 missionary members of their newly created "Société de Notre Dame de Montréal" under the leadership of Paul de Chomedey, Sieur de Maisonneuve. The new mission was to be established for the sole purpose of convert-

world, controlled the court of Louis XIII with a mixture of guile and terror.

At Richelieu's urging, Louis granted title to all land in New France to a group of shrewd French businessmen known as the Company of One Hundred Associates. Unable to exploit all the territory themselves, the Associates granted subleases to likely settlers. The title to the island of Montreal was granted by the Associates to two fervent believers, Jean-Jacques Olier, later founder

Left, fur trappers ravaged Quebec's beaver population. **Above**, 19th-century campfire supper.

ing Indian souls to Catholicism, and Olier specified that the Notre Dame settlers "should have nothing to do with the fur trade." There would be difficulty enough, they cautioned Maisonneuve, in "planting the banner of Christ in an abode of desolation and a haunt of demons."

Maisonneuve, a tough ex-soldier and Knight of Malta now driven by religious fervor, founded his colony, "Ville Marie," on Champlain's Place Royale site after a hard Atlantic crossing. Reaching shore, he fell on his knees and gave thanks. A rough palisade was quickly erected, and the first

Mass of the new settlement was said on August 18, 1642.

The consecrated host was displayed all day on the altar to show that this place had been claimed for Christ; at nightfall the altar was lit by firefly lanterns. Father Vimont, Superior of the Jesuits at Montreal, told his small congregation, with unusual prescience: "You are a grain of mustard seed that shall grow till its branches overshadow the earth. You are few, but this work is the Word of God. His smile is on you, and your children shall fill the land."

Life was extraordinarily hazardous and arduous for the settlers. Attacks by Indians

The Iroquois raids were a more constant and nagging danger and, until his men learned canoeing skills sufficient to meet the Indians on the water, Maisonneuve was forced to adopt a defensive posture. Nevertheless, Iroquois ambushes, often of workers returning to the palisades after a day in the fields, killed more than 50 people between 1643 and 1650 – this in a community that numbered fewer than 150.

To guard against ambushes, the settlers employed guard dogs who warned the French of stalking Iroquois warriors and prevented many deaths. Most famous of these was Maisonneuve's dog, Pilote, whose

were a daily danger, crops refused to take in the soil, and the melting snow caused disastrous annual floods. In December 1642, the confluence of the St Lawrence and St Peter rivers rose violently, lapping at the edges of the fledgling settlement. Maisonneuve, in great fear, planted a cross on the threatened bank and vowed to erect another on Mont Réal if the waters receded – which they did, on Christmas Day. On the feast of Epiphany (in early January) a procession, with a grateful Maisonneuve himself at the rear bearing a heavy wooden cross, scaled the hill and planted this token of thanks for God's mercy.

nose frequently detected approaching Indian warriors before they were visible. The dog is immortalized along with Maisonneuve in a statue located in old Montreal.

The first baptism of an Algonquin child occurred at Ville Marie in 1642, a great victory for the embattled missionaries. This, after all, was their reason for enduring the hardships of life in New France. But as they gathered around the rough baptismal, their thoughts might have turned to the great cost of salvation. How many more would have to die so that a few Indian souls could be saved? So many of the Indians did not want them there at all, and many others simply did not find the prospect of eternal life with God a joyful one. Would this first native Christian child find itself an outcast, or an apostate, in later life? The devout could banish such doubts, but not all of the Ville Marie company were as stout in their faith as the ascetic Récollet priests and the grim Maisonneuve himself.

In 1644, fed up with Indian harrassment, Maisonneuve walked out like a Western gunslinger to meet the leader of the Iroquois in single combat. It wasn't exactly a fair fight (Maisonneuve being armed with two pistols) but he succeeded in killing the chief at what

services. In 1644 the young nurse Jeanne Mance opened Montreal's first hospital, l'Hôtel Dieu, which was also the first building outside the palisades. The pale, slim Mance, who had almost died on the voyage from France, regained her strength to tend to those less fortunate.

The schoolmistress Marguerite Bourgeoys, another deceptively frail Frenchwoman, founded the settlement's first chapel, Notre-Dame-de-Bonsecours – still standing, after several rebuildings, on its original site in Old Montreal. This "Sailors' Church" welcomed generation after generation of weary river-goers to the safety of

is now Place d'Armes and a statue of this dedicated founder of Montreal stands there today.

Despite the religious fervor of some at Ville Marie, the settlement flourished more as a French outpost than a center of conversion. The quick wealth of the fur trade brought more people, including the so-called *filles du roi*, young Frenchwomen brought to Montreal to marry the male settlers. With a larger population came the need for new

God's house. Bourgeoys's order of nuns, Le Congrégation de Notre-Dame-de-Bonsecours, was authorized by Louis XIV in 1671, the first native Canadian religious order. The Notre-Dame Congregation was, into the 20th century, one of North America's most influential institutions for the education of Catholic women, and Bourgeoys was raised to sainthood in 1982 by Pope John Paul II.

Montreal was now North America's premier Roman Catholic city, and remained so for almost two centuries. Dominated in early days by Franciscans and Jesuits, the city later

Left, tranquillity in 1791. **Above**, Paul de Chomedey de Maisonneuve lays down the law.

welcomed Jean-Jacques Olier's St Sulpice fathers, and the so-called Gray Sisters (more formally known as Les Soeurs de la Charité de l'Hôpital Général de Montréal), who tended to the poor and derelict. The Oblates, Christian Brothers, and Sacred Heart Sisters also found their way to the city.

All the schools of Montreal and many of its most impressive buildings are the result of the church's great hold on Montrealers. When the Notre Dame Cathedral of Montreal was built in 1829, it drew visitors from across Canada and the United States; it was then the largest church in North America and remained so until St Patrick's Cathedral was built in New York in 1879.

In 1874 there were 74 churches of all denominations in Montreal – one for every 2,000 inhabitants. Even at this date they were still largely Catholic, but with several tasteful additions from the Church of Scotland and the Anglican Church. Harriet Beecher Stowe, author of *Uncle Tom's Cabin*, wrote in 1860 that "Montreal is a mountain of churches," while Mark Twain took a more jaundiced view: "This is the first time I was ever in a city," he wrote in 1881, "where you could not throw a brick without breaking a church window."

Muscular Christianity: During the 1660s, the governing spirit of Ville Marie was the energetic Superior of the Sulpicians, and keen amateur historian, François Dollier de Cassons (1632–1702). He was a strapping, 6' 5" (2.2-meter) ex-soldier who, with cassock tucked up for greater freedom of movement, surveyed the town's first street plan, planned a canal to bypass the Lachine rapids, and built the first parish church and a seminary for the Sulpicians, still the official owners of the island.

In 1663, however, Louis XIV took formal possession of all the land and trade of New France, and land parcels and trading licences henceforth were granted only by the Crown and its representatives at Quebec. The island of Montreal was divided into land packets known as *seigneuries*; the owners, or *seigneurs*, subdividing their land into tenant parcels farmed by *habitants*. For a nominal rent – "half a sou plus a pint of wheat per acre" was the going rate in 1667 – the *habitant* was given the land to work, on which he built a dwelling for himself and maintained a road. He was also bound to grind his grain at the *seigneur's* mill.

Seigneuries were typically divided up, not in chunks but in long strips so that every *habitant* could have some river access. This division is still evident in Quebec estates. The *habitant*, with his dyed wool cap (*toque bleu*), blanket-cloth coat and tasseled sash, remains a ubiquitous, if somewhat clichéd, symbol of rural Quebec. Bonhomme, the snowman symbol of Quebec's annual winter festivals, also wears the toque and sash of the *habitant*.

The landowners themselves built grand stone houses on estates away from the riverbank. Named after their owners, some of these châteaux are still standing: Château de Ramezay, one of the first, served later as the seat of Montreal's government; De La Salle House can be found in the suburb of Lachine (named rather hopefully as a stage on the road to China, *La Chine*). But while Ville-Marie seemed to be gaining a foothold on the island, the Indian threat did not lessen. On August 4, 1689, the worst Iroquois raid yet left 200 people of Lachine dead. Another 100 were captured and never returned.

There followed 10 years of sustained fighting with the Iroquois which effectively halted the fur trade on which Montreal's prosperity depended. The early Montrealers entered the 18th century on a pensive note, but the diplomatic new Governor-General of Montreal, Hector de Callières, managed to negotiate a peace treaty with the Indians. In 1701 more than 1,300 Indians, representatives of 40 different nations, were persuaded to come to Montreal and camp outside the city's walls for peace talks. De Callières, skilled in smoothing over old grievances, circulated among the assembled chiefs and hammered out a deal all could accept. Surveying the hundreds of tents, camp fires and milling Indians and Frenchmen, de Callières cried: *"Voici la paix. Oublions le passé."*

Peace had come, yes. But it was not to last for long.

Right, ruthless Iroquois raids were common until the mid-1600s.

RELIGIOUS ROOTS

If faith can move mountains, it can also settle them, as the establishment of Montreal shows. In 1642, approximately 50 members of the *Associés de Notre-Dame pour la conversion des sauvages de la Nouvelle France en l'île de Montréal* crossed a capricious ocean to found the Ville-Marie mission near the "royal mountain" looming over Montreal's landscape. (Unfortunately, they didn't receive a formal invitation from the Iroquois, the *sauvages* who were their object of conversion.)

The religious fervor of 17th-century France, marked by the creation of numerous religious orders and lay evangelizing groups, spilled over into New France, which soon became populated by old and new religious congregations.

As history painfully shows, however, colonies do not live by faith alone. In Montreal, Catholicism combined with fur and the *fleur-de-lis* to form the defining triptych of the city's early history, and this medley led to an ecclesiastical power and control unprecedented in North America, a power that remained relatively undiminished until the "Quiet Revolution" deep in the 20th century.

Ever since Sieur de Maisonneuve planted a towering crucifix in thanksgiving for Ville-

Marie's survival of a flood in 1643, Montreal's visage has been Janus-faced, characterized by both political and religious profiles. New France was envisioned as both a source of wealth for France and as a North American beachhead for the Counter (or Catholic) Reformation – an attempt by the Roman Catholic church to respond to the rapid and lasting emergence of the Protestant reformers.

The Jesuits were among the first missionaries to brave the frigid but fertile colony of New France. Their missions in South America, Ethiopia, Russia, India, and China were well-known, largely through the publication of their exploits in *Relations*. Their fame led not only to a steady flow of vocations, but also to handsome donations from well-endowed patrons.

Called "Black Robes" by the Native Americans, the Jesuits sought converts among the ag-

gressive Iroquois and more pacific Huron peoples. For many of these missionaries, their vocations ended in martyrdom. During the 1650s, the Iroquois attacked Quebec City, Trois-Rivières, and Montreal, the three centers of the French fur trade along the St Lawrence River. Montreal, which was a natural "command center" for the fur trade, was saved from decimation by the efforts of Adam Dollard and 16 companions, who perished in a stand against several Iroquois war parties on the Ottawa River. Upon learning of these attacks, Louis XIV, the "Sun King," bestowed his radiance upon his valuable but besieged colony. In 1661, he made the small community of under 2,000 settlers a royal province, and dispatched 1,000 troops to protect the colony.

All public appointments were from then on handled by the crown, and the governor, the "intendant" (who maintained the royal authority and oversaw economic development), joined with the Roman Catholic bishop to form a sort of triumvirate called the Sovereign Council. In New France, therefore, unlike the British colonies, cross and sword united to block inchoate democratic initiatives.

Bishop Laval was quite happy to pick up the political mantel proffered him by the king. As chief prelate from 1649 to 1688, this ascetic cleric secured vast lands for the church, established a seminary (the forerunner of Quebec's Laval University) and controlled education in the colony. (The separation of church and state was as heretical an idea as predestination in New France.)

A major figure in the ecclesiastical educational system of Montreal was Marguerite Bourgeoys (1620–1700), Canada's first female saint. A dramatic amalgam of courage, compassion, and conviction, Marguerite set sail for Montreal in 1657 with M. de Maisonneuve, 100 men, and a handful of girls and women. During the undulating passage, she served as both nurse, prelate, and mortician, nursing the eight men who died of plague during the voyage and preparing them for watery graves.

Marguerite, who eventually founded the Congrégation de Notre-Dame, counselled, catechized, and cared for many of the 1,000 *filles du roi* who streamed to New France between 1665 and 1673. In a French colonial version of "Here Come the Brides," King Louis XIV sponsored the migration of young girls to the colony, "entirely free from any natural blemish or anything personally repulsive," to help populate New France.

In a further effort to increase the number of (French) mammals on its few snowy acres, the crown granted baby bonuses, penalized bachelors, and provided handsome pensions for fecund parents. Parents were also required by law to have their sons married by the age of 18 or 19, and their daughters had to be betrothed by 14 or 15.

In many ways, the church was attempting to build a more *Catholic* France in North America, a new "city on the hill" that would somehow be more pristine than its European counterpart. Marguerite Bourgeoys was the church's "trump card" in this enterprise.

Dubbed "mother of the colony," Marguerite, in addition to chaperoning the *filles du roi*, recruited French and Canadian girls as teachers, organized a boarding school, established a school for Indian girls on the Sulpician reserve of *La Montagne*, as well as a domestic arts school. As a guardian of virgins, Marguerite was well aware of the dangers of the opposite sex. While travelling to Nantes, en route to the New World, Marguerite was accosted by scores of aggressive men. She recounted in her diary, "I could not leave

the coach... all these men said many insulting things to me… I closed the door and barricaded it with everything I could."

Marguerite's survival skills would serve her and her charges well in a colony where women were a scarce and precious resource. Although Bishop Laval refused to allow her and her coworkers to take religious vows, they were eventually permitted in 1698 to become a non-cloistered religious community. Considered by her peers to be a saint when she died in 1670, Marguerite was not officially canonized by the church until October 1982.

Today you can see where Marguerite welcomed the King's wards at Maison Saint-Gabrielle (on

Favard Street). Built in 1688, this served a farm center, elementary school, and, finally, the first school of domestic arts for young women in New France. Part of the present-day structure dates to 1698.

Perhaps no one more epitomized the strength of the missionary church than Abbé Dollier de Casson, Superior of the Sulpicians in Montreal. A towering figure, he could apparently lift two men simultaneously, one in each hand.

While praying on his knees one evening by the Bay of Quinté, it is said, Dollier de Casson was harangued by a young Indian, who mocked him with obscenities. Without getting up, the forceful cleric shot out his right arm and sent the brave sprawling. He finished his prayers uninterrupted.

Abbé Dollier de Casson built the Suplician Seminary, which you can still visit today on Rue Notre-Dame at Place d'Armes. Begun in 1680, this is the oldest building in Montreal and one of North America's oldest.

The work of religion, in education at every level, and in ministry for the sick, the impoverished, orphans, and elderly has been of central importance to Montreal's history. Throughout the city, religious schools, hospitals and seminaries are among the oldest, most enduring institutions.

The tenacious grip of medieval Christendom on Montreal began to relax, however, after 1950. Government intervention in the areas of health and education brought radical changes to the complexion of Catholicism in Montreal and the province of Quebec in general. The "Quiet Revolution," followed quickly by the Second Vatican Council (1962–65), led to a major exodus of many of the Quebec church's vowed members and to a substantial loss of its power and authority. Between 1967 and 1983, the ranks of religious congregations in Quebec dropped by 40 percent.

Perhaps more than any other North American city, Montreal exudes the ambience of a community where church and state were long and enduring bedfellows. As you pass by Montreal's numerous churches, centuries-old hospitals and houses for the religious, pause, for a moment just to recall the lives affected by the faith and fervor of 17th-century Catholicism.

Left, Jesus lives in St-Denis. Above, Tiffany window in Erskine and American Church.

After the peace of 1701 between the French and the Indians, Montreal rebuilt itself, dropped the name of Ville-Marie, and concentrated on becoming the trading center its location seemed always to promise. The pursuit of the beaver pelts was furious, sometimes unscrupulous, and almost always at the expense of Indians on the lookout for European liquor, guns, and utensils. Traders typically exchanged goods for pelts at far below market price, reserving the massive profits for themselves and exploiting the Indian trappers who had risked life and limb to bring in the pelts.

The lure of quick wealth was too much for most early Montrealers to resist, and "everyone turns trader" a contemporary traveller noted. The aging Dollier de Casson wrote of the fur trade gloomily, describing "the diabolical attractions" of quick wealth and the resulting *"perdition générale"* of Montreal. Even Montreal's clergymen ventured out to the trading stalls beyond the city gates to barter their utensils and equipment for furs that would bring massive profits in Europe.

The Indians, however, were not the only ones to pursue the beavers into their habitat. Toughened *coureurs de bois* – French woodsmen skilled in the arts of paddling and trapping – steered fur-heavy canoes into Montreal harbor and looked for a good price. Some of these hardy souls had "gone native" and barely appeared French to the civilized denizens of Montreal. Their supplies sold off, they and the Indians would proceed to get roaring drunk on cheap liquor, collapsing in dirty heaps or copulating, fighting, and drinking until dawn.

In 1721, the town fortifications were improved with 18-foot stone walls, bastions, a citadel, and more cannon. The wooden buildings inside the walls, always at risk of

fire, were replaced in accordance with building regulations that called for stone walls and roofs of slate, tile, or tin. "The town has suffered by fire very materially at different times," the traveller Isaac Weld wrote some time later, "and the inhabitants have such a dread of it, that all who can afford it cover the roofs of their houses with tin-plates instead of shingles. By law they are obliged to have one or more ladders, in proportion to the house, always ready on the roofs."

Drama and dancing: For almost five decades the little town boomed, its *seigneurs* and traders gradually becoming wealthier as the demand for beaver furs grew in Europe. In the long winter months, leisure time was unlimited and the Ramezays, Vaudreuils, and other prosperous families of Montreal enjoyed amateur theatricals, dancing, and sugaring-off picnics in which a festive party sledded out to the maple stands to collect sap for maple syrup.

The more prosaic *habitants*, at least as protrayed by sentimental artists such as Cornelius Krieghoff (1812–72), loved to

Preceding pages: Queen Victoria, ever watchful of her rebellious French subjects. **Left,** after Wolfe's defeat and death in 1759, British troops took decisive control of the town. **Above,** the exiled Québécois leader Louis Joseph Papineau.

dance, play cards (a pursuit officially banned by the church), and drink heavily. Krieghoff is perhaps the best known of the artists who chronicled the scenes of daily life in early Quebec; his paintings are seen frequently on posters, postcards and, memorably, the label of a brand of Canadian whisky.

It was 1756 when the Seven Years' War brought an end to the prosperous peace. Armed conflict, this time between French and English, once more ruptured Montreal. The English, long eager to get a foothold on North America and the riches it promised, ran up against the well-oiled imperial designs first proposed by Richelieu. Neither

on the part of France to keep its colonies. Richelieu's influence was long gone, and the desire for imperial might was waning in a France wracked by internal difficulties and facing battles with English and Prussian soliders on its own land. (The satirist Voltaire conveyed one prominent attitude to France's colonial adventure when, in *Candide*, he famously dismissed New France as "a few acres of snow.")

The English and French forces met in a decisive battle at Quebec in 1760. The French commander, Montcalm, defending a stout fort, did not reckon on a flanking manoveur. The English went upriver past

side had any illusions about their colonial ambitions, despite the rhetoric of religious conversion habitually used by the French.

The English, after several abortive attempts to oust the French, massed their efforts in the middle of the 1750s, attacking first at Ticonderoga. Louis Joseph, Marquis de Montcalm, ruled the French forces from his headquarters in Montreal and scored an impressive short-handed victory at Ticonderoga.

The English forces were superior, however, and not hampered by the political machinations that prevented an all-out effort

Quebec, scaled the cliffs there, and surprised the French forces from the rear. Montcalm was defeated and killed on the Plains of Abraham by the British general, James Wolfe, who was also killed. In September 1760, the British general Lord Jeffrey Amherst entered Montreal through the Récollet gate and was met by Vaudreuil, the governor of New France, who formally surrendered.

The British flag flew over Montreal for the first time on September 9, 1760. In 1763, under the Treaty of Paris, France ceded its territories to Britain. So ended the era of French control in Montreal.

Despite this enormous change in political direction, daily life did not alter much for the average Montreal inhabitant. The British Governors were sensitive to the fact that several generations of Frenchmen were responsible for whatever European civilization, trade and development the colony enjoyed. No land was stripped from the *seigneurs*, and the Quebec Act of 1774 accepted the French language and Roman Catholic religion as essential parts of Quebec culture.

A cosmopolitan mix: But by this time one could hear a broad Scottish burr on the streets of Montreal, or the haughty bleat of influence of English bureaucrats on Montreal. In 1765, the price of a four-pound white loaf (a "brick") was fixed at eight coppers; bakers could not charge more than 10 coppers for the heavier brown loaf, usually of six pounds. Slavery was also a prevailing concern, and the governors thought it best to distance themselves officially from the buying and selling of humans so widely practiced in parts of the republic to the south. It was decreed that "no tavern, ale-house or innkeeper do receive, harbour, or entertain any bond or servant slave or slaves, drinking, gaming or loitering in their houses, under a penalty of £5."

English nobility. The demographics of the city changed radically during the next generation, and the population exploded with an exuberant commercial eagerness. Montreal was still a boom town, on whose streets leather-clad *coureurs de bois* (woodsmen), fresh from the river portages and Indian camps, rubbed shoulders with Scottish merchants, English soldiers, and aristocratic French *seigneurs*.

New civil regulations also marked the

Trade rapidly became brisk in ice blocks (left) and timber (above).

From this time on, and especially in the decades immediately before the American Civil War, Montreal was a frequent destination of slaves trekking toward freedom on the so-called Underground Railway.

The strategic position of Montreal – Dollier de Casson had called it "the dyke of Canada" – made it a desirable military target, and during the American Revolution (1775–83) the city once again came under attack. The first American overture was a failure. In 1775 the garrison at Montreal heard that Ethan Allen and his famous "Green Mountain Boys" were marching along the Longue

A Woman's Lot

The law making marriage a co-partnership, and creating *communitié de bien*, is sanctioned by the code of French law, called *Coutûme de Paris* which indeed is the text book of the Canadian lawyer; the wife being by marriage invested with a right to half the husband's property; and, being rendered independent of him, is perhaps the remote cause that the fair sex have such influence in France; and in Canada, it is well known, that a great deal of consequence, and even an air of superiority, is assumed by them…

—A British View of French Canada, 1807

Many 18th-century male observers of women in New France were struck (not always favorably) by the taken-for-granted independence women enjoyed and the potent influence they exerted in the colony, no matter what their cultural background.

Although 18th-century French attitudes toward women were more flexible than those of the British, they were far from being, in modern terms, "progressive." Under French laws, wives were expected to follow their husbands, even if that meant traveling to an entirely new country. So French culture alone can't take credit for this remarkable phenomenon.

A look at the female immigrants themselves offers better answers. The two main types to immigrate to the colony were the *dévotées,* dedicated religious women or nuns, and the *filles du roi*, government-sponsored immigrants. Most of these women were highly educated and, significantly, were self-motivated in their decision to try life out in New France.

The *dévotées* rapidly developed badly needed hospitals and schools. As a result, they secured for themselves an important place in the social structure of the colony. Moreover, they permanently established the education of girls as a part of colonial culture, hence passing on to these women two extremely important assets for an independent lifestyle: an education and a trade.

Most of the *filles du roi* were originally urban dwellers and were trained in a wide variety of skills. Many of these women also brought dowries with them that they, though modest in France, were small fortunes in the New World. Since wives were a scarce resource among the men of the colony, those women with property were highly coveted.

The inhabitants of New France seem to have been distinctly unhindered by the Puritanical attitudes toward sex that established such a firm foothold in New England. These more "open" colonial attitudes stemmed from a parent culture that viewed human sexuality both with tolerance and interest. Marriage ceremonies tended to be more public than private, and kinfolk as well as the larger community had a penetrating voice in deciding who could marry whom. In French Canada, marriage contracts were often signed by not only the bride and groom's extended families, but also by *all* those attending the wedding.

The involvement of this wider community in the marriage reflects the family effort to protect a bride's property. As a result, many a wedding resembled a business deal rather than a sacrament. The European medieval tradition of *charivari* (wedding night riot) was also transplanted in New France. If the community disapproved of a marriage, they staged a *charivari*, a noisy boycott of the couple's home, which could last several days.

Family life among the *habitants* and *habitantes* of colonial Lower Canada was distinguished by one significant feature: the home and place of work were not separate realms. Women worked as bonesetters, bookbinders, woolfillers, laundresses, wigmakers, pedlars, greengrocers, moneylenders, auctioneers, educators, and nurses. They toiled in the fields next to their menfolk and some were active in less expected areas such as arduous bricklaying and backbreaking stonework. In addition, many children were sent out of the home at an early age either to a nursemaid or to learn a trade, hence freeing many mothers from the exhausting and time-consuming task of raising children.

The combination, then, of a French cultural heritage and the unique roles they played in New France, provided many women with an unusual degree of independence.

Pointe road, just east of the city. A small force of English and French soldiers advanced to challenge the invaders and Allen was easily defeated and captured.

The garrison commandant, an old soldier called Prescott, threatened to cane the arrogant Allen and had to be dragged off by his men. Allen was imprisoned on board the ship *Gaspé*, moored in harbor, and Montrealers rejoiced at having "caged the great New Hampshire incendiary." But the jubilation was short-lived, for in the autumn of 1775 General Richard Montgomery advanced on the city with a much larger force and the governor, Sir Guy Carleton (later Lord

deliverance and its agents. The Americans, on the other hand, found Canadian notions of liberty "monstrously ill-digested" and soon regarded the Montrealers as "rascals and enemies" and even "dam'd Tories."

Peace breaks out: Benjamin Franklin arrived in June 1776 to smooth over these rough spots but his overtures were rejected. The Americans left in 1783 when Britain massed a large army near Montreal, and a peace treaty was signed with the new United States republic the same year.

Perhaps the only palpable benefit of the American occupation was that one of Franklin's associates, a propagandist called

Dorchester), was compelled to surrender without resistance.

The attitude of the Americans was then, as it is now, that the occupied people should be overjoyed to be freed from the shackles of colonial rule. Montrealers were invited to "seize the opportunity presented to you by Providence itself" and join the not-quite-Continental Congress. But the Americans failed to reckon with other ideas of freedom; Montrealers were happy and prosperous under the British and mocked the American

Above, sawing ice on the St Lawrence Seaway.

Fleury de Mesplet, decided to stay on and ply his printing trade in Montreal. In a shop on Rue de la Capital, a narrow lane off Rue St François-Xavier, he began printing Canada's first newspaper, *La Gazette du Commerce et Littéraire*. In 1788 the paper was produced in English as well as French, a concrete indication that English had arrived in the city. You can still pick up a copy of the *Gazette* today – it is now Montreal's major English daily – and find some of those "monstrously ill-digested ideas" that offend American sensibilities.

Many other commerical enterprises began

in these decades to serve the needs of the wealthy fur traders and their employees, and the influx of United Empire Loyalists fleeing the anti-monarchist revolution to the south swelled Montreal's population. The focus of the town shifted away from the harbor settlement and toward what is now downtown Montreal.

The city's new aristocracy was largely Scottish in origin, and it included many enterprising rogues who had taken advantage of the wide-open colonial life to make their vast fortunes in fur trading. Simon McTavish, Joseph Frobisher, William McGillivray, James McGill, and Simon

the Nor-Westers left their mark on their home base of Montreal. The city's main English-speaking university is built on land bequeathed by Edinburgh University graduate James McGill, who wanted the colony to have "an English college on a liberal scale." With $10,000 and the 46 acres of land known as Burnside, the university was begun. When classes began in September 1843, the college site was still countryside, and its 20 hardy students tramped across fields full of crops and grazing cattle to reach the fount of wisdom. They had to dress "in plain, decent and comely clothes, without superfluous ornament" and wear gowns to their lectures on

Fraser were the stars in Montreal's social and commercial firmament in this era. Their names also dot the rivers and regions of western Canada which they were the first to explore.

In 1783 a group of them founded the North-West Company, a fur-trading cooperative begun in order to challenge the hegemony of England's Hudson's Bay Company. The Nor-Westers were absorbed by the Hudson's Bay Co. in 1821, but for decades raced them to the fur trade in the west and north of Canada.

Just as their names filled in the maps there,

medicine, classics and mathematics.

Beaver Hall Hill, site of Canada's first men's club, also owes it name to the Nor-Westers. Membership in the Beaver Club was limited to those who had wintered in Canada's wilderness, *le pays d'en haut*, and during the long Montreal winters the adventurers would gather here to tell tall stories, drink whisky, and sing the canoeing songs of the old *voyageurs*, paddling away for all they were worth with their walking sticks, fire tongs, or dress swords. The minutes of one dinner meeting, for February 28, 1809, show that the 24 attending members drank 38 bottles of wine and 26 bottles of beer in what was surely an extremely rowdy evening.

The grand houses of the new fur lords, dwarfing the châteaux of the early *seigneurs*, were sited away from the town in the elevated environs of Westmount and Mount Royal itself. The name Westmount is still synonymous with privilege and old money in Montreal's society lexicon.

While these Scottish "lords of lake and forest," the "hyperborean nabobs" of the fur trade (as Washington Irving had enthusiastically called them), spoke English among themselves, most were bilingual, the result of necessary traffic with their *voyageur*

for almost 13 years, so presumably drama did not agree with the tastes of these northern hearties.

In the same year, 1786, the Englishman John Molson opened his brewery on the banks of the St Lawrence; he also began a small shipping-line that was to grow quickly in the next 50 years. Molson, a great favorite of the French *habitants* along the river, is a suitable emblem for this golden age of commercial Montreal: he made his vast fortune from almost nothing in the new colony by working hard to meet the simple needs of its inhabitants. He is reputed to have said that "An honest brew makes its own friends" – a

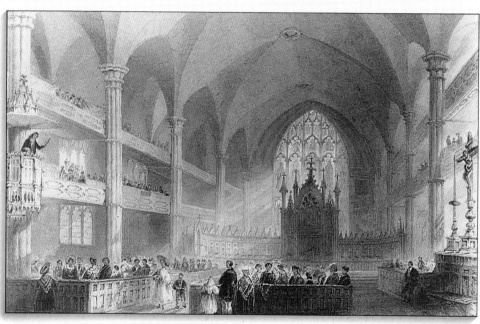

paddlers and, in some cases, of Scotland's Auld Alliance with France against the English.

Many, including McTavish, McGill and Frobisher, also married French Canadians. They were models of biculturalism in action, happy in a city still essentially French. It was not until the spring of 1786 that an English play, Goldsmith's *She Stoops to Conquer*, was performed in Montreal by a professional troupe from Albany, New York. No other play is mentioned in the history of Montreal

Left, and <u>above</u>, Notre-Dame Cathedral.

slogan found on his family's beer bottles to this day.

When his brewery first opened, a bottle of strong beer cost nine cents, mild ale went for seven cents a bottle, and small or table beer cost five cents. Molson also built Montreal's first hotel and its first commercial theatre, the Théâtre Royale. Molson's brewery was the first in North America and, while the steamship line that used to run his ships the *Accommodation* and the *Swiftsure* between Quebec and Montreal is long since gone, you can still enjoy a bottle of Molson's lager or ale in any Canadian tavern.

THE HABITANTS

There are some who love good food,
Beans with pork, and small green peas;
Or plenty of pork also with beans,
There are some who eat, others who don't.
The spoiled gherkins in the salad,
There are some who eat them and make them-
selves sick.
But to eat pea soup
The Canadiens are always ready!
Ah! ah! the Canadiens are always ready!
          —French Canadian Folk Song

Imagine yourself a very long way from home, so far away that the prospect of returning is next to impossible. You are in a strange land, known for its fierce winters and covered by a tenacious, seemingly impenetrable forest. You will be the first to settle the new colony – you will plan your settlement without really knowing much about the country, taking risks, experimenting, and desperately hoping that all will turn out well.

You will give birth to your children on the kitchen table, perhaps with the help of a midwife, and each day you will toil to provide the necessities of life: preparing meals, making soap and candles, mending and washing clothes. At the end of your days your face will betray the marks of a rough life outdoors and of bearing too many children, and your hands will show the scars of many harvests. But you will have lived an honest life, even a prosperous life – the life of a French Canadian *habitant* or *habitante*.

"To be always ready,"as the above folksong proclaims, seems more appropriate for the Boys Scouts of America than for fledgling colonists, yet it is an apt shibboleth for the first European inhabitants of Canada.

No one could possibly envy the hardships the first French Canadians faced, the bitter and lonely winters, unpredictable crops, and the relentless necessity of becoming self-reliant. These are all things that every Canadian pioneer confronted, but the French managed to settle along the St

Lawrence in a unique fashion and, in so doing, founded a truly distinct society.

New France's first permanent homesteads (evidence of which can still be seen today), were uniquely linked to the available and oh-so-crucial water sources. The original plots were very long, narrow strips of land with one terminus facing the St Lawrence River. In the original settlements, water frontage was usually 600–750 ft (200–250 meters) wide and had a depth of several miles. Following a French feudal model, colonization in French Canada used *seigneurs* – usually merchants, soldiers, priests and gentlemen farmers – as principal real estate agents for frontier properties. Usually a large tract was granted to a *seigneur* who had to promise the French crown that he would settle the land. Once *habitants,* farmers, were found, they were given tenancy on the land and had to build a house, harvest crops each year, pay a rent (*cens*) and fringe benefits (usually a yearly ham or tub of butter) to the *seigneur,* and agree to the *corvée* (feudal service) that most often involved construction and road work. In return, the *seigneur* erected a mill and oven, handled disputes, and tried to nurture an environment of bucolic prosperity.

A typical stretch of farmland was usually divided into several tiers: close to the house (and water) was a vegetable garden, a broad band of cultivated land followed, then meadows and pasture lands, and finally a timber reserve or wooded area used for fuel, tools and building material.

In the 18th century when New France's population expanded dramatically, a second row of backlots (and eventually a third) were joined to the first band. Each cluster of these lots, referred to as a *rang*, had its own council house, school, chapel, butter and cheese dairies, and frequently a rural women's circle. The poor in each community were cared for through *guignolées* (collections) and communal working projects were organized for building, moving, woodcutting, harvesting and land clearing.

The narrow plots along the river became the fundamental social unit of early French Canadian culture and profoundly influenced the way in which New France emerged. The linear settlement pattern with houses clustered along the waterfront established a compelling solidarity among the *habitants*. Few other colonies in Canada developed this kind of built-in interdependency. As one historian has noted, the uniformity of these narrow lots created a "peculiar social equality among households" with mutual assistance playing a key role in the community. As a result, French Canada never suffered from the rise of the large estate and the divisive social stratification associated with it.

One institution reflecting the importance of neighbors was the *premier voisin* (first cousin), usually the head of the next-door family. Invited to most family functions and included in all important decisions, the *premier voisin* helped out with any major project and was called upon for help when any emergency arose. In return, his family always received a loaf of bread on baking day or a slab of meat during the slaughter season.

The life of the farmer in France was, in many ways, remarkably suited to Canada. Both France and the St Lawrence region were good dairy countries with few milk-souring heat waves and possessed soils suitable for growing *légumes*, root crops, hay, and fruits rather than cereals. The core diet of the *habitants* strongly echoed the typical fare of a French peasant, with a few changes: peas and pork became central ingredients in many dishes, particularly a daily staple: pea soup.

One 18th-century trader recorded the recipe for this now famous French Canadian dish: "The tin kettle in which they [a group of fur traders] cook their food would hold eight to ten gallons. It was hung over the fire, nearly full of water, then nine quarts of peas – one quart per person, the daily allowance – were put in; and when they were well bursted, two or three pounds of pork, cut into strips, for seasoning, were added, and allowed to boil or simmer until daylight when the cook added four biscuits, broken up, to the mess, and invited all hands to breakfast. The swelling of the peas and biscuits had now filled the kettle to the brim, so thick that a stick would stand upright in it... The men now squatted in a circle, the kettle to the mouth, with almost electric speed, soon filled every cavity." (From Edith Fowke's *Folklore of Canada*).

In New France, the *habitants* were able to supplement their diet with game, particularly wild hare and venison, as well as an abundant supply of fish from the St Lawrence River. Eels, considered a delicacy in France, were more readily available and were eaten raw, smoked, dried and stewed. Folklorist Edith Fowke notes that the *habitants*, following an old French recipe, simmered molluscs in cream along with cider, salted pork and onions – British colonists to the south exported this recipe where it became New England clam chowder.

In the new colony, milk became a core part of the French peasant's diet and was used the the preparation of almost every meal. In one popular dish, milk was boiled; then chunks of bread were thrown into it along with great quantities of maple sugar. The soggy mixture was spooned out into bowls and eaten as a kind of bread pudding in the evening. These game and milk dishes were rounded out by wild berries, garden vegetables, especially carrots, onions, cabbage, turnips and eventually potatoes. (Cabbage dishes were popular because, according to French folk medicine, cabbage cured venereal diseases, increased a mother's milk, and prevented hair from falling out.)

The *habitants'* daily menu consisted of a breakfast of pancakes, bread, salted pork, and cider (until replaced by coffee and tea). A noontime lunch of pea soup with fried potatoes and a garden vegetable followed. At around 4 o'clock in the afternoon, leftovers from lunch would be consumed along with a cucumber salad and bread smeared with either pork fat or butter. The final meal of the day was eaten at eight or nine in the evening when a bowl of bread cooked in milk and sugar would be served along with cider.

Although today's French Canadian diet has changed drastically from that of the *habitants*, many of the old foods associated with holidays are still remarkably popular: *tortières*, meatball stew, sausages, onion sauce, maple sugar candies and doughnuts among them. Even by today's health-conscious standards, Canada's first European settlers had a healthy diet, well balanced in calories and protein, and, with few exceptions, pleasing to the average palate.

With the bumptious Americans to the south, peace was unlikely to endure. War came once more in October 1813, when 5,000 troops under Major-General Hampton advanced on Montreal from the west. A decisive battle was fought at Chateauguay, where fewer than 1,000 Canadians commanded by Lieutenant-Colonel Charles de Salaberry defeated the Americans.

Although Montreal was the first city of Canada, both commercially and strategi-

their throats cut by savage Irishmen. One of their marching songs gives a better idea of their motives, and mien:

We are the Fenian brotherhood, skilled in
the arts of war
And we're going to fight for Ireland, the
land that we adore,
Many battles we have won, along with the
boys in blue
And now we're going to conquer Canada
– because we ain't got nothing else to do.

cally, the main battles of the War of 1812 were fought in Ontario. But Montreal did feel the effects, if only psychological ones, of the unrest in the threat of "Fenian raids." The Fenians, Irish Americans whose name comes from the Irish motto *Sinn Fein* ("Ourselves alone") – today the name of the Irish Republican Army's political wing – harassed settlers along Canada's southern border during the 1812 war and after America's bloody Civil War (1861–65).

The sallies of the Fenians never amounted to anything like an invasion, but timorous Montrealers lived in daily fear of having

But the Fenians did have some bite, as Canadians learned in the early morning of April 7, 1868. Thomas d'Arcy McGee, one of the Fathers of Confederation, was returning from an all-night meeting when he was shot and killed outside his home in Ottawa by agents who claimed to be connected with the Fenian cause. This has the dubious distinction of being the first political assassination in Canadian history. When news of the death travelled, a huge crowd of mourners gathered to wait for D'Arcy McGee's body at Montreal's Bonaventure Station.

A salutary effect of the War of 1812 was

that its threat to Canada's economy hastened the founding of the colony's first bank, the Bank of Montreal, which was chartered in 1817. The war had also indicated the very real danger of moving men and supplies past the Lachine Rapids when time was of the essence; nobody had successfully navigated the rapids that had stopped Cartier and they remained extremely arduous. In 1821, with money "panhandled" from the provincial and British governments, the Lachine Canal

Montreal was incorporated and its first mayor, Jacques Viger, elected. Viger completed a grand term in office, performing Montreal's first census and donating the land for Viger Square, Montreal's most popular park between the 1860s and 1890s. He also coined the city motto, *Concordia Salus* (Health lies in Concord), giving it the distinctive coat of arms that conjoins the national symbols of France, England, Scotland and Ireland. The Societies of St Jean-Bap-

was completed – almost 200 years after a canal had first been suggested by the far-sighted Dollier de Cassons.

Improvements were also evident on the city streets, lit from 1815 on with gas lamps; the purpose of this innovation was mostly social – a decree said the lamps were installed so "that ladies might be induced to visit their friends much more frequently."

Also in this period (1825), the City of

Preceding pages: fashion was as important in 1897 as it is now. **Left**, and **above**, Cornelius Kreighoff's portraits of French-Canadian life.

tiste, St Andrew, St Patrick and St George were all founded at this time. "Concordia Salus," certainly, but old ties still die hard.

The prosperity and optimism of the 1820s were shattered by events that shook Montreal in the 1830s. The 1837 rebellions in Toronto and Montreal indicated that not everyone was satisfied with the colonial government and its wide-open opportunities for the rich to get richer. In Montreal, reformers known as *les Patriotes* and led by, among others, Louis Joseph Papineau demanded reform of a system that was in large part controlled by a clique of family interests. Representative government was a radical notion in these times, of course, and the majority found the demands of the *Patriotes* unpalatable.

Britain refused to acknowledge the 92 resolutions drawn up by Papineau and his associates which demanded, among other things, the dissolution of the appointed governing Council of Lower Canada, known as the *Château Clique* (the reference is to Château St-Louis, Quebec's Government House). Papineau called for a council of elected representatives to replace the in-bred and self-serving clique, which, like the Family Compacts controlling Upper Canada, doled out privilege and contracts with the arrogant disdain of absolute monarchs.

The atmosphere in Montreal was ripe for violence: cholera epidemics in 1832 and 1834 had ravaged the population, and political clubs and duelling societies fomented the unrest by meeting publicly to argue and fight. On November 6, 1837, a fierce riot broke out on peaceful St James Street and spilled into Place d'Armes; after dark, the house of Papineau and the offices of the *Vindicator*, a newspaper supporting him, were wrecked. Two weeks of uneasy silence were broken by the imposition of martial law when Sir John Colborne, the commander-in-chief, set up his headquarters in the Château Ramezay and dispatched troops to hunt down the *Patriotes*. Many, including Papineau, fled to the United States.

Others were not so resourceful. Twelve captured *Patriotes*, most of them young men who had worn the white "O'Connell" top hat with a jaunty tilt, recognized badge of the radical, were publicly hanged by the authorities. Sixty or 70 more were banished, and Montreal's last sight of the Rebellion was a chain gang of forlorn prisoners being marched down to the Bonsecours landing stage, there to embark on their long journey to New South Wales or Tasmania.

The sentences may seem harsh, but despite its new metropolitan status, Montreal was still a frontier town, and magistrates felt obliged to judge stiffly. In 1817, the crimes

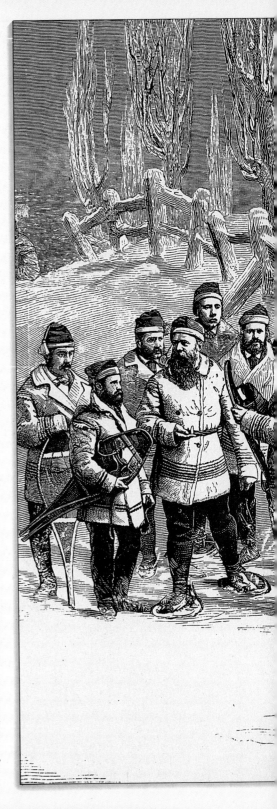

The men's snowshoe club turned essential winter footwear into an excuse for social activity.

of sacrilege and shoplifting were still punishable by execution, as was the even more serious crime of horse-stealing. Petty crimes were typically punished with humiliation in the stocks or the pillory, but judges were also in the habit of having small-time criminals branded on the palm of the hand with a heated iron. The brand, in the shape of a crown, was held to the flesh for as long as it took the convicted criminal to repeat "*Vive le roi!*" three times. It was more likely to be "God save the King!" however, since the session lists from these times show that the vast majority of tried criminals in Montreal were British or itinerant Loyalist Americans,

and not francophone Québécois.

Britain's reaction to the trouble in the colonies was to dispatch the Earl of Durham to survey the state of public affairs there. Lord Durham's famous *Report on the Affairs of British North America* was the first document to isolate French-English tensions as a source of political worry in Canada. In 1841, partly as a result of Durham's suggestions, the provinces of Upper and Lower Canada (today Ontario and Quebec) were joined in an Act of Union that was the beginning of modern Canada. In 1843 Montreal was made capital of the new united Province of Canada, but enjoyed that honor for all too short a time: only five years.

In 1848, while revolution was sweeping Europe, the reactionary element of Montreal sacked the Parliament Building and burned it to the ground after the legislators approved a bill to pay reparations to *Patriotes* punished in 1837. The members of the house fled in alarm, leaving the building to be destroyed. The vandals, carrying the Speaker's ceremonial mace, ran through the streets and attacked the residences of the parliamentarians, including that of the governor-general, Lord Elgin.

After this debacle, the Canadian parliament was moved to Toronto and alternated between there and Quebec until a permanent site was chosen in Ottawa, on the banks of the Ottawa River. A Boston newspaper gave a gloomy picture of the city in the 1840s: "Montreal wears a dismal aspect… the removal of the seat of government caused some 4,000 inhabitants to leave… every third store seems to want an occupant and empty houses groan for tenants." If that weren't enough, typhus brought to the city's harbor in 1847 killed more than 6,000 people; the Great Fire of 1852 – only the worst in a long series – lasted for 26 days, destroying 1,200 buildings and leaving 9,000 people homeless.

Despite these setbacks, Montreal was well on its way to becoming what one contemporary called "the first city in magnitude and commerical importance in British America." The fur trade was waning, but the enterprising rich of Montreal had diversified and Molson's steamship line was doing a good trade between Montreal and Quebec. A guidebook of the time also recommended the city's brisk weather. "The climate," it said, "though severe in winter, is exceedingly conducive to health and longevity and the average mortality is much less than many other cities in North America."

The old harbor had been renovated by energetic young builders, including Englishman John Ostwell, who, at the age of 19, designed the new Customs House. The new Bank of Montreal building was erected in Place d'Armes by the Scot David Rhind, who based it on Edinburgh's grand Bank of

Scotland building. The railways came to Montreal in 1853 when the Grand Trunk Railway Co. began service to Portland, Maine, following it with a line to the still provincial city of Toronto in 1856.

A final event symbolizes this era of expansion and commerical vigor, when Montreal was the New York of Canada, its St James Street as important as Wall Street. In 1860, Albert, the 19-year-old Prince of Wales (later King Edward VII), opened the magnificent Victoria Bridge.

The stage was now set for Montreal to assume primacy of place in the new confederated Canada. In the 1860s, as suggested the prospects for a united Atlantic Colony. The leaders of Upper and Lower Canada, hearing of the conference to which they had not been invited, decided to crash the party and plead their own case. At the head of this group was John A. Macdonald, the wily, alcoholic Scotsman destined to be Canada's first prime minister, whose slightly irresolute portrait now adorns Canada's $10 bill.

Macdonald and his cohorts chartered the *Queen Victoria* in Quebec City, loaded her with $13,000 worth of champagne, and steamed down the St Lawrence to Prince Edward Island. Despite a very modest reception – a single oyster boat – Macdonald was

earlier, the American Civil War and Fenian aggression reached the minds of Montrealers. Blacks fleeing slavery were now to be seen on the city streets, and a defeated Jefferson Davis sheltered for a time in a house on Mountain Street. Fear of growing American influence made confederation a popular notion among Montrealers.

In 1867, representatives of the Atlantic colonies decided to meet in Charlottetown, capital of Prince Edward Island, to discuss

Left, watching the ice break up on the St Lawrence. **Above,** the leisured classes soon created parks.

able, with the aid of his precious cargo, to persuade the Atlantic colonists that Canada should be part of any union. The rough terms for confederation were agreed upon at what one disgusted New Brunswick editorialist called "the great intercolonial drunk." They were later ratified at a conference in Quebec and on July 1, 1867, the British North America Act created modern Canada by joining Nova Scotia, New Brunswick, Ontario and Quebec.

The new country was embroiled in scandal almost from the beginning. MacDonald quickly became involved in the Métis Rebellion scandal, an uprising that occured when the government purchased Rupert's Land out west but neglected to take into account the indigenous population living there. The Métis were a mixture of French and Amerindian and their leader, Louis Riel, won the sympathy of many Montrealers. When MacDonald decided to have Riel hanged, he was quoted as saying: "He shall hang though every dog in Quebec should bark in his favor." Riel's death only served to entrench French-English hatred.

In addition, to hasten a rail link to western Canada and the Pacific, Macdonald and his colleague from Lower Canada, Georges-

today it houses the Neurological Institute of the Royal Victoria Hospital.

With the CPR deal cut, Macdonald's ailing campaign was bolstered by "anonymous" gifts of money, first $60,000 and then $35,000. His campaign in its final days, Macdonald foolishly wired Sir Hugh for more: "I must have another ten thousand. Will be the last time of calling. Do not fail me." Sir Hugh considered the political financing simple good business, but the public did not see it that way. His solicitor's Montreal office was ransacked late one night by a confidential clerk and the incriminating telegram appeared on the front page of Mon-

Etienne Cartier, had accepted party contributions from a group of Montreal businessmen who wanted the contract to build it. The Canadian Pacific Railway (CPR) Bill was passed by Parliament in 1870 but the backroom dealing reached public attention soon after. Focus of the scandal was Sir Hugh Allan, a prosperous Montreal shipper frequently to be seen walking the streets in a tartan waistcoat, his bushy beard well-groomed, or surveying the grounds of his massive estate, Ravenscrag. The estate's mansion, a self-congratulatory tribute to Canada's then richest man, is still standing;

treal's newspapers. Macdonald and Cartier had to resign, and a despairing Cartier died the following year. Macdonald, a more accomplished political survivor, outlasted the public's short memory for wrong-doing and was back in office in 1878.

The railway was delayed, but not stopped. On June 28, 1886, with bands playing, the first passenger train steamed out of Montreal's old Dalhousie Station, bound for Port Moody, British Columbia.

St Jean-Baptiste Day celebrations. June 25 has always embodied a marked French nationalism.

GAMES FOR IDLE HOURS

Most people today, faced with so many leisure pursuits, can scarcely imagine a time when no organized recreation existed. Yet such was the case for the first French Canadians who, especially during the long winter months, had, to put it plainly, time on their hands. They talked away the evenings, of course, played cards, and sometimes held dances; but a common amusement, which now all but died out in North America and Europe, consisted of parlor games.

Folklorist Maurice Tremblay has recorded several Québécois parlor games, decendants of colonial French Canada's indoor recreation. He divides these games into two categories: games that test strength and skill; and games that fool or mystify one of the players.

Because the games stem from the experiences of a predominantly Catholic and agricultural society, they can tell us much about early Québécois rural life. Many of the games draw on physical endurance, emphasize a battle of wills, and incorporate the imagery of farming. Others (such as "The Last Judgement") poke fun at the church and are a kind of risqué satirizing of popular religious myths. While some of the games are moderately indecent and others are downright crude (such as "Breaking Wind"), all combined a sense of mischievous fun and high spirits.

The games probably also functioned as important social tools since they taught a kind of practical folk-wisdom to each participant: recognition of one's limitations, humility, a sense of humor, determination, endurance, and good-natured competitiveness. As Tremblay writes of these intriguing parlor games, just as "peasant wisdom encourages ambition and appreciates real worth, it endeavors on the other hand to teach humility in success, a knowledge of one's shortcomings, and the acceptance, with equanimity, of the vexations as well as the joys of life."

Below is a sampling of how many of Montreal's first *habitants* "bided their time" through indoor frolics. Most of the games listed are mens' activities, although some (like "Asking Favors of the Holy Virgin") have special roles for women.

Games of Strength and Skill

Smacking Bottoms: Two players sit on the floor, the feet of one between the legs of another, each holding a towel in his right hand. While one rolls on his back the other slaps him on the buttocks with the towel. The players take turns until one cries out for mercy.

Kissing the Thumb: A player hangs himself by the arm to a pipe in the ceiling or beam; he then must raise his body to kiss his thumb.

Loading the Sheep: A player lying on the floor makes himself go limp as if dead; a second player tries to lift him onto his shoulder.

Threading a Needle Sitting on a Bottle: A bottle is laid on its side and a player sits on it cross-legged. The player must then thread a needle while trying to keep the bottle from rolling.

Duelling Forks: The feet of two players are tied together; then their hands are tied together under their thighs. Both hold forks between their hands and try to prick each other's buttocks. This goes on until one gives up.

Pulling the Stick: Two players, sitting facing each other on the floor with the soles of their feet together, grasp a broom horizontally. Each pulls the broom towards him until the stronger pulls the weaker up off the floor.

Games of Mystification

Asking for Favors from the Holy Virgin: A woman puts a veil over her hair and sits on a chair, playing the role of the Holy Virgin. Other players bring her someone who wants to ask her for a favor. After listening to the request, the Holy Virgin makes the applicant come close to her and sprays him or her with water, previously held in her mouth.

The Last Judgement: A table is set in the middle of a room and covered with a large rug, one corner of which falls to the floor. Another rug is placed on the floor facing the judge, but with one end of it extending under the table. One player is the judge and sits on a chair behind the table. Another player hides beneath the table, and is hidden from view. The people to be judged are kept in a separate room and are brought in one by one. After being questioned, each one is condemned to hell and the player hiding underneath the table pulls the rug from under the condemned. Surprized (and hopefully frightened), the condemned person falls to the ground.

Nursing the Sick: The person playing the doctor is sent out of the room. He is then called in to nurse a sick child but is given a spoon whose handle has been previously heated.

Weighing the Bacon: The player to be weighed has a blanket put over his head. While two other players pretend to weigh him by lifting him under the arms, a fourth player places a basin under the one being weighed and they let him fall into it.

Breaking Wind: Two men lie down with the head of one near the feet of another. One man places his seat against the other who tries to break wind if he can. The game goes on in turns.

Shooting the Rapids: Several people sit astride a long bench. The first player grips the ends of the bench while the others cross their hands over the eyes of the person in front. The game is supposed to consist of the first player not losing his grip as the others pull him backwards but, unbeknownst to him, the player covering his eyes has had his hands covered with soot which is smeared all over the first player's face.

These were heady times for Montreal. It was now indisputably the center of the unified Canada, a Canada optimistic about its coast-to-coast railroad and its imminent entry into the 20th century. It was also arguably the most beautiful city in the country.

In 1868 an American visitor marvelled at the fine architecture of the town. "I am much struck," he said, "by the continued rapid growth of this now great northern city... The buildings everywhere in course of erection would dignify any city. There are none in the United States which present finer specimens of street architecture than are found, not isolated here and there, but in long blocks and throughout the city."

The newly developed harbor was one place where this excellent aspect was visible, with a terrace of newly erected buildings in the then popular neo-classical style. Wealthy merchants from the old town moved their premises to larger lots on Ste-Catherine and Sherbrooke Streets. In 1891 Henry Morgan, a dry goods merchant, opened Canada's first department store, the Colonial House – a four-storey effort later taken over by the rapacious Hudson's Bay Company.

Morgan's colleague Henry Birk has lived on, however; the jewelry store he moved uptown in 1894 was just the first of a fine chain now extending across the country. Other temples of trade and travel followed, among them the Canadian Pacific Railway's new Windsor Station. As its colorful president, William Van Horne, insisted during the 1880s: "Beats All Creation, the New CPR Station."

But the glow of these golden years was dimmed by social inequality and industrial hardship. Montreal contended with several desperate, disease-ridden slums. Point St Charles was the largest of these, a jumble of houses and shacks that sheltered the workers

from Robert Griffin's soap factory and so known locally as Griffintown, a name it retained well into the 20th century.

Immigration was, from the late 19th century on, Montreal's combined blessing and curse. The cheap source of labor immigrants provided for booming industry (now including huge grain elevators on the waterfront and heavier shipping) was welcome; but the population explosion posed serious difficulties for Montreal's housing and sanitation

resources. In 1825 the population of Montreal had been just 26,000; by 1850 it had doubled. By 1865, it had doubled again and the city passed the 100,000 mark.

By 1910, Montreal's population was more than 500,000 and growing fast. The lot of many people was unremittingly hard: dirty, back-breaking factory work, tiny shacks to live in, and the constant threat of deadly epidemics.

The new Montrealers came from everywhere: from Ireland, fleeing famine, from eastern Europe, from China, from Greece, Italy and Portugal. And they followed the

Preceding pages: the 20th century brought a building boom. **Left**, the ultra-modern BNP building. **Above**, the Olympic Park Tower.

pattern then being established in cities all over North America. While the older inhabitants moved farther and farther from harbor and train station – in the case of Montreal, farther up the hill – the new Montrealers put down their battered suitcases wherever, and as soon as, they could.

Today one can walk up Boulevard St Laurent, the fabled "Main" of Montreal, and map the ethnic neighborhoods with ease: a kind of striatic record of Montreal's immigration waves, with the Chinese on La Gauchetière, the European Jews near St-Urbain, the Greeks along Avenue Park. Here, along with some of the best restaurants

Canadian and the Mount Royal, and moved around Canada's business counters from inside buildings that rose higher and higher from the downtown streets.

Few bothered to learn French as their grandfathers had, and the gap between rich and poor, English and French, widened. The French still played the dominant role in Montreal's daily life, but the English minority controlled a slice of the city economy disproportionate to its size.

The animosity between French and English Montreal, an increasingly serious problem since at least the 1837 Rebellion, was exacerbated by the conscription controversy

in the city, you can find people sitting on their terraces and balconies, retaining traditions from the turn of the century.

With this new diversification of Montreal, the old moneyed families began increasingly to shut their doors. In the 1890s Montreal was known as "the city of merchant princes," but the princes were haughty. No longer did the aristocrats of Montreal walk the streets like James McGill, or even the garrulous Sir Hugh Allan, had done in a simpler era. Instead they stayed inside the walls of their Westmount estates, found others like themselves in exclusive new men's clubs like the

of World War I. The Québécois men of Montreal had no quarrel with Britain's enemies, and many objected to being forcibly enlisted in the war effort. These so-called "zombies" became the scourge of Canada, villified in the national press and publicly accused of cowardice.

Not surprisingly, following the period of economic depression that affected Montreal no less than anywhere else, the same issue arose during World War II. Whereas the war seemed to offer many English Canadians relief – and a job – after the depression of 1929–38, the Québécois perceived themselves as once more bullied by imperial aggression overseas. The premier, Maurice Duplessis, spoke for many when he argued that the federal government did not speak for French Canadians.

There was no easy solution; jailing objectors was one option, but it risked creating martyrs. The federal government's inability to meet this crisis with effective measures became a sign of its ongoing problem with separatist sentiments among the Québécois.

The early English governors of Lower Canada had not seen fit to face the French fact squarely; now the easy mix of French and English that marked Montreal's early

Moreover, by the 1950s, Montreal was no longer riding the wave of industrial and commercial success that marked its entry into the new century. Canada's focus was shifting away from the river ports and toward the Great Lakes, especially Toronto. The strong axis that had existed between Montreal and New York – since John Jacob Astor had entered the fur trade in the 1820s by wooing ambitious Montrealers away from the Hudson's Bay and North-West companies – began to shift as well.

No longer did the wealthy of Montreal hire New York's celebrated architects to construct their massive monuments to them-

history, and that of Quebec more generally, was no longer available. Economic disparity, the sense that control rested with a few privileged Westmount families, and the reality of Canada's growing anglophone population all contributed to the feeling among French-speaking Canadians that they were second-class citizens, a nuisance, and in danger of being assimilated forever.

Left, Prime Minister MacKenzie King, center, with wartime leaders Franklin D. Roosevelt and Sir Winston Churchill. Above, Pierre Trudeau (left in picture) brought style to government.

selves. Montreal was still a desirable place for a patrician New Yorker to visit, but now on pleasure jaunts rather than on business. The sidewalk cafés and brasseries of Paris could be found here now, populated by black-clad existentialists puffing on Gitanes and looking as though the weight of angst was just too, too much. But if the high-rollers from New York wanted to talk turkey, they straightened their cravats and headed for dour, provincial Toronto and the gleaming towers of Bay Street.

So, like all Quebec, Montreal was in some disarray in the post-war period. In the 1950s and '60s the so-called "Quiet Revolution" (*see page 76*) transformed the massive, mostly rural province from an almost feudal Catholic society into a confused 20th-century democracy. Change, once slow to arrive, now worked its double-edged magic.

The church, no longer able to exert extensive daily control, retreated in sulky seclusion. The descendants of Quebec's *habitants* were radicalized, and radicalized themselves. Montreal and Quebec city, site of the provincial government, became hotbeds of intellectual activity as the thinkers of Quebec society tried to find their footing in the shifting international terrain. Separatism fo-

mented in the seminar rooms of Université Laval and Université de Montréal, and then in the cafés of Grand Allée and Rue Ste-Catherine. The prevailing feeling was simply that Quebec was culturally French, and always had been. Why were the people of Quebec enduring a federalist government policy that failed to protect the uniqueness of that culture and forced them, in effect, to become English?

Ottawa was conciliatory and threatening by turns, but matters did not come to a head until October 5, 1970 when the *Front de Liberation du Québec* (FLQ) captured the British trade commissioner, James Cross. Five days later the FLQ kidnapped the Quebec labor minister, Pierre Laporte, whose brutally strangled body was found in the trunk of a car two weeks later. These acts of terrorism followed an extensive FLQ letter-bombing campaign, and frequent calls for "Independence or Death!"

The Prime Minister, Pierre Trudeau, himself a Québécois and product of Laval's radical law faculty, invoked the War Measures Act (Canada's equivalent of martial law) for the first time during peace in this "October Crisis." The revolution, expected daily by the students on Montreal's streets, never came; instead came the soldiers – 10,000 of them, ordered into Montreal on October 16.

But separatism was not quelled. The Parti Québécois (PQ), formed in 1968 by the dynamic René Lévesque, gained power in Quebec on November 15, 1976 and worked to bring the matter to a vote. The PQ's 1979 referendum on "sovereignty-association" failed with the voters, but succeeded in driving many of the strong English minority from Montreal, where they had clustered for 300 years. Businesses quietly left Montreal during the 1970s and '80s, setting up shop in Toronto instead, thus sealing Montreal's commercial fate. Between 1976 and 1981, an estimated 100 head offices left Montreal, taking about 14,000 jobs with them. If Montreal business had been sputtering in the '50s and '60s, it was now in a tailspin.

The separatism issue brought Montreal and Quebec generally to the attention of the world. When, in 1967, General Charles de Gaulle stood on the steps of Montreal's City Hall and cried *"Vive le Québec libre!"* it was a slogan heard not only from coast to coast in Canada, but around the globe.

Yet other features of the city to achieve world fame have been less polemical. In 1967, to coincide with Canada's centennial celebration, the World's Fair was held in Montreal, mainly on Île St-Hélène and Île Notre-Dame. Expo '67 brought millions of visitors, foreign and domestic, to Canada's most culturally diverse (if no longer most powerful) city. Aggressive politicking on the part of Montreal's legendary mayor, Jean

Drapeau – the Huey Long of Canadian municipal politics – brought the city the Summer Olympics of 1976.

After the disaster of Munich in 1972, when terrorists slaughtered members of the Israeli team, the Montreal Games were a massive success. And most of the Olympic visitors cared little not only that the city had overspent vastly on the facilities, but also that the Oympic Stadium is still unfinished according to the original plans (though now modified and home to Montreal's major-league baseball franchise, the Expos).

With the defeat of the Parti Québécois in the 1980s, Quebec's political focus shifted

have been seized, Harris tweed imports have been stopped until a French translation was supplied, and people's windows may be broken if they use "Wet Paint" signs.

So the future of the city of mountain and river is unclear. Can it become a financial and manufacturing capital once more, challenging the dominance of Toronto? Or will it remain a cultural museum, surviving on service industry and the tourist trade? Will English Canadians feel drawn to live here once more, or will Montreal become a French-speaking enclave that treats English-speaking visitors with the disdain of Parisian waiters? Will separatism resurge and undo

away from strong separatism to a more demanding participation in Canadian confederation. The 1988 Meech Lake constitutional accord guaranteed Quebec's right to "a separate and distinct culture" – its failure to be ratified in 1990 revived hostility between French and English Canadians.

Under Quebec's restrictive language laws, known as Bill 101, merchants are no longer allowed to display English signs in their windows. Unilingual doughnut bags

Left, the old-style Windsor Station. **Above**, the new-style Mercantile Bank Building.

Canada's confederation?

One tentative answer is visible daily. Quebec's license-plates bear the province's aggressive slogan: "*Je me souviens*" – and what they remember specifically is the 1763 conquest by the English. Quebec is a place where, perhaps more than anywhere else in Canada, people do remember: ancient grievances and defeats, old victories and ambitions. Whatever shape Montreal's future takes, it will be a future deeply tinged by history, the old scars, long-standing hates, and the force of 400 years spent between river and mountain.

THE QUIET REVOLUTION

Despite its many historic sites, Montreal will strike the visitor of today as a quintessentially modern place, a city of glass towers, busy streets, and cosmopolitan population. It was not always so. In the years immediately following World War II, when most of North America was chugging happily towards the Space Age, the province of Quebec still resembled something like a medieval society. Montreal, its urban jewel, was run like an isolated city-state. Church interests dictated public policy from backrooms, political corruption was rife, and the people lived in ignorance of a wider world.

The events that changed the face of modern Quebec, and made Montreal's reputation as Canada's most interesting city, are called in Canada "the Quiet Revolution" – an appropriate label in a country with little history of civil violence. Quebec's revolution *was* quiet, but it changed the province in profound ways. If in today's Montreal you notice keen political debate in the newspapers and cafés, people taking advantage of the city's cultural opportunities, remember that it was not always possible. If you notice, less charmingly perhaps, fewer black cassocks on the streets and more churches sinking into disrepair – this, too, is the legacy of Quebec's social revolution.

Change, when it came, was swift. Quebec moved wholesale into the 20th century in just a few years (roughly 1960–65), with a handful of journalists, intellectuals and disaffected workers challenging the stagnation of the *ancien régime* with articles, debates and labor action. And what was the focus of these quiet revolutionaries of Quebec? The answer is not surprising. Reformist feeling on the streets of Montreal, as on the streets of Paris two centuries earlier, focused on two targets: church and state.

The Roman Catholic church, long a powerful force among Montreal's French Canadians and Irish, had found new strength in the mid-century influx of eastern European immigrants. It continued to play a role in Quebec life not significantly different from days in the 18th century, when prelates banned card-playing and sacrilege was a capital crime. Rural and small-town inhabitants of Quebec lived in grinding poverty, deferring to the wisdom of parish priests and corrupt politicians, looking on Montreal and Quebec City as though they were foreign capitals instead of their own cities.

The Church did little in those post-war years to dispel the ignorance and backwardness that held most of Quebec in thrall. The province's parish priests controlled most aspects of daily life, ruling rural Québécois with a combination of moral terrorism and personal authority.

Rebellious parishioners, even schoolchildren remiss in their catechism, were likely to be isolated and accused during Sunday sermons. Also, many of the province's most corrupt politicians learned their politics, as well as their theology, at the hands of Catholic educators, and were schooled early in the practice of annexing the moral high ground in debates on social policy.

Until the 1960s, political control of Quebec was lodged firmly in the hands of premier Maurice Duplessis (1890–1959) and his Union Nationale party. With a stranglehold on the provincial parliament – known as the National Assembly – Duplessis and his cronies were able to barter public works for votes, sell liquor and building licenses for huge profits, and stretch their political tenure into a graft-ridden 16-year dynasty.

Duplessis had first been elected in 1937 and had guided disgruntled Québécois through the conscription crisis of World War II, articulating the isolationist stance most Québécois found persuasive. But from 1944 to 1960 the Union Nationale enjoyed absolute power in Quebec, and as a result allowed themselves the luxury of absolute corruption.

A royal commission investigating the Union Nationale in 1961 estimated that more than $100 million worth of graft had been paid out to companies doing business with the provincial government in these years. The going rate for Montreal liquor licenses (later to be had for about $100) was $30,000. Duplessis, a hysterical anti-communist, busted strikes with glee, enjoyed publicly humiliating his own ministers, and taunted his hapless opponents who could not promise the roads and hospitals he traded for votes.

Through all this, Quebec's powerful English minority remained unmoved; it was the journalist André Laurendeau who first suggested that they were actually supporting Duplessis as the province's *roi nègre*. The complicity of the English economic czars of Montreal suggested to Laurendeau, and to many others since, that Duplessis was a puppet – a "black king" allowed to rule a profitable colony by imperial interests jealous of their investments. While Duplessis was denouncing English businessmen in public, his tyrannical government was providing them with a very stable investment environment.

meshed with new liberal feeling that found the moral totalitarianism of the Church outmoded and offensive. And the casual nexus between church and state was one of the first targets of the newly radicalized thinking, ending an era in which the parish priest would inform his parishoners of the "morally right choice" – the Union Nationale candidate – in provincial elections. Economic changes were also underway, and as Quebec's abundant natural resources (hydro-electric power, uranium, timber) became more valuable than ever in world markets the Québécois began to experience fledging fortune.

The nation, too, was changing. In 1965, to signal that the country had broken its firm ties with the British Empire tradition, the old Canadian flag,

Still, the voters of Quebec have their own complicity to answer for; Duplessis did not stay in power because of the tacit approval of a few dozen powerful Montreal anglos. René Lévesque, who served in the Liberal government that finally overthrew the Union Nationale after Duplessis's death, called his reign *la grande noirceur* (the great darkness) and said Quebec had been "cursed" and "damned" by the dictatorial premier's tenure.

Duplessis's death in 1959 proved a catalyst for change beyond the walls of the provincial parliament. Rural Québécois discovered that ignorance and poverty were not divinely-ordained conditions. The resentment building against the Duplessis government, in the universities and elsewhere,

Left, jazz in St-Denis. **Above**, Human Steps typify the modern dance style.

modeled on the Union Jack, was replaced by the Maple Leaf Flag.

By the late 1960s, the new political feeling had gelled into strong Quebec separatism, the Church was either retreating into sullen isolationism or embracing the reforms of Vatican II, and the people of Quebec were enjoying a level of economic prosperity unimaginable a decade before. As befits a *quiet* revolution – there were no barricades, no storming of prisons, no guillotine – Montreal today shows few signs of massive social change. But, seen in religious, political and economic terms, the revolution in Quebec's daily life was real enough: *le roi nègre* was dead. The *joi de vivre* that many Montrealers experience and express today has its roots in this "quiet" death of a quasi-theocracy that has dominated their culture for close to three centuries.

Who lives in Montreal? Well, the city has more than its fair share of luminaries. Anybody who's anybody in French Canadian politics and culture can be found here. Not, perhaps, in the phone book, but at the theaters and cinemas, the chic St-Denis eateries and late-night cafés.

Pierre Trudeau sightings are a popular topic of conversation. The former prime minister, still suave and commanding in his seventies, is a famous downtown dweller. The streets of Outremont, an exclusive inner-city neighborhood, are packed with present and past political figures whom most Canadians would recognize, if not exactly remember.

The French Canadian entertainment industry is also firmly ensconced in Montreal. Television and film stars frequent the restaurants around the Canadian Broadcasting Corporation (CBC) headquarters in the east end, while the more famous, such as comedian Michel Coté and director Denys Arcand, choose cafés nearer their residences. Rock stars Misou Misou and Robert Charlebois, beloved athletes Maurice "Rocket" Richard and Jean Beliveau, plus the central figures in the Quebec literary scene, Michel Tremblay, Yves Beauchemin and Réjean Ducharme all call Montreal their home. Those well-known French Canadians who *don't* live in the city are, more often than not, residents of the "other" center of French culture – Paris, France.

The English community, though much smaller, also boasts a few notables. Poet and songwriter Leonard Cohen is associated indelibly with the "Plateau" neighborhood, while novelist Mordecai Richler has immortalized the former Jewish area along Rue St-Urbain. Aspiring federal Liberal Party leader Paul Martin is also a Montrealer. Likewise the tycoon business family the Bronfmans. Other minority communities in the city, including Asian, African, European and Caribbean, all claim their own rich and famous, all have their venues in which to see and be seen, their newspapers and magazines where stars rise and fall. Montreal is not only a large center but a cosmopolitan one. Diversity is its principal wealth.

Clichés and generalizations only serve to drain vitality from the group being portrayed. In fact, the city is so diverse that finding the "ordinary" Montrealer could be difficult. It is not always possible to say

where he or she eats, or even shops. The "average" Montrealer doesn't exist, because this is a city of 3 million exceptions. Nevertheless, one can venture a few observations about the urban resident. People, after all, *are* Montreal. Buildings and landmarks are mere markers of the will and personality of a population.

French-style: Our fictional but typical French Montrealer is named Madeline. She lives with her husband in a condominium one street east of Outremont. The apartment is a second-storey walk-up with the standard exterior staircase. The building, located so

Preceding pages: young Montreal. Left, a ride at La Ronde. Above, taking it easy.

near the classy neighborhood, was recently renovated; prices went up, poorer people moved out, and Madeline moved in. Buying a condominium makes sense in Montreal, a city where nearly 40 percent of the population live in apartments. Buying an apartment "almost" in Outremont makes dollars and sense; resale value is helped by location. The apartment is, by any standard, spacious; long corridors, high ceilings, with a balcony overlooking the street. The couple, both in their early thirties, are childless. They have space in abundance.

Madeline's husband works near the airport, she in a government office in Old Mon-

eating a muffin and glancing over the entertainment listings in the newspaper. There are literally hundreds of things to do – music, theater, night clubs – but she ends up making a reservation at a restaurant that is favorably reviewed. It is the end of the week. Her husband will be tired; she too wouldn't mind a quiet meal. The restaurant is moderately priced and allows customers to bring their own wine. That is more economical. With the mortgage, taxes, payments on the car...

Because it is Friday – pay day – Madeline and two colleagues have lunch in a restaurant. The waiter, who is an anglophone, addresses them in French, but Madeline of-

treal. He takes the car; she rides the number 80 bus down to Rue St-Antoine. Leaving at eight o'clock, she barely manages a cup of herbal tea and a piece of fruit. While waiting for the bus Madeline buys *La Presse* newspaper, for lighter reading during the ride, but hopes her husband will pick up the more serious *Le Devoir*. In her heart, though, she suspects he will opt for the tabloid *Le Journal de Montréal* – there was a Canadiens hockey game last night, and *Le Journal* has the best sports coverage.

At work, where she is a department supervisor, Madeline spends a 15-minute break

ten answers in English, or English *and* French, just as she and her friends, one of whom is Italian, switch easily from language to language amongst themselves. She orders a salad. What do they talk about? Work. Husbands. The figure skating competitions on television. One colleague, who is reading a Michel Tremblay novel, offers to get tickets for his new play, opening in Montreal next week. They agree in principle to attend a Sunday performance. All three women smoke and order decaffinated coffee.

Later in the afternoon Madeline gets off the bus at Rue Laurier to do some shopping.

She spends 15 minutes in a book shop admiring Milan Kundera's new novel and a collection of Québécois fiction, but decides to just pick up a few magazines for the weekend. Besides, she has work from the office in her briefcase: who has time to read? At the bakery she buys croissants for breakfast and delectable cakes for a late-night snack. At the *Société des Alcools* she lingers over the wines, finally selecting a three-year-old Chablis for dinner. A bit of window shopping follows. But it is still too cold, even in April, and she walks quickly home. The car is nowhere to be seen along the street.

Her husband returns shortly afterwards

Later that evening they eat the cakes and sip cognac while watching the last 20 minutes of the CBC news. Then they go to bed, too tired to watch the video.

English-style: Our English Montrealer is named John. He is a bachelor who lives in NDG (Notre Dame de Grâce), a predominantly English-speaking neighborhood north of Westmount. His apartment is a "3½," meaning one bedroom with a kitchen and living room, and is rent-controlled – the only reason he still lives there. John drives a five-year-old Honda that he finally paid off six months ago, exactly two weeks before a garage bill left him $600 poorer. The com-

with a *Le Journal* rolled under his arm. Traffic on the Metropolitan was even worse than usual, he complains, and he stopped to rent a video – *Batman*, dubbed into French – for midnight viewing. After changing, chatting with Madeline's mother on the phone – her parents live in Chicoutimi, where she grew up – the couple slip the wine into a paper bag and recheck the address of the restaurant. Her husband, on learning that the cuisine is a mix of Thai and Chinese, hopes it won't be too spicy.

mute from NDG to the Sherbrooke architectural firm where he works is 15 minutes, traffic permitting. This morning the traffic does not permit, however, and he arrives at the office a little late.

The firm is composed of French and English speakers. Fifteen years ago, when John first started working there, most business was conducted in English; today, French predominates. John, who was raised in Westmount and NDG, is fluent, though some of the older anglophone employees speak French only haltingly.

At lunch John hops onto a subway and

Left, playing in the park. **Above**, two's company…

rides to Place des Arts. He hopes to buy tickets for that night's concert at The Spectrum, but arrives to find that it is sold out. Instead he picks up *The Gazette* and spends his hour in the record shops along Rue Ste-Catherine. He buys two CDs for his system and a cassette for the car stereo. Montreal is a great city for music. Listings for the weekend alone include classical concerts, jazz in bars, lots of rock bands, a Senegalese singer at Concordia University, and a group of Pakistani musicians in a converted church in Côté-St-Luc. The previous December the Rolling Stones played at Olympic Stadium.

Back at the office he returns a phone call from his friend Marc, a francophone friend from his McGill University days nearly 20 years before. Most of his friends are anglophones. Though a few have left Montreal – including his parents, who were relocated to Toronto in 1978 – most continue to live in Westmount, NDG, or Pointe Claire, and continue to work for downtown firms and companies. At parties his friends often talk about the political situation and about moving away, but only rarely do they turn their words into action and uproot themselves. Montreal is, after all, their home.

Marc has great news: tickets for the Canadiens game the next night. It is April, and April in Montreal means hockey playoffs. Tickets for playoff games are impossible to get without connections. How did Marc manage it? John doesn't ask.

To celebrate he invites his friend to dinner. They meet at seven o'clock to enjoy a fiery Indian meal at a tiny restaurant off Rue Queen-Mary. The restaurant owner conducts business in English, which Marc speaks flawlessly. Afterwards the two men go for a few beers in an old college haunt near U de M (Université de Montréal). John orders and begins to tell his friend about work, a woman friend, his plans to buy a fancy new car. The band, a horn-driven R&B ensemble, is from Toronto. They are well worth the cover-charge.

Different worlds? Hardly. Same city? Clearly. The city can be "home" to anyone. Anyone can, likewise, call it home.

Left, acquiring the right image.

It's difficult to find a level shelf in Nat Levine's grocery shop on Rue St-Viateur. Cans lean at odd angles, boxes waver and teeter. But if you're looking for a second-hand kettle or a pair of old boots, Nat's the person to see. Walk past the old-fashioned scale, past the bins of vegetables and fruits. Worn paperbacks and salvaged toasters jostle for shelf space in a dusty, cluttered corner. Paintings hang on the wall, crooked and unframed, and very affordable.

At one time, Nat's shop was down the street, on the corner of Jeanne Mance, just east of Avenue Park, across from the bagel shop warmed by the wood-burning oven and from the kosher butcher where Hassidic Jews carefully eye cuts of meat. A popular Greek restaurant expanded, and Nat was forced to move. But he still provides home delivery – free of charge – to long-time customers such as the elderly woman on Hutchison Street who phones in her order, being too frail to make the trip.

When Levine's grocery first opened for business almost 50 years ago, most of Montreal's Jews could have strolled to the shop in minutes. They lived around the Main, or Boulevard St-Laurent, a Yiddish-speaking world framed by French street names like Cadieux, Esplanade, and Marie-Anne.

Multilingual mix: Today, the city's Jewish community is no longer shaped by the alleys and winding staircases of one neighborhood, but by the textures of many. Yiddish swirls along the streets of French-speaking Outremont as Hassidim prepare for Friday night services. Elderly Jews shuffle through the streets of Côte-des-Neiges and Snowdon, stopping to catch their breath or exchange gossip. Their bilingual grandchildren (that's English and *French*, not Yiddish) play in distant, grassy suburbs like Dollard des Ormeaux.

And still they come back to the old neighborhood, the Main, the children of par-

Left, catering for a demanding community which values its traditional cuisine.

ents from Poland, Hungary, Lithuania. Their children, too, make a modern-day pilgrimage to the street described as "the funnel through which repeated waves of Jewish immigrants entered Montreal." Tucked between the fashionable boutiques and trendy cafés on the Main are bits and pieces of the old community, scattered fragments along St-Laurent.

The old community is there as you step onto the wooden floor at Schreter's dry goods store: walls clothed with suits and sweatshirts, shorts and shoes. Once there, it's only a few blocks south to Schwartz's deli: open the door and walk through a curtain of smoked meat that local gourmets claim is second to none. ("When I die," a framed tribute proclaims, "I want to go to Schwartz's.") And catering to those Jews who prefer a slice of heaven is Berson's monuments just across the street. Granite tombstones, polished and blank, rest waiting to be carved.

Migrations and exodus: An epigraph for Montreal's Jewish community would be premature. Just under 100,000, the community is alive and well, rooted in a history committed to survival. By standing on the corner of Rues Notre-Dame and St-Jacques, you can hear the echoes of the city's – and country's – first synagogue, which was built in 1777 by the Sephardic community, descendents of the Jews expelled during the Spanish Inquisition.

Geography and history unravel in an inseparable knot. Distant countries have shaped the city's Jewish community. Tensions in Russia altered the face of Montreal, particularly when the assassination of Czar Alexander II in 1881 sparked a series of pogroms, the Russian word for devastation, a synonym for organized massacres. Jews were the targeted scapegoats and Canada was regarded as a hand filled with promise, Montreal being its palm.

The Russian pogroms triggered the first large wave of Yiddish-speaking immigrants. Until then, Montreal's Jewish community was small. In 1847, when Jews numbered less than 200, the first Jewish society was organized to provide relief to the community's poor and needy, particularly the newer immigrants. In the last two decades of the 19th century, some 13,000 Jews arrived in Canada. Owing to the circumstances which forced them to flee, they were aware of the very sense of Jewishness that had cost lives in Russia. Customs and a way of life that existed in the *shtetls* (small Jewish towns) of old Europe were adapted to the streets of Montreal.

Docks to sweatshops: Through the funnel of the Main the wanderers streamed. Poor and

displaced, they relied on mutual aid societies such as the first Hebrew Sick Benefit Society, founded in 1892. The need for financial help and medical benefits was acute. For some, it was a short trip from the docks to the sweatshop. They worked under deplorable conditions in the garment industry, toiling in cramped sweatshops wedged into old buildings, with little air or light. Days were long, wages were low.

One testimony from the period recounts: "One cloakmaker turned his four rooms into a shop and supposedly kept the other three as a home for his wife and seven children. But the shop was all over the place... A woman was making bread on a table, upon which there was a baby's stocking, scraps of cloth, several old tin cans and a small pile of unfinished garments. In the next room was an old woman with a diseased face, walking the floor with a crying child in her arms. Such conditions were typical in all garment centers."

The poor working conditions proved to be fertile turf for Jews in a labor movement committed to social change. Ideologies developed in eastern Europe by such groups as the Bund, a Jewish socialist party founded in Russia in 1897, were renewed in cities like Montreal with the drive to educate and unionize exploited workers. The Workmen's Circle saw itself not just as a mutual benefit society but as part of the larger labor movement which was struggling to end capitalist exploitation.

Sidewalks became stages for social change. Corner stores turned into political arenas. Bookshops were transformed into debating dens. "Elstein's bookshop on Ontario Street was more than a store," reported one account. "It was virtually a club where anyone who read books would meet to argue politics and orientations."

The expanding community: Politics stretched far beyond the Main. Three-quarters of the federal riding of Montreal-Cartier, centered around the Main, was Jewish. (In August 1943 they made history by electing the first communist, Fred Rose, to the House of Commons.)

Amidst the dust of the depression, small cottages sprouted into prayer houses. Hebrew resounded through forgotten lofts and spare rooms in industrial buildings. By 1940, 40 of Montreal's 50 synagogues were located within a mile of each other. Rue St-Urbain alone – immortalized in the novels of Mordecai Richler – had six. Richler writes of the Jewish district, it was "an all but self-contained world made up of five streets; Clark, St-Urbain, Waverley, Esplanade and Jeanne-Mance, bounded by the Main on one side, and Park Avenue on the other... On each corner a cigar store, a grocery, and a fruit man. Outside staircases everywhere. Winding ones, wooden ones, rusty and risky ones. An endless repetition of precious peeling balconies and waste lots making the occasional gap here and there."

Row after row of winding staircases, of cold-water flats, nurtured a generation of Jews who went on to make significant contributions to the arts and sciences in Canada, from poet A. M. Klein to David Lewis, one of Canada's most eloquent politicians, who learned English poring over Dickens. Others have made a quiet difference, like political activist Leah Roback, white-haired and tireless, a "Bread Not Bombs" button pinned to her coat.

As their lot improved, Montreal's Jews

of what has now become a French school.

Time stands still a few blocks away at the Hassidic prayer houses on Jeanne Mance, just round the corner from Nat Levine's grocery shop. But for the small signs outside, they look like any other house on the block. The similarities end at the door. Inside, the rituals of an 18th-century religious philosophy continue.

The everyday world: Daily life for the city's Hassidic community, Canada's largest, is wrapped in Yiddish. Cohesion is one of the distinguishing marks of Hassidism, as is charismatic leadership of the various sects. The *zaddik* (leader) is seen as a healer, con-

moved out of the streets around the Main and into better homes and neighborhoods. A revitalized wartime and postwar economy created what one social critic called "the social and economic conversion of the Jews."

Jews left the old neighborhood and built synagogues in the new ones. Few of the original synagogues around the Main remain. Where there was once a synagogue there is now a church or a parking lot. On Fairmount Avenue, Hebrew letters arch across the sky and disappear into the facade

Left, doing business. **Above**, going shopping.

fessor, moral instructor and practical adviser. Central to Hassidism is a belief that they persist in their devotion to God and should not be distracted by the secular world.

Insular by choice, the Hassidim are an enigma not only to the French Canadians of Outremont, but to the many Jews who are unfamiliar with their ways. The men walk along streets in their *kapotes* (black silk coats) and *spodiks* (fur hats), locks of hair curled around their ears. Women dress discreetly in modest clothing, children in tow.

Hassidism and secularism clashed in 1988 in a zoning dispute that pitted a sect that wanted to build a new synagogue against a town council that balked at making the necessary re-zoning changes. Tensions flared when a newspaper article spoke of the "Jewish Problem" in Outremont. For many of the city's Jews, especially Holocaust survivors, the phrase rekindled memories of Nazi Germany. Others recalled the anti-Semitism of Quebec in the 1930s. Insensitive descriptions about how the Hassidim dressed and fear-baiting references to their growing numbers only made matters worse. Both French and English Montrealers were quick to denounce the paper's careless journalism.

Immersed in their Yiddish world, the Quebec nationalism and the Quiet Revolution in the 1960s: a period in which French Canadians, after enduring centuries of discrimination at the hands of an English minority, began to reclaim their past and their status as a majority.

A shifting political scene: Shifts in the Quebec political scene coincided with changes in the Jewish community. A new wave of Jewish immigrants arrived in Montreal, bypassing the Main. Political instability in North Africa led French-speaking Sephardic Jews to seek a new home. (The majority of Montreal's Sephardic community, now over 20,000, come from Morocco.)

Hassidim are a minority within a minority. More than half of the Jews of Montreal claim English as their mother tongue. The immigrants who arrived in Montreal earlier in the century arrived in a society dominated by an English-speaking minority. By virtue of a provincial school system separated on religious grounds, Jewish children were forced to attend English Protestant schools. The doors to French-language schools were closed to them.

As members of the anglophone minority of Montreal, many Jews found themselves on the wrong side of history during the rise of

Through the Sephardim, some of the city's Jews saw the "French fact" of Quebec. The Sephardic community's desire to preserve their culture and identity mirrored the goals of French nationalists. Yet many Jews found it difficult to adapt to the new politics, particularly the elderly, accustomed to a time when French was not the official language that it is today.

Anglophone Jewish concerns were heightened with the election of the Parti

Watching the parade go by: many Jews still preserve their old traditions.

Québécois (PQ) in 1976, elected on a platform committed to a sovereign Quebec. In the aftermath of the PQ's victory, many of the city's younger Jews left for Toronto. But they still gather at reunions featuring slabs of Montreal's smoked meat, and smuggle bags of bagels to Ontario after periodic trips to their native city.

An aging population: By 1986, over 20 percent of the Jewish community was over 65. Many Jews, particularly women, live below the poverty line. That there is a "Jewish poor" in Montreal would probably come as a surprise not only to those who hang onto caricatures of Jewish wealth, but also to many in the community itself who associate poverty with Jewish life at the turn of the century.

Yet, as in the past, the community has responded. Services have been created to meet the needs of the elderly. Kosher meals are brought to homes where the infirm can't cook for themselves. In the heart of Côte-des-Neiges, a low-income neighborhood where many Jewish elderly still live, Project Genesis provides storefront services to clients flustered by a French document or frightened by a rent increase

The Jewish Immigration Aid Service, created in the wake of World War I, continues to help new arrivals. Auberge Shalom is a shelter for battered women where even the most Orthodox Jewish woman can find refuge, as it is run according to Judaic laws. At the Golden Age Association, stooped seniors move to Tai Chi and sculpt stone.

The Jewish Public Library, now in its 75th year of community service, features exhibitions, films, and concerts that celebrate the city's Jewish heritage and links to Israel. Here, grey-haired men scour Yiddish newspapers next to racks of Hollywood videos.

Preserving language: Across the street, next to the YM-YWHA, Yiddish bounces off the stage at the Saidye Bronfman Center. Dora Wasserman's Yiddish theater group has become an integral piece of the fabric of Jewish Montreal, helping to preserve a dying language. Internationally acclaimed, it performs before thousands of Montrealers annually, including works by Nobel laureate Isaac Bashevis Singer, who once wrote "If the Yiddish language is dying, it should only keep dying for the next thousand years."

In a still room at the Montreal Holocaust Memorial Center, candles cast solemn shadows on a wall inscribed with place names etched in the collective memory of Jews. Founded in 1979, it is Canada's first Jewish historical museum and Holocaust educational center. The museum examines not only the destruction of Jewish life during the Holocaust, but also European Jewry as it existed before Nazism wreaked its havoc. Local Montrealers donated most of the artifacts in the museum.

Between one-fifth and one-fourth of the city's adult Jews are Holocaust survivors. Continuity is an important theme: many Jews preserve and continue their traditions and way of life before and during the Holocaust, and continue to link European Jewry with the community today. A new permanent exhibition, *Splendor and Destruction: Jewish Life that Was, 1919–1945* was one recent effort to maintain this link.

Contemporary Jews: The Jewish life that was in Montreal is no more. But though demographics and the political landscape have changed the complexion of the community, it still has plenty of color and warmth. The city is home to the Canadian Jewish Congress, a Jewish "parliament" that is national in scope. Fluently bilingual Jewish Montrealers sit as city councillors. They are leading academics in universities like McGill University, where they were once restricted. Each year Jews take to the streets in a fund-raising March for Jerusalem. Bonds with Israel are strong, with many projects linking the city to the country. True to a history of diverse opinion, others quietly promote a dialogue with Palestinians.

When two Jews get together, an old joke goes, there are three opinions. What fate awaits the Jews of Montreal? Some speak of the writing on the wall and nervously point to the resurgence of Quebec nationalism. Others are committed to staying, adapting to a new Quebec as they maintain a religion thousands of years older than the city itself.

Meanwhile, back at Levine's grocery store, it's business as usual. Nat takes another order over the telephone.

Politics are politics and people are people. Contrary to popular opinion, the Québécois are not obsessed with the machinations of independence; newspapers refrain from spouting invective against confederation, cafés fail to hatch midnight cabals, and every day is certainly not *jour de la révolution*. Lives may contain a heightened level of consciousness about the structures of government, but lives remain private and voluntary. Politics can be variously a pastime, passion, or obsession; it need never be a birthmark, a chain around the neck. Though tensions surrounding language and culture exist, Montreal is neither Beirut nor Belfast. This is worth remembering.

And the city streets are gouged with potholes. And the highways, designed for carriages, discourage the obedience of laws inadequate to the challenges of surviving the commute home. The St Lawrence River is treated like a sewer, the police department maintain their headquarters in donut shops, and zoning laws permit free-for-alls in neighborhoods whose preservation is in doubt. Montrealers are elected to the municipal government to reform or *not* reform, to overhaul or conserve; and citizens, if they are organized and learn how to frame their demands, can usually affect policy in a desired direction.

These are the issues and players of city politics. The mayor, councilors, citizen's groups, the media, children in primary school who use art class to agitate for pollution control: ordinary people dealing with substantial, concrete issues – homelessness, taxes, recycling facilities – in the hope of improving the quality of life in Montreal. Their voices are modified, in proportion to the scale of both the problems and prosperity endemic to Canadian society.

The same cannot be said for the voices

currently debating the "large" questions that are reverberating throughout the country. For many Canadians, and most outside observers, "politics" in Montreal and Quebec means rampant fratricide and divisions in a nation unable to reconcile its linguistic and cultural duality. Politics means language laws, majority rights, Quebec's meandering toward some form of independence from confederation and shouting matches. Moreover, in the 1990s, in the wake of the

Meech Lake Accord and English-Only Ontario towns, politics means being impatient, ill-tempered and wishing the mess would resolve itself, for better or worse, and leaving people in peace.

How did the situation deteriorate so rapidly? How did the evolution of Quebec suddenly become a source of implosion for the entire country? Answers to these questions are easy; explanations remain elusive.

First, a word about Canada. To describe the nation as "massive" is accurate but inadequate. If anything, Canada is *several* massive countries bookended by oceans to the

Preceding pages: Montreal projects a good-time image. Left, shamrock, fleur-de-lys and British uniforms mingle in a St Patrick's Day parade. Above, putting out the flags.

east and west, a polar cap to the north and the United States to the south. These massive countries, called provinces, are home to strikingly small populations – a total of 25 million – who cluster near the extreme southern borders to benefit from milder weather and warming trade breezes.

The term "country" is not being used too loosely here. In 1867 the architects of Canada's political house proposed a "confederation" of the various regions to defend against American territorial ambitions and strengthen their economic potential. No one envisioned a unified nation-state grounded in ideology and chauvinism. How could they

have? At the time of the pact British Columbia wasn't even accessible to Ottawa by overland transportation. (Nor would it be until the cross-Canada railway was completed in 1881.)

If the 4,000 miles (6,400 km) that separate Montreal from Vancouver seem long in an age of jetliners and fax machines, imagine how long they seemed in 1867. Confederation was an exercise in political moderation. Realism, too. Canada could *not* be like the United States. But it still could function and its individual members, granted considerable autonomy over their affairs, could be at

once self-sustaining *and* loyal to the large "collective."

How does Quebec fit into the picture? Uneasily. It is at once a founding province and a conquered state. Though the conquering pre-dated the confederation by 100 years, the legacy – English domination of commerce, discrimination against the Québécois and their language – built into the infrastructures of business and government, lingered until barely a decade ago.

Quebec joined the confederation in 1867 because it hadn't much choice. It has remained a part of the country for far more diverse reasons. More than any other province, Quebec *is* unto itself; it is psychologically, if not literally, a nation, possibly even a nation in the American model. Those who would deny Quebec's exceptional status – an attitude implicitly dismissive of tremendous cultural and economic achievements – only coarsen the debate. Besides, Canada was designed to accommodate diversity. How much diversity, though, and at what cost to existing structures, was never resolved. Quebec's nationalist aspirations have highlighted this ambiguity in the design.

It should be mentioned that Canada's political system, based on representation by population, heavily favors the country's most populous provinces: Ontario and Quebec. Two-thirds of all voters reside in these two provinces. A federal party cannot win an election without the tacit support of Ontario and the full backing of Quebec, whose voters tend to cast their ballots *en masse*. As a result, most of the Canada's prime ministers have come from the central regions and many of the major leaders have been Québécois. These include the two most recent prime ministers, Pierre Trudeau and Brian Mulroney.

Ironies abound. First, literally speaking, it is not Quebec that suffers from a lack of power and influence. Such a fate belongs to the smaller provinces, especially those in the west. Second, disagreements aside, the English-Canadian political establishment is obliged to pay great attention to Quebec's demands. By voting in one direction and thereby offering a party the guarantee of a full quarter of the seats in the House of

Parliament, the province has become the country's king-maker; governments are elected or rejected and policies – like the recent Free Trade Agreement – are secured or squashed based on the will of the Québécois. In a democracy, this is genuine political power.

Finally, it is worth pointing out that a number of Canada's leading proponents of federalism are themselves French Canadians. Trudeau, Mulroney, and the heir-apparent to the federal Liberal Party, Jean Chrétien, are but a few examples. The ranks are far from closed inside Quebec. There is still plenty of room for alternative voices.

nation of a 20-year "quiet revolution" (*révolution tranquille*), a period of ferment, marked by outrage at paternalistic English control of Montreal business, and by the intellectual and spiritual assertion of Quebec's "self-hood."

Lévesque fired the imagination of French Canadians when he cried: "We are nothing more than an internal colony which lives at the will of another people." The logical next step, argued the Parti Québécois, was independence. *Sovereignty-Association* were the buzz words in those days, an abstract relationship between the new nation of Quebec and Canada that would make for an eco-

Trudeau, Quebec's philosopher-king, tellingly described French Canadians in 1956 as "a people vanquished, occupied, leaderless, kept aside from business life and away from the cities, gradually reduced to a minority role and deprived of influence in a country which, after all, it had discovered and explored, and settled."

Quebec elected its first – and so far only – separatist government in 1976. The Parti Québécois of René Lévesque was the culmi-

nomically painless withdrawal from the bower of federal funding.

In 1980 Lévesque's government held a referendum asking the Québécois to decide the matter. They did; 60 percent voted to remain in Canada. Ironically, the very middle-class the quiet revolution helped to create regarded independence as too extreme, an unnecessarily radical measure to protect their culture and language. The Parti Québécois, deflated by the defeat, failed to win the 1985 election and was replaced by Robert Bourassa's Liberal Party.

The deciding factor in the 1970s inde-

Left, the French have never appreciated English queens. **Above**, Hôtel de Ville.

pendence movement was Pierre Trudeau. As prime minister from 1968 to 1984 (excluding a brief interruption in 1979), Trudeau forged a Canada of his own imagination and intellect. René Lévesque met his equal in this prime minister. For Trudeau, Canada was the sum of its linguistic diversity. He set about recasting confederation through the introduction of a mandatory bilingualism on all levels of the federal government.

Vancouver to Halifax, Windsor to Yellowknife, Trudeau's Canada would be home to both languages, both cultures, a country where tolerance was automatic and, all being equal, no one particular group

needed special protection. Trudeau was determined to twist the arms of Canadians until even a Calgarian who'd never met a French Canadian, or an inner-city Montrealer whose English consisted of pop-song lyrics, would have to acknowledge both the value *and* the necessity of bilingualism. He was also, of course, subtly undermining the Parti Québécois freedom cry.

It worked well, kind of. When Trudeau introduced a Charter of Rights and Freedoms to Canada's patriated constitution in 1981, the charter steadfastly ignored any conciliatory gestures toward Quebec's "two nation"

ideal, and Quebec steadfastly refused to sign the document. Combatants settled into their respective trenches, and for a few years animosities were left to simmer while the inevitable evolutions occurred: Trudeau retired from politics, Lévesque died, and the Conservative government of Brian Mulroney came to power in Ottawa. Those commentators who felt that the withdrawal of Trudeau and Lévesque from the scene would deflate tensions were, unfortunately, proved wrong. When the "Quebec Question" flared again in 1988 it was with a ferocity that took most Canadians by surprise, and which left the country reeling.

The spark was the Meech Lake Accord, the Mulroney government's 1987 attempt at a conciliatory constitutional agreement. The accord, which increased the powers of all the provincial governments in relation to Canada's national capital Ottawa, also included a "distinct society" clause that would allow Quebec to opt out of many federal programs and override any supreme court decisions that threatened its security. Meech Lake argued for a different vision of Canada, and though not especially popular west of Ontario, it appeased Quebec and the federal government, and seemed a reasonable compromise. All of Canada's provincial leaders signed the preliminary agreement.

The fraternity was short-lived. Within a year Quebec's Bourassa government placed the accord in jeopardy by exercising its privilege and overriding a supreme court decision. Why such a grave matter? The controversy was linked to concerns over previous legislation, Bill 101, the polemical 1977 *Charte de la Langue Française* (Charter of the French Language) that gave the French language primacy in Quebec through several stringent measures, including the barring of English-language schools to new immigrants.

There is no question that Bill 101 is unconstitutional under the terms of the BNA Act, since it denies English Quebeckers any right to use English in commercial situations. The law has also been known to produce risible results, with the so-called "tongue troopers" (agents of the *Commission de Surveillance de la Langue Française*) changing long-standing Quebec place names or fining merchants who put English "Merry Christmas" signs in their windows. English Canadians were enraged.

In 1989, Bill 178, Bourassa's replacement law, forbade the use of *any* English on outdoor signs in Quebec, even those that also featured French. The measure was necessary, claimed the government, to preserve the "rights of the majority." English Canadians were, once again, furious.

The result was a backlash against Quebec. Premiers withdrew their support for Meech Lake, jeopardizing ratification. As well, cities and towns in Ontario began to declare

tribalism that displayed with pride a "become like us, or leave" mentality.

The issue has all to do with language. Quebec is a society that thinks, reads, and writes in French. Eighty percent of its citizens subscribe to different magazines and watch different television programs than do the rest of Canadians. Group identity is bound up inherently with language. Defending the language, therefore, through means like Bills 178 and 101 and enforced French education is a defense of identity. Says writer André Belleau: "We do not need to speak French: we need French in order to speak."

themselves "English Only," and the resentment toward both the Quebec sign laws and the Trudeau-sponsored bilingualism intensified. Some people began to question the "two languages" model. Canada, they argued, was a multicultural society, not a bilingual one. Canada was also a society grounded in tolerance, a land of "live and let live." Quebec, on the other hand, was, according to some, becoming more and more an ideological nation-state, an enclave of

Gallic preferences predominate in Atwater market (left), and in all public signs.

"How can English Canadians understand this?" the Québécois argue. Security and power are birthrights for native English speakers. Privileges are assumed. Not so for French Canadians; they are obliged to create their own political, social, even historical space both within the country and the North American continent as a whole. *Je me souviens* (I remember) is the province's elusive motto. Remember what? The answer: who the Québécois were, who they are and who they will be.

How does all this affect Montreal? The city is the heart of Quebec. It is where the major linguistic skirmishes are being fought. Most of these frictions appear silly. Banning bilingual signs, changing street names, the "language police," Parti Québécois youth leagues that comb the city to seek out offending merchants: this kind of behavior flatters no one. Far more encouraging is the level of discourse in the media, where commentators from *Le Devoir*, *La Presse*, *Le Soleil*, and *The Gazette* criticize intransigence on all sides and call for clearer thinking.

In the 1989 elections, the Liberals returned to power, the Parti Québécois was strengthened in opposition, and a new voice emerged – the Equality Party, an anglophone

English or French? According to the Trudeau model for Canada, the choice should be up to the individual; schools, social services, and all government bodies must be available in both official languages. According to the Quebec government, English is a dominating language that devours other cultures; hence the choice has been predetermined: to live in Montreal is to become a French speaker.

These are very distant views. Common ground is, in one sense, becoming harder and harder to find. A third view wonders if linguistic and cultural exclusivity contradicts the very ethnic wealth of Montreal. In these

group that elected four members from predominantly English-speaking Montreal ridings. Although the Equality Party may prove evanescent, its presence in the assembly was seen as a healthy development.

One need only wander Montreal for a few hours to realize that it is an ethnically diverse city. Besides English Canadians, the "allophone" community includes Italians, Greeks, Jews, the Indian subcontinent, the Caribbean and Africa. Each of these communities function first and foremost in their native tongues.

But what will be their second language –

days of dissolving orthodoxies, as seen in Eastern Europe, and emerging polyglots, such as a "United" Europe, when nations are being virtually reinvented by their newest citizens, is the "two solitudes" approach to Canada's problem itself a relic from the past? It seems that, while certain elements of the French and English communities may want their old solitude, it is doubtful that they can have it. Things are changing. And thinking is bound to change too.

Above, bikers cross ethnic and linguistic barriers.
Right, René Lévesque.

Intellectuals Versus Streetfighters

Received wisdom sorts Quebec politicians into two types: the intellectual or the streetfighter. Pierre Elliott Trudeau, ex-professor of jurisprudence from Université Laval and Canada's former Prime Minister, personified the former; his arch-foe René Lévesque, chain-smoking *capo* of the Parti Québécois, typified the latter.

The dichotomy is misleading, obscuring the fact that the two flavors are invariably swirled together in Quebec's political figures. Pragmatic, even Machiavellian, arrogant but charismatic – these are the qualities of Quebec's most talented politicians. But, no matter how able, all have been hamstrung by the issue of language, with its anglophone undercurrents.

Trudeau, Quebec's philosopher-king, staked his political life on constitutional reform and federal bilingualism, but in 1968 his elaborate courting of Ottawa seemed to many Québécois simple collaboration.

Lévesque, a journalist, foreign correspondent and broadcaster, entered the provincial scene as a Liberal MP in 1960 and dramatically fired the imagination of French Canadians when he declaimed: "We are nothing more than an internal colony which lives at the will of another people."

Lévesque emphasized *not* federalism (in which power rests with the national government), but sovereignty-association; *not* bilingualism, but preferential treatment for the Québécois tongue. The hard-talking Lévesque swept into power in 1976 and challenged Trudeau, then Prime Minister, on the destiny of Quebec.

Though separatism is still a live issue in Quebec, the revolutionary fervor of the 1970s is gone, Lévesque is now dead, and the Parti Québécois, which advocated an independent Quebec, is out of power. The most palpable effect of their term is the controversial language law, Bill 101.

The underlying contradiction is rarely examined, however: if French-Canadian language and culture is as vibrant as some claim, why is it necessary to have these extreme measures to en-

sure a hothouse protection? A simple answer: a great deal of the long-standing animosity between the Québécois and their English-speaking conquerors still has to be worked out.

Robert Bourassa, the bureaucratic leader of Quebec's Liberal party, has been hoist several times on the petard of language. Shoved aside by Lévesque's 1979 conquest, Bourassa is now back in power, a long-term survivor. But he is at the mercy of linguistic radicals, and his position on Bill 101 is wishy-washy at best and he has failed to woo back the big business interests that left Quebec during the highly charged PQ reign.

So the Liberals cling to power in Quebec's provincial parliament. At the same time, the federal votes of Quebec, traditionally Liberal even when the province was ruled by the PQ or Maurice Duplessis's iron-fisted Union Nationale party, have swung over to Canada's Progressive Conservative party. An Irish Quebecker from Baie Comeau, Brian Mulroney, elected to a second prime ministerial term in 1988, took the controls in Ottawa, delivering Quebec to the Conservatives like a gift.

Mulroney, like Trudeau, risked being upstaged by his wife. Mila, the immaculately poised daughter of a wealthy Yugoslav-born Montreal psychologist, effortlessly put other political wives in the shade at international shindigs such as the 1991 world economic summit in London. She also had a pronounced liking for shopping and was soon dubbed by some "Imelda the Second". "In Montreal shopkeepers bring her things to see at her hotel," said biographer Claire Hoy. Unlike Margaret Trudeau, however, she did not shrink from making political speeches, and her husband was thought to value her opinion when contemplating cabinet changes.

Mulroney's likely opponent in the next general election is the federal Liberals' heir-apparent Jean Chrétien, an old Trudeau man from Shawinigan, Quebec, whose mangling of the tongue of Louis XIV is legend. Chrétien is also one of the purest examples of the streetfighter strain of Quebec politics. He talks out of the side of his mouth like a self-parodying gangster, and the columnist Peter Newman has described his face as "looking like someone had practised taxidermy on it."

THE LIFE AND TIMES OF PIERRE TRUDEAU

What was it about Pierre Trudeau that fired the enthusiasm of so many Canadians? What did this arrogant, balding law professor from the radical seminar rooms of Quebec tell the nation about themselves? Whatever it was – something about the Canadian ability to be great? – Canadians responded in a way no prime minister before or since has dared to dream of. Trudeau was, if only briefly, a genuine national hero in a country largely without them, a rock star of a politician who made crowds swoon and ran the country on sheer force of personality.

And what a personality it was. Behind the inscrutable mask of the Jesuit-trained intellectual lay a consummate jokester, given to sliding down banisters, playing with yo-yos and frisbees, and keeping the exhausted press corps guessing about his next move.

His wife Margaret ("Maggie"), pictured opposite, was almost 30 years his junior, a former flower child who embarrassed Canadians with her own unplanned exploits: running around in a bathrobe at the Rolling Stones' hotel after a Toronto concert, dancing at Manhattan's Studio 54, giving candid interviews in *People* and *Playgirl*. This was the prime minister's wife? But, despite their oddball aura, Pierre and Maggie proved an irresistible pair for normally cautious Canadian voters. Trudeau was the longest-serving prime minister of this century, and only exited the national political scene on his own terms in 1984: a king taking leave of his subjects.

In many ways, Trudeau reflects the uniqueness of Canada. He was born in 1919 to a Québécois father, Charles-Emile ("Charlie") Trudeau, and a Scottish mother, Grace Elliott. The first Trudeau had come to Canada in 1659, and Charlie was a scion of the family, a shrewd businessman who left all three of his children million-dollar legacies at his death in 1935. Grace was a quiet woman from whom Pierre learned deportment, reticence, and the keen regard for discipline he carried into office. A bachelor until his fifties, he lived with his mother in their old house in Montreal until he was nearly 40. She died in 1973 when her son was in his second term of office.

Trudeau came on the national stage abruptly, rising quickly from his professorship at the Université de Montréal law school to become, in 1967, minister of justice under Liberal prime minister Lester B. Pearson. When Pearson retired, Trudeau – young, charismatic, an attractive French intellectual – stepped smartly into the Party's power vacuum, winning a stunning upset at the chaotic leadership conference.

That was perhaps his luck, being in the right place at the right time; his *skill* lay in holding onto power, acquired so effortlessly, for more than a decade. Through some of Canada's most exciting political years, Trudeau was a national fixture: the man the Toronto *Sun*, western Canadians, and Bay Street gray suits loved to hate; the man Canadian children, Québécois, and everybody else loved to love. The media called it "Trudeaumania" and, while Trudeau never claimed (like John Lennon) to be more popular than Jesus, he could have done so.

The social exploits of Trudeau are legendary. Before his 1971 marriage, he was seen with a variety of "beautiful young things" on his arm. After the marriage, he had well-publicized arguments with the gallivanting Maggie, a free spirit who hung out with Andy Warhol and took photos of New York celebs. (She even had a brand of designer jeans named after her.) Despite the trouble brewing in their marriage, the Trudeaus were devoted parents, with a unique talent for having children on Christmas Day – the first two of their three sons (Justin, Sasha, and Michel) were born on December 25.

That little quirk of fate seemed to bode well for Trudeau. The gods were smiling on him. Even the media circus of the marriage break-up in 1977 did not scar Trudeau publicly, as Canadians – by then disposed to suspect the flashy political magician – gave him new credibility as a single father and martyr to responsibility. But who knows how much he suffered behind the well-crafted public statements?

Much of Trudeau's celebrated arrogance, his unwillingness to suffer fools, whether in the House of Commons or the press corps, stemmed from his own severe mental self-discipline. It was learned early, at the Collège de Brébeuf in Montreal, where Trudeau was known as a scrapper who never backed down in a fight, verbal or physical. He shone at the Université de Montréal, and success took him to Harvard, the Sorbonne, and the London School of Economics. He came to Ottawa in 1965 as one of Lester Pearson's "Three Wise Men" – a trio of Quebec intellectuals of which Trudeau proved himself the ablest. He was arguably Canada's most brilliant leader.

But Trudeau's refreshing frankness in debate sometimes appeared merely willful, as when he told a House of Commons colleague to "Fuck off," explaining later that he had actually said "Fuddle

the disco-age leisure suits. For *Sun* readers, no clothes horse could be considered a serious leader.

But these dismissive second thoughts are not necessarily born of mature reflection. And they cannot be allowed to nullify Trudeau's early success, and the value of the national vision on which it was based. The Jesuit-educated overachiever, a child of strict but loving parents, had risen to international fame. He hob-nobbed with royalty, rock stars, and international political meteors.

Yet, unexpectedly, behind the facade of fashionable living and easy brilliance there lived a hard-working scholarship boy, a clever Québécois bookworm who deeply loved his country and his province (in that order) and simply wanted to keep them alive and thriving. Richard Gwyn, author of

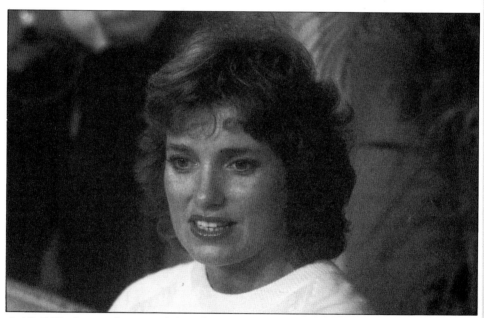

duddle." His dreams of a strong federal Canada had a coercive flavor to many Canadians when he sent troops into Montreal during the October Crisis. ("Just watch me," he told reporters who had asked how far he was willing to go in keeping Quebec in line.)

Late in his series of terms as prime minister, Trudeau's celebrated arrogance took a decidedly peevish turn, and the mania that had fired his early campaign victories was far from fashionable any longer. Indeed, the fashionable thing through the late 1970s was to mock the naivete that had found Trudeau such a compelling figure in 1968. The *Sun*, the reactionary Toronto tabloid long given to hate-filled attacks on anything smacking of reform, consistently referred to Trudeau as "PET" and delighted in reporting on his sartorial fussiness: the flashy jackets, the fresh rose in his lapel,

the biography *The Northern Magus*, said succinctly of Trudeau's character: "Ambiguity is the only consistency."

And Canadians – before they indulged in the patently Canadian put-downs, the second guessing of anyone who does well, the "Who does he think he is?" demand they learned from the Scots – before all that, they loved Trudeau for the national visionary he was. He showed them who they could be: influential and envied players in the international stage. He showed them what a true national leader, rather than a mediator of regional interests, looked like.

Briefly they followed the lead, relishing his notoriety and the international status it bestowed on them. But, in their ultimate reaction to Trudeau's vision, Canadians showed him (and themselves) that they were not ready to embrace greatness.

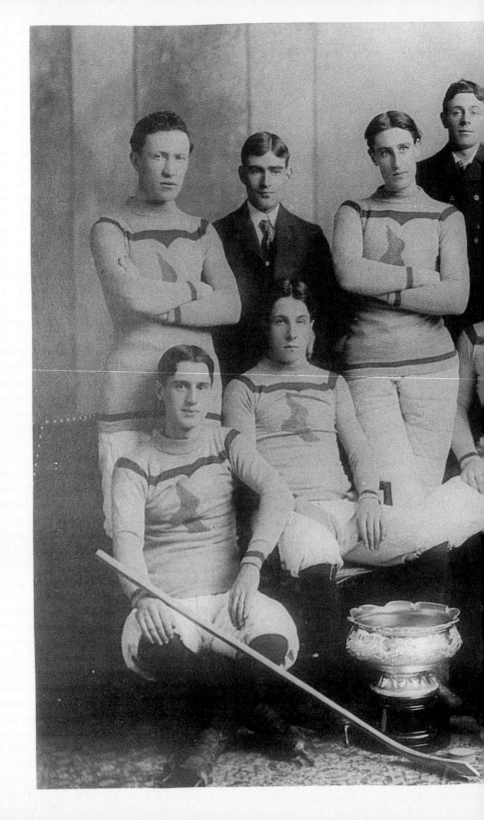

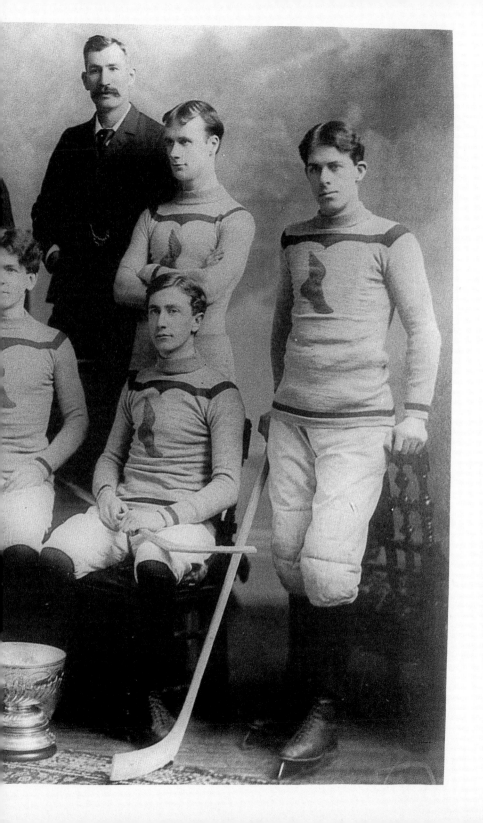

To understand ice hockey is, in some sense at least, to understand Canada itself. Across a frozen expanse, enterprising individuals dodge or fight off vicious obstacles, searching for the narrow openings that will bring them glory. And yet the individual cannot succeed alone – only the team, working together, can consistently send the puck home.

Hockey is raucous but also rule-bound: when individuals flout the laws of the game, they are physically removed from their fellows, placed in the penalty box – the "sin bin" – and the team must struggle on. Fighting is part of the game, but only when it is fair and obvious; dirty play (provided the referee can see it) will draw the penalty every time. Hockey is wide-open, honest, at once rough and graceful, team and individual, a swirling mixture of bone-rattling hits and the poetry of fast skating. It is like nothing else on earth, and it is Canada's game. It *belongs* to Canadians, in a way little else does.

Hockey Night in Canada: Legend has it that Canadians are notoriously self-effacing, finding little to boast about in their own achievements, and not much inclined to boasting anyway. But when the talk comes around to hockey, Canadians can rightly claim the laurels. Let the propositions be clear: Canadians are the best hockey players in the world, and Canadian fans are the most loyal and discerning. Come Saturday night – "Hockey Night in Canada," as the CBC broadcasters so accurately call it – Canadians of all ages are glued to their sets, even their radios, dissecting plays and performances in joyous technical detail.

While many Americans view hockey as a cross between all-star wrestling and roller derby on ice, for Canadians the game is an expression of national aspiration. Our game, our league, our players. What Canadian child has not "skated" around the living

Preceding pages: hockey in its more genteel days. The game is now a brutal contact sport (left) but attracts fans young (above).

room, dumping an imaginary puck into the corner? What youth has not spent an eight-hour day chipping tennis balls into a foldable net in the back lane, playing until it was too dark to see, too cold to feel toes, and ignoring the call to dinner? For all of them, the hockey announcer's traditional cry, "He shoots... he *scores!*" is a dreamy mantra, a call to glory.

Of course there have been times – desperate times – when the Russians, Swedes, Czechs, and even the Americans put Cana-

da's hockey supremacy to the test. Take 1972, the first Canada-Russia series: it was supposed to be a cake-walk, a mere workout, for Team Canada. But the Russians came to the Forum in Montreal, the Sistine Chapel of Hockey, and beat "our boys" seven goals to three. Over the next few weeks, Canadians watched in stunned silence as this eight-game foregone conclusion suddenly became a live issue. Teachers wheeled clunky school TVs into classrooms so kids wouldn't miss the day games. Canadians gaped as it took Paul Henderson's goal with 34 seconds left in Game 8 to save their national pride.

But a watershed had been passed. The novelist Mordecai Richler accurately expressed the feeling that swept from coast to coast after that first series. "We already knew that our politicians lied, that our bodies would be betrayed by age," he wrote. "But we had not suspected that our hockey players were anything but the very best… After the series, nothing was ever the same again in Canada. Beer didn't taste as good. The Rockies seemed smaller, the northern lights dimmer."

There have other series since then, and Canada has acquitted itself well enough. Canadians also know (don't they?) that the

Montreal's place in the history of hockey is, like its place in the history of Canada, unparalleled. There is a lively dispute about the invention of hockey, with at least three cities – Kingston, Halifax, and Montreal – claiming to have witnessed the first game. In fact hockey closely resembles *kalv*, a stick-and-ball game played in the Netherlands as early as the 16th century.

Kingston claims to have been the site of the first North American hockey game on November 25, 1855, but the evidence is a little sketchy. Montreal's claim, though coming 20 years later, lies on firmer ground: on March 3, 1875, two teams gathered to

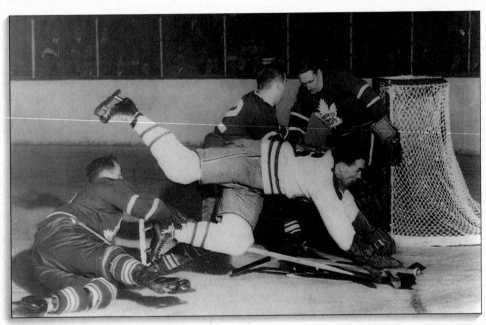

best Canadian players never play on Olympic or series teams because they're too busy earning a living in the National Hockey League (NHL). They know that the best players in the world still come from funny places like Brantford, Parry Sound, Chicoutimi and Fredericton. They know there is still a large majority of Canadian players in the NHL, the American Hockey League (AHL), even the American college leagues. They go south of the border, they take their money and their education, and that's just fine with most people. Hockey still belongs to Canada, always has and always will.

play on the city's Old Victoria Rink. The assembled hearties were mostly winter-idle rugby players, who muscled their way up and down the long rink using (according to one report) "a flat piece of board" as a puck. No record survives of the final score.

Hockey was not popular in Montreal at first, competing with well-established games like rugby football, lacrosse and even cricket. Lacrosse, a game borrowed from the Indians, was by the far the most popular sporting pastime in 19th-century Montreal. *Les toques bleus* – the blue-hatted members of the Montreal Amateur Athletic Association – were often to be seen playing the Indian game in the fields around Montreal. During the 1850s and '60s regular clubs such as "the Alma Mater" and "the Hochelagas" took on "the Shamrocks," "the Montrealers" or "the Crescents."

The Canadians who played the first games of hockey probably borrowed many of the game's features from field lacrosse, as well as from the English game of field hockey. And like lacrosse, as first played by Native Americans, early hockey had no official boundaries or rules: an indeterminate number of players could range far and wide to set up their goals. They had better be fit,

going. Imagine clearing a field every time you wanted to play lacrosse or soccer.

These difficulties were overcome during the 1880s when two enterprising undergraduates from McGill University, R.F. Smith and W.F. Robertson, codified the rules of hockey. They specified the approximate size of the playing surface, limited the skating players to eight a side (later six, and now five), and generally gave shape to the game as we know it today. Smith invented the puck by cutting the sides off an India rubber ball, which he found bounced too much for good play on the ice. Permanent winter skating rinks – invariably uncovered

however, since goals were often placed as far as a mile apart. (In this respect the early game also resembled primitive forms of English football, games of which often involved entire towns and ranged for several days over half a county.)

The most common setting for a game was some shoveled patch of the frozen St Lawrence River. One reason for the game's early failure to fire the interest of Montrealers was the sheer effort involved in getting a game

Left and **right**, the Canadiens fight it out with their arch-rivals, the Toronto Maple Leafs.

– were built to make the task of finding suitable ice less hit-and-miss.

Writing the rulebook: It was not until 1907 that the International Ice Hockey Federation was formed to govern a game that was becoming more popular by the year. The National Hockey League did not form until 1917 – six years after the Canadiens, the joy of Montreal, had been organized. There were seven teams in the early NHL: the Canadiens and Maroons of Montreal, the Toronto St Patricks (later the Maple Leafs), Chicago Blackhawks, New York Rangers, Boston Bruins, and Detroit Red Wings. From the beginning *les bons Canadiens* were a power-ful force.

Le Club de Hockey de Canadiens (as they are officially known) have won more NHL titles than any other team, taking possession of Lord Stanley's Cup 23 times since the old Governor-General donated the trophy – at a cost to himself of $48.67 – in 1926. The Cup has grown, sprouting bottom layers like a tree grows rings, and *les Glorieux* have been there every step of the way. Their Montreal temple, the Forum, is so thickly festooned with NHL title banners that opposing players feel distinctly woozy at the sight of its crowded rafters.

As the Cup has grown, so has the league, and the current expanded league has bal-looned to over 20 teams that represent cities unthinkable as hockey centers a few decades ago: Los Angeles, Washington, even East Rutherford, NJ. The bloated league has also had more malign effects, extending the sea-son to a ridiculous length and making the playoff procedure an annual league joke. These days the Stanley Cup finals are not likely to begin until sultry mid-May, and it is not uncommon for playoff games to be de-layed by fog caused by condensing warm air near the ice.

For purists, modern play has deteriorated as well. Forwards are today as likely to dump the puck heedlessly into the corner, letting their linemen scramble, as they are to carry it into the enemy zone on the stick. There may be fewer fights than in the days of "beat 'em in the alley if you can't beat 'em on the ice," but dirty play – vicious hooking, cross checks – has become more common.

Laments like this are legion, they are the daily currency of sports pages in fact, but they do point to something real. The NHL is probably reaching the limits of its growth: already some of the players turning pro don't belong anywhere other than in the war-like junior leagues. In their drive to push rev-enues higher and higher, the leaders of the NHL may be selling the league's glorious legacy down the road.

The Canadiens have not exactly been above all this: they've produced their share of bad play, goon rookies, and the rest. But they are still the example many fans turn to for peace of mind when all else in hockey seems tarnished; they represent what pro hockey was, and can be again. Such wide-spread support cannot obscure the fact that the Canadiens are also very much a local product of Montreal, an 80-year family af-fair between city and club. Indeed, the "H" on their old-fashioned sweaters is popularly taken to initial "*Habitants*," the team's af-fectionate nickname, when it probably just means "hockey" (as in "Club de Hockey").

Les Habs are the team that young Montrealers, indeed youngsters from across Quebec, dream of playing for. There is no other team, and the home-town fans know it. A few of those wide-eyed French Canadian kids grow up to claim that birthright: don-ning the red and blue sweater, skating out onto the holy ice of the Forum, and putting one away for *les Canadiens*. The rest just keep dreaming.

Many of the best players ever to lace up skates have worn the Canadiens' sweater. First and best, perhaps, was Howie Morenz, the legendary "Stratford Streak." An Ontario boy, Morenz anchored the club's high-scor-ing 1920s line with two Québécois shooters, Billy Boucher and Aurel Joliat. In the inau-gural game at the Forum, on November 29,

1924, the Morenz line pushed in six goals in a 7-1 defeat of the Toronto St Patricks. The stonewall in the Montreal goal was another legend, Georges Vezina ("the Chicoutimi Cucumber") who rose to glory at the Forum from a small-town family of 22 children and incidentally gave his name to the trophy for goal-tending excellence in the NHL.

In the 1940s Maurice "The Rocket" Richard, who skated like the wind and handled the puck like it was glued to his blade, captained the Flying Frenchmen of the Forum. In those days, Richard's power-play team was so effective – it included Big Jean Beliveau, Dicky Moore, and Bernie "Boom

Canadiens entered their greatest-ever period of glory, the epic five-year dominance of the Stanley Cup from 1956 to 1960. They have won the Cup many times since then, including a hard-fought four-year streak in 1976–79, but the team of the late '50s was probably the best ever assembled by the venerable old club. The roster includes many of hockey's most illustrious names: Beliveau, Henri "Little Rocket" Richard, Geoffrion, Jacques Plante (one of the best goalies ever, and the first to standardize a face mask), and the coach, a former player called Toe Blake.

There will be arguments about the merits of the two streak teams – the late-1970s club

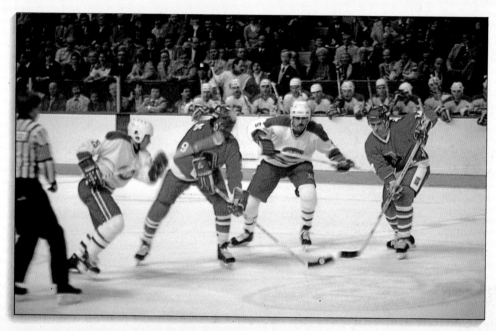

Boom" Geoffrion – that the NHL was forced to change its rules. With Beliveau and Richard circling the net like angry hornets and Geoffrion unloading thundering slapshots from the point, the Canadiens could score two or three goals in the course of a two-minute penalty. The League altered the rules so that any power-play goal would automatically end the penalty, putting opposing goalies out of their misery.

The Rocket was a fading blast when the

The game's best seen live (above) but the next best way is on television (left).

included Ken Dryden, Jacques Lemaire, Serge Savard, Bob Gainey, and Yvon Cournoyer – but there is something elemental about that 1950s dynasty. Before the World Hockey Association (WHA) expansion, before league-parity rules, before the Canadiens ceased to be a family affair and became just another business in the NHL, before *English* became the language of their dressing room: for five years this team, composed almost entirely of Quebec boys, could not be knocked off by the best hockey players in North America.

Something else was different in 1976, of

course: the Parti Québécois had gained power in the province, deflating the powerful metaphor *les Canadiens* had always provided for downtrodden Québécois. Here was real, not symbolic, power. Hockey was suddenly for many Montrealers just a game, no longer a national place-holder capable of provoking the riots on Rue Ste-Catherine that greeted the suspension of Maurice Richard in March 1955.

The villain of the suspension was NHL president Clarence Campbell, just the latest example of a Scot shafting a Québécois. Sportswriter Tim Burke of the Montreal *Gazette* called the riot "the opening shot of the

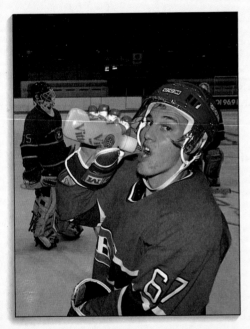

Quiet Revolution." But by November 15, 1976, the revolution was over and won, and *les Canadiens* (many of them federalist, not separatist) skated through a game dominated by election results coming across the scoreboard, proclaiming the Parti Québécois's stunning victory.

These events, dramatized in Rick Salutin's play *Les Canadiens*, show why the 1956–60 dynasty is a more potent symbol of what *le Club de Hockey* means to Montrealers – a source of fierce cultural pride – when all else seemed beyond reach. Salutin's play, set in a miniature rink, reads

Quebec's history through the lens of hockey. The musket that kills General Wolfe becomes the first hockey stick. Events are described by a commentator: "the shut-out of the French Canadians at the Plains of Abraham," "the sparkling teamwork of the Patriotes in 1867," "the power play of 1867." But in the play's second act, the mythologization of the Canadiens ends when metaphors for power and Québécois aspiration are no longer necessary. Hockey is hockey; power is in the benches of the National Assembly, not the seats of the Forum.

But hockey is still a powerful element in Québécois culture, and the melding of hockey with drama continues. A similar mini-arena setting, complete with commentator, organist and referee, is now used by the *League National d'Improvisation*, which pits teams of uniformed actors against one another in the competitive acting-out of improvized themes. (Penalties may be called for hamming it up.) Many of Quebec's best actors start their careers here, moving up from junior leagues to the televised national games, and then on to even bigger things.

Unfortunately, the other great team of hockey's early years, the Toronto Maple Leafs, has fallen on rocky times in recent years. They have not weathered expansion and the modern game as well as the Montreal gods. Sure, the Washington Capitals have been known to beat the Canadiens once in while, and the Stanley Cup has lately eluded them. But they have never haunted the basement of their division like the hapless Leafs, winners of 11 Stanley Cups (the last in bygone 1967).

It is perhaps a little hard to imagine now, but there was a time when the Montreal-Toronto hockey rivalry was one of the most exciting in sport. If one were a Canadian, allegiance had to be pledged – Leaf or Hab, and no fence-sitters allowed. And hockey was clearly not the only thing at stake: there was civic pride, the least often examined undercurrent of racial and linguistic enmity.

The writer Roch Carrier fingered these issues brilliantly in his short story *The Hockey Sweater*: a Quebec kid, a desperate Maurice Richard fan, needs a new hockey sweater and his mother writes away to

Eaton's, the famous Canadian department store, to get it. But when the parcel arrives it contains a *Maple Leafs* sweater. *Quel disastre!* But his mother will not send it back because it fits him. He is shunned by the other little Rocket Richards, a traitor to Mother Quebec, *les Habitants*, and the Rocket himself. A young priest sends him to confession.

Torontonians have never been quite as hockey-mad as their counterparts to the east, nor have they ever invested so many of their personal and collective ambitions in one team. Toronto hockey has produced its share of heroes – Francis "King" Clancy, Frank

died. Legend has it that Ballard's tight-fistedness is what has kept the Maple Leafs from returning to their rightful place atop the NHL, firing his coaches with abandon and paying sub-par salaries to his players. A battle is raging even now over who will control the ailing but still immensely profit-able club.

No, the Canadiens, not the Leafs, are Canada's national team. Or they ought to be anyway. Boorish western Canadians have been known to boo the (required) French sections of the national anthem when *les bons Canadiens* are in town. "Some of the players were so angry they didn't want to go

Mahovlich, Red Kelly, Darryl Sittler, Dave Keon, Lanny Macdonald, coach Punch Imlach – but recently it has been known for a less glorious personage, the crochety owner of the Leafs, ex-convict Harold Ballard. Ballard, who went to jail in the 1970s for defrauding his own hockey club of $200,000, is so offensive to everyone that local sportswriters even started a Ballard-Watch pool when he was hospitalized for heart trouble an ailment of which he recently

Left and **above**, hockey now incorporates helmets and body pads to prevent serious injury.

out on the ice," Serge Savard said on one such occasion in Vancouver in 1980. The fans in Winnipeg have had a better appreciation of what *Le Club de Hockey de Canadiens* represents: the first time the Canadiens visited Winnipeg after the Jets joined the NHL, all the fans wore tuxedoes and gowns.

All in all, they deserve, at the very least, our respect. The old-fashioned red and blue uniforms, as they glide across the ice, represent not ust the best in hockey, but a window to the tough and tireless teamwork inherent in all of Canadian history.

"I remember." This was the refrain of French troops as they, along with grand hopes of New France, perished on the Plains of Abraham in 1759. *"Je me souviens"* remains Quebec's shibboleth, and is ubiquitious throughout the province, gracing cultural icons from flags to license plates.

Montreal remembers in a special way the language and culture of its "New France" heritage. As the world's second-largest French-speaking city, Montreal has long been considered the commercial and cultural pivot of Canada, and, perhaps more importantly, the garden of Quebec's social and political identity.

From its origins as the first French foothold on a vast and punishing land, to its present status as Canada's most urbane and exciting city, Montreal is a colorful swirl of people, politics, language, and culture. It is here where faith and fur joined hands to transform irrevocably Canada's First Peoples. It is here where Quebec's intellectual and artistic vigor has its most potent expression, and where pride, politics, and the past merge in a brilliant and ever-changing tapestry.

Montreal has been called a "phonic" city, with "francophones" (French-speakers) in the majority, "anglophones" (English-speakers) and "allophones" – those whose first language is other than French or English. While the "phone" lines sometimes get crossed, and communication among these sundry cultures occasionally falters, the city has remained, remarkably, a cohesive, vital, and peaceful social network.

To the surprise of many, London's influential *Sunday Times*, at the beginning of the 1980s, reported that "Montreal now surpasses San Francisco as the most interesting North American city... There is a swagger about the city that one used to find in San Francisco before it went limp in the early '70s."

But has Montreal, in the 1990s, fulfilled that promise of excitement to come? Proving that it has, the Places section of this book guides you through the European charm of Old Montreal, the dynamic modernity of Downtown, the astonishing Underground City, and then through the parks and out into the countryside surrounding Canada's most exciting city.

Preceding pages: today's high rises; view over McGill University; winter wonderland. **Left,** invitation to fitness near the waterfront.

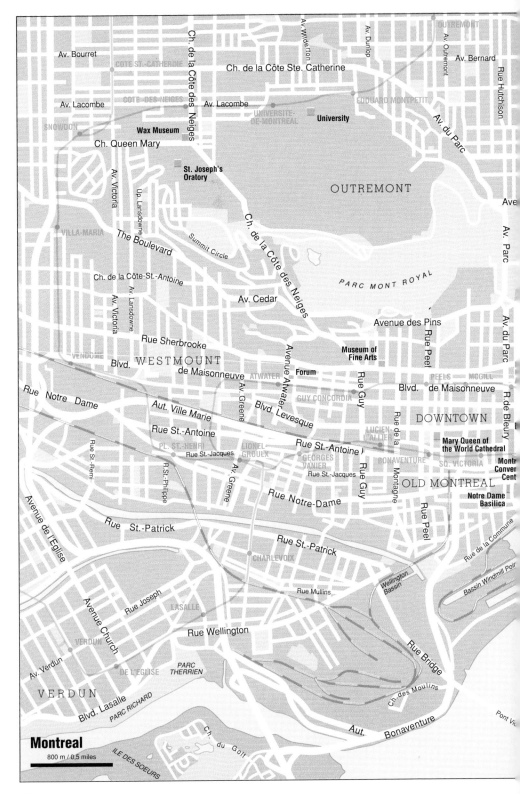

Montreal

800 m / 0,5 miles

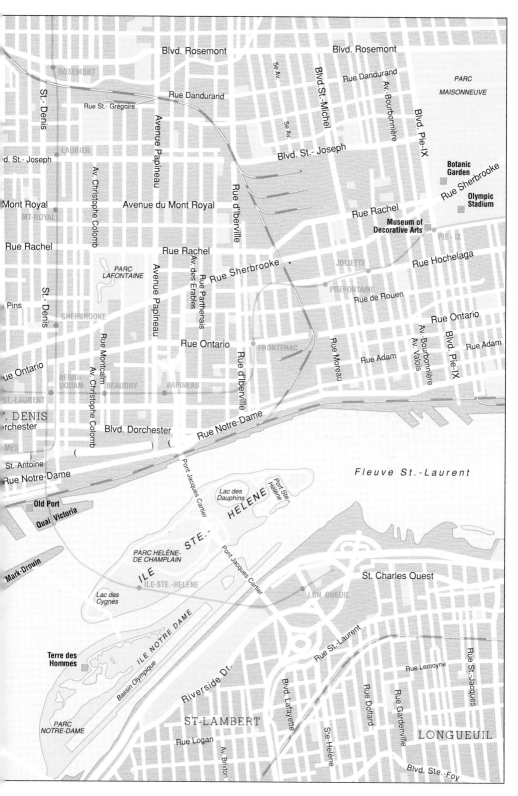

MAISONNEUVE

OLD MONTREAL

Old Montreal is back. Exploring this area that once was the entire city of Montreal, and functioned as its business center until late in the 19th century, it is hard to imagine that in 1960 the streets were deserted, the buildings derelict and slated for demolition. So near did Old Montreal come to extinction that its current prosperity seems almost evanescent, a movie-set to be torn down once filming is completed.

No need to worry now. In 1962 the Viger Commission declared the area historically invaluable; houses were restored, buildings gutted and renovated, and restaurants, shops and clubs began to spring up in proportion to the renewal of vigour and invaluable street traffic – both tourists *and* Montrealers alike. Every city, like every family, is an inheritance of styles and traditions, heirlooms bequeathed to the next generation to share – and celebrate – a sense of continuity. Old Montreal is modern Montreal's inheritance, and thanks to foresight and initiative it is by and large a *living* one.

The area is also a provocative blend of commercialism and history. An 18th-century building finds itself housing a late 20th-century business; banks of computers line a four-foot rubble wall, printers and fax machines operate inside stone vaults. Architects can focus their creativity on pre-existing shapes and dimensions, and still do excellent work. Electricians wire rooms that smell faintly of paraffin; painters strip and varnish narrow staircases with cross beams that force tall people to slouch. Old Montreal welcomes modern entrepreneurs to make history contemporary while making profits for themselves. Atmosphere is in abundance and the location can't be equaled. Why *not* set up shop in Old Montreal?

But there is another side to the restorations. Most Montrealers and tourists descend to the old city to sightsee during the day and dine in the evenings. Afterwards they return to their homes or hotels, leaving the cobbled streets quiet and melancholy. Efforts to make the area a functioning neighborhood have met with limited success. Condominiums and apartments are beginning to appear, but more slowly than anticipated. Bustling in daylight, ghostly in darkness: a double life that is, one hopes, temporary.

And Old Montreal *was* once a neighborhood of houses, shops, and churches. It is an area of public squares – four major ones in a nine-block radius – and these, until recently, served as community centers, where people gathered to gossip and discuss the business of the day. Their presence reminds the traveler of a vibrancy behind the impressive buildings. What better way to explore Old Montreal than by using the squares as axes?

Stand in **Place Jacques Cartier** and try to imagine yourself a citizen. The

Left, the great man forever faces L'Eglise Notre-Dame. Right, Château Ramezay.

year could be 1790 or 1990; the principal structures still stand, the churches and seminaries still function; the St Lawrence still borders to the south and the mountain to the northwest, and while the walls that protected Montrealers until the early 19th century are gone, the area remains distinct and indivisible. During the summer you may find yourself sitting on a square for hours watching the merriment. If it is winter, though, be advised that a seat in a café has its advantages.

Heart of tourism: Place Jacques Cartier is the obvious place to start your visit to Old Montreal. Rectangular in shape, lined with Victorian-style street lamps and cobblestones, the square has a grace and charm that conjures images of strolling women with parasols and men playing absently with pocket watches. The heart of tourist Montreal is here. Restaurants and terrace cafés abound. During the summer, sidewalks, already crowded, dissolve into hives of onlookers gathered around the jugglers,

mimes, and acrobats. Artists and *chansoniers* are also plentiful, along narrow Rue St-Amable, Rue St-Vincent, or any alley where the acoustics are sonorous.

The square slopes up from the St Lawrence River to **Rue Notre-Dame**. Excellent views of the port, the behemoth freighters being bunkered and provisioned, are available on any but the foggiest days. During winter, however, Place Jacques Cartier is subject to the quirky imagination of a city hall decorator who festoons **the Green** with giant helium-inflated Christmas trees. The trees come in all colors – white, green, polka-dotted, blue – and would curtail the view even more severely were they not prone to sagging like abandoned tents.

The Green is also the launching point for Montreal's annual **Fête des Neiges** in late January, a brisk but lively winter festival that features, among other things, ice sculptures in the **Vieux-Port** and ski and snowboard demonstrations

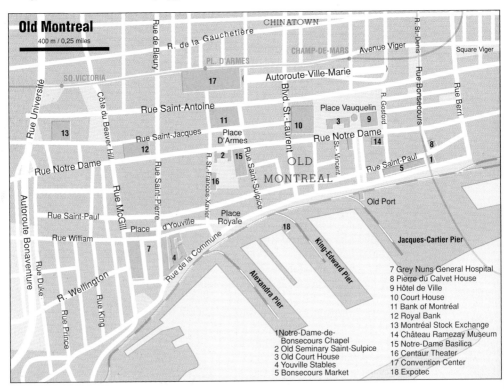

Old Montreal

400 m / 0,25 miles

CHINATOWN

Rue de Bleury
R. de la Gauchetière
PL. D'ARMES
CHAMP-DE-MARS
Avenue Viger
Square Viger
R. St-Denis

SQ. VICTORIA
Autoroute-Ville-Marie
Rue Université
Côte du Beaver Hill
Rue Saint-Antoine
Blvd. St-Laurent
Place Vauquelin
R. Gosford
Rue Bonsecours
Rue Berri

11
10
3   9
13
Place D'Armes
Rue Notre Dame
14
8

Rue Saint-Jacques
12
2   15
Rue Saint-Paul
5   1
Rue Notre Dame
R. St-François-Xavier
16
OLD MONTREAL
R. St-Vincent
Rue Saint-Sulpice

Rue Saint-Paul
Rue Saint-Pierre
Rue McGill
Old Port

Autoroute Bonaventure
Rue William
Place d'Youville
Place Royale
18
Jacques-Cartier Pier

R. Wellington
7
4
Rue de la Commune
King-Edward Pier

Rue Duke
Rue King
Alexandra Pier

Rue Prince

1 Notre-Dame-de-Bonsecours Chapel
2 Old Seminary Saint-Sulpice
3 Old Court House
4 Youville Stables
5 Bonsecours Market

7 Grey Nuns General Hospital
8 Pierre du Calvet House
9 Hôtel de Ville
10 Court House
11 Bank of Montréal
12 Royal Bank
13 Montréal Stock Exchange
14 Château Ramezay Museum
15 Notre-Dame Basilica
16 Centaur Theater
17 Convention Center
18 Expotec

right in Place Jacques Cartier itself.

At the top of the Square, towering above the buildings and plastic trees, is **Nelson's Monument**, an imposing if odd tribute to England's naval hero. Imposing because it stands 105 feet (35 meters) tall and dates from 1809. The statue is odd both because the Admiral faces *away* from the St Lawrence and, more to the point, because he is there at all. Little in public Montreal escapes the political: a memorial to the English conqueror of a French navy is lucky to have escaped intact.

Nelson squares off with a less grand statue of **Vouquelin**, an early French administrator, in the tiny **Place Vouquelin** at the crest of the incline. From this square, once the site of the town jail and the public flogging ground, the "new" Montreal sprawls in all directions. Vouquelin, it should be noted, *is* facing the river, though his position may have more to do with keeping the bitter north winds to his back than anything else.

Place Vouquelin is bookended by important buildings. To the west is Montreal's former **Palais de Justice**. The old court house, dating from 1856, was designed by John Ostell, the man responsible for the magnificent twin towers of **Notre-Dame Basilica** on **Place d'Armes**. The style, known as classical revival, was extremely popular in Montreal at the time, particularly the thick columns and, when it was added later, the cupola dome. Recent restorations of the building focus on the 1890 dome, and the court house is now occupied by government offices.

Across the street, at 100 Rue Notre-Dame, is the new(er) bastion of canon and code. This massive, suitably dour building was used until recently for criminal cases, and features massive columns fronting a lovely bronze door. Above the door are bas-reliefs detailing the history of criminal law, while the Latin inscription over the cornice reads: "He who transgresses the law shall seek the help of the law in vain." Hardly

Old Montreal skyline.

comforting words for a defendant! The **Nouveau Palais de Justice**'s current function involves showcasing the talents of Quebec's finest young artists. It is home to both the art and drama conservatories, where aesthetic laws are transgressed daily.

East of Place Vouquelin stands Montreal's stately **Hôtel de Ville**, a second-empire structure with slender columns and the mansard roof so predominant in Québécois architecture. The building, which dates from 1860, survived a major 1922 fire and today boasts an extra storey. During the holiday season, enormous red bows lend the city hall the appearance – not intended, one suspects – of a demurely-wrapped gift. It was from a second-storey balcony that Charles de Gaulle addressed a crowd packing Place Jacques Cartier in 1967. De Gaulle roused the Québécois with his cry *"Vive le Québec libre!"* The crowd heeded his words.

Château Ramezay, across from the city hall, is the most famous of the many restored houses around the square. Built in 1705, this low-lying fieldhouse has served as the offices and warehouses for the *Companies des Indes*, official residence for British governors, court house, school, seat of government, even the headquarters for the American army under Montgomery and Benedict Arnold during their brief occupation of Montreal in 1775.

Benjamin Franklin stayed in the house on his mission to persuade Lower Canada to join the American revolution. The Château survived these incarnations nicely, and still boasts the three-foot walls and deep stone vaults ordered by its namesake, Claude de Ramezay, the 11th governor of Montreal. Today, it is a museum of life in 18th-century Montreal.

The rooms of Château Ramezay are worth exploring. Among the more curious artifacts on permanent display are stern portraits of pioneer officials, religious icons, maps of North America, a 1750 manuscript of liturgical chants

Fête des Neiges at Jacques Cartier Square.

translated into an Amerindian language, rugs, chandeliers, business ledgers, even a reproduction – for obscure reasons – of the head offices of the *Companie des Indes* in Nantes, France.

As well, a series of rooms recreate the interiors of diverse living quarters in New France. These include the offices of the governor, a dining room, kitchen, and servants' quarters. All the rooms contain period furniture; some of the pieces, especially the cabinets, are very fine. Special exhibits are mounted regularly, including a recent display of Goya's drawings.

In the whitewashed vaults and narrow passages of Château Ramezay's basement is an attempt to do justice to the Amerindians who inhabited the region before the Europeans. The predominant feature of the exhibit are 19th-century photos of "civilized" Indians smoking pipes in suits and ties. The displays are modest, but still valuable.

Two other prominent examples of restoration include the **Maison du Calvet** (1770), with its distinctive high chimneys and steep roof to prevent snow from accumulating, and **Maison Papineau** (1785), known for its wood facade painted to look like limestone. Both houses are also famous for their historic namesakes.

Of the two, Calvet is more notorious. Pierre du Calvet was an administrator who betrayed the French, first to the British in 1759 and then to the Americans in 1775, for which he was duly imprisoned. Upon his release several years later Calvet sought financial compensation from the Americans for his trouble, but was refused. Next he sailed to England to protest his term in prison. Tragically, his ship sank en route, and Calvet was consigned to the status of traitor for perpetuity.

The Papineau family, in stark contrast, is among Quebec's most honored. Louis-Joseph Papineau, the leader of the 1837 rebellion in Lower Canada, was born in this house, and a total of six generations of the family, including

Civic pride blossoms forth.

many distinguished politicians and businessmen, have occupied it.

Maison Papineau was also the residence chosen by Eric McLean of the Vigor Commission to begin the renewal of Old Montreal. In the early 1960s, **Rue Bonsecours**, where both houses are located, was dreary and vaguely disreputable, hardly suitable for gracious living. When workers began to restore Maison Papineau, they eliminated two brick storeys and replaced all the windows. They also stripped the walls of 19 layers of wallpaper. The refurbished Maison du Calvet even offers a quaint coffee shop.

Arguably the most charming street in Old Montreal is **Rue St-Paul**. Cobblestoned, the air smacking of the St Lawrence River 100 yards to the south, and lined with 18th-century buildings that currently house restaurants, shops and government offices, the street is authentic without being precious, at once current and deeply historic. The three most prominent structures are **Rasco's Ho-**tel, the **Marché Bonsecours**, and **Notre-Dame-de-Bon-Secours**.

In its day, **Rasco's Hotel** at 295 Rue St-Paul was considered among the finest hotels in North America. Named after an Italian, Francisco Rasco, who emigrated to North America in the early 1800s, it was constructed in 1836 and featured a lavish restaurant that was "the place to be" in 1840s Montreal. A ballroom and concert hall were also available for the cultured and/or wealthy.

In 1842 Charles Dickens, on the visit that would eventually produce *American Notes*, stayed at the hotel with his wife. Dickens's observations about Montreal, though simple, ring true even today: "Montreal is pleasantly situated on the margin of the St Lawrence, and is backed by some bold heights, about which there are charming rides and drives. The streets are generally narrow and irregular."

Rasco's Hotel, abandoned for decades, was restored in 1982 and currently

Trotting out in St Paul's Square.

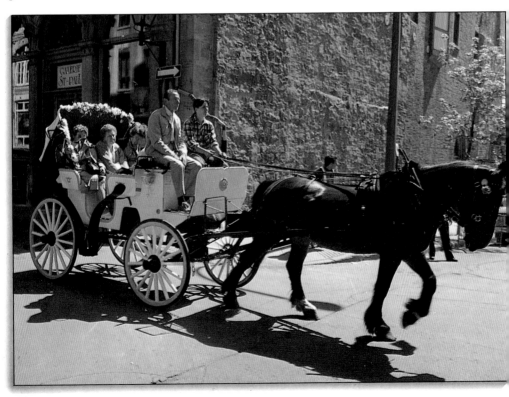

houses the proverbial government offices. Look for the name between floors of a simple, almost spartan, greystone building.

The **Marché Bonsecours** was once the most photographed edifice in Montreal. It boasts attractive facades, especially on the river side, and a Renaissance-style dome (1864) that was the first to be erected in the city. Remember that Montreal was, and still is, a port; ships moving down the St Lawrence from Quebec would have spotted the dome and Notre Dame church before anything else. For a sailor, riding an autumn storm and fatigued from months at sea, these markers became emblems of security and shelter, visible even in his dreams.

The Marché functioned primarily as a market and exhibition center. The vagaries of history, however, forced it to function briefly as both house of parliament (1849) and, between 1852–78, the city hall.

Marché Bonsecours.

No symbol of Montreal's maritime heritage is more poignant than **Notre-Dame-de-Bon-Secours**. One must stand at water's edge in the **Vieux-Port** to appreciate the church's impact. Rising above the clock tower is a statue of the Virgin Mary, her outstretched arms welcoming ships into port. Little wonder that for hundreds of years seamen shipping out of Montreal made a pilgrimage to Notre-Dame-de-Bon-Secours to pray for safe passage.

Little wonder, too, that the lively and busy interior of the "sailor's church" has a decidedly nautical look: votive lamps shaped like vessels, carvings of ships – many donated by seamen – hanging from the ceiling. The word *secours* translates as "assistance" or "help." The English translation of the church's name – Our Lady of Divine Assistance – lacks all the resonance of the original.

The first church was founded in 1671 by Marguerite Bourgeoys. Various incarnations followed, the current building dating from 1772. Typically

A LIVING LANGUAGE

The leading French dictionary, *Le Petit Robert*, defines linguistic purism this way: "The excessive concern for the purity of language, in accordance with an intangible and idealistic model." It is characterized by a desire to freeze a tongue at a certain stage of its evolution. Purism is autocratic. Worse, it is uninteresting.

Québécois, the French spoken in Montreal and throughout the province of Quebec, is anything but pure. Major French dictionaries published in Paris once took it upon themselves to denounce Québécois as a bastardization of the original tongue.

They couldn't have been more misguided. Montreal French is a language crackling with vitality. Anglo-Canadians, Greeks, Africans, Asians, even the occasional transplanted American, seize the French tongue and contort, distort, and otherwise twist it into new, unimagined shapes. Compound this with the ribald, earthy, but always original *joual* of the Québécois themselves, a street-wise dialect bursting with word-puns and wit, and the linguistic climate is far from dull.

A major concern of linguistically sensitive francophones, however, is that the verbal climate is a bit too interesting, Québécois French, they sense, is being overrun by anglicisms: English words incorporated into day-to-day vocabulary. Where else, for example, do people go for drives on *le weekend* as long as *le traffic* isn't too heavy and they can *faire du parking* with success. In Quebec such an excursion would occur at *la fin de semaine* – as long as *la circulation* isn't too heavy, of course, and they can *faire du stationnement* with success.

Yes, Montreal French is rife with English expressions. Many people are, after all, fluently bilingual; such a gift leads inevitably to a casual mingling of languages, especially with so much of the popular culture emanating from just across the border in the United States. A musician is *super-cool* if *le mood* that night is good. In the mornings people eat *les corn-flakes*, slip on their *sportwear*, and go *faire du shopping*. A *rough and tough* guy usually wears *son tee-shirt* or *son-pull* (pull-over sweater), and will spend evenings at a friend's *living* (living room) drinking *les Ex* (Molson's Export beer). At work, especially in an age of technology, one attends *un briefing* or *un meeting* to do some *planning* or perhaps engage in *un autre brainstorming* session. Later on the executive will relax with *un coctail* at *un night-club. C'est OK* to stay late to *voir le show*.

Even persons are stirred into the linguistic stew. An Englishman in Quebec? Easy: *un rosbif*! And in certain parts of English Canada, a Québécois is known as a *peasouper*, in honor of the province's love of pea soup. We are, apparently, what we eat.

Quebec French is also characterized by certain expressions. Besides the accent, a Parisian will usually be able to identify a Québécois by phrases like *nous autres* (the rest of us), *J'ai-pas* (I don't know), the musical *binbin* (*bien, bien*: very, very good) plus the bookend greeting *Salut!* (Hi/Bye) instead of the more formal *bonjour* and *au revoir*. There are also literally thousands of words that are unique to Quebec. Experts estimate that, of the 200,000 active French words, 8,000 to 10,000 originated in North America. Of those, however, the average Montrealer may incorporate 300 to 500 into his or her vocabulary. A few samples will whet the appetite: a *bête puante* (smelly animal) for a skunk, a *p'tit blanc* for a whiskey, *une sacoche* for a handbag, a *char* for an automobile. How about a *chanteur de pomme* (singer of apples) – a playboy who seduces women using glib, sickly-sweet language!

The Montreal accent is particularly noteworthy. Many visitors to the city, both French and those who've learned the language in school, are shocked at first by what they hear. More precisely, the shock is with what they don't *understand*. A thick Montreal accent is a marvel. It is skitterish, lightening-quick, and sounds initially as if the speaker is using his or her nose rather than mouth. The tone is harsh but decidedly musical. Listen closely, extract the odd words of dialect, and what will emerge is a gregarious and engaging tongue almost totally lacking in the pretense of Parisian French. Québécois French doesn't sound like a textbook. It sounds like people!

Québécois features of Notre-Dame-de-Bon-Secours include the arched door, wooden belfry, and the *oeil-de-boeuf* (a small round window in the gable). Interestingly, Saint Marguerite – she was canonized by Pope John Paul II in 1982 – returned from a visit to France in 1672 with a tiny wooden statue of the Virgin Mary. Against all odds the statue survived numerous fires and is now kept in a house on Rue Sherbrooke.

Marguerite Bourgeoys is a legend in Quebec. The museum dedicated to her life in the basement of Notre-Dame-de-Bon-Secours is a site of veneration for many Catholics, especially older people who can recall an era when the Québécois were among the most devout and pious in Christendom. Her life is, naturally, shrouded in myth and folklore. The museum is modest, and consists largely of showcases that use miniature dolls to re-enact the key scenes of Saint Margeurite's long and active life. The dolls wear traditional costumes and smile sweetly. A more interesting activity, included in the ticket price, is a climb up the creaky wooden staircase to the aerial chapel and observation tower.

The view of the harbour is impressive. Visible to the south, astride the St Lawrence, are Expo 67's two most famous, or infamous, landmarks: Buckminster Fuller's 20-storey geodesic dome, now a skeleton after a fire, and architect Moshe Safdie's cubic apartment complex Habitat. The latter, a startlingly ugly and awkward living space, consists of 158 units hoisted into place like building blocks. The panorama north of the mountain is also fine, weather – and wind – permitting. The tower and museum keep regular hours; Notre-Dame-de-Bon-Secours is open to visitors every day of the year.

Finally, a tour of Place Jacques Cartier would be incomplete without a walk along the sweeping arc of **Rue de la Commune,** once Montreal's waterfront, and a glance inside the Vieux-Port. Little remains of interest in the old port, except a curious art-deco clock

Amphibus leaves the Old Port.

tower and, at the far end of Old Montreal, the final **Harbour Commission Building**. Notre-Dame-de-Bon-Secours and the harbour commission building frame the entire area.

Rue de la Commune – once a bustling thoroughfare lined with carriages and transport wagons, with a promenade where strollers could watch the ships unload onto railway cars as thickets of mist swayed in the pitch like compass needles – is now a quiet, largely inactive street. But history is painted on the facades of the warehouses: J. Alfred Ouimet: Importater; Borque: Wholesale Grocer, Standard Paper Box. Condominiums are beginning to take root in some of these derelict buildings.

Place d'Armes: The expansion westward from the houses of Place Jacques Cartier to the skyscrapers of **Place d'Armes** represents, in broad terms, the transformation of Old Montreal from an 18th-century French colonial outpost to a 19th-century English business center. Keep in mind that pre-1759 Montreal

was a walled city, even though the hilly topography of the region left many of the taller buildings, including both churches, fully exposed to cannon fire from the St Lawrence River.

The ramparts had four main gates, including one off Rue Notre-Dame, and featured walls that were 18 feet high and 4 feet wide (5.5 by 1.2 meters). Historians emphasize their flimsiness and it is generally accepted that, had the city ever been attacked, this line of defense wouldn't have slowed the enemy for very long.

When the ramparts came down in the early 1800s, the symbolism was inescapable. No longer defensive, no longer insular, Montreal was now open for business with the rest of Canada and, thanks to the St Lawrence, the outside world. Place d'Armes was where the major transactions occurred.

But first a word about the cluster of streets between the two squares. For many tourists, and most locals, Old Montreal in summer is the sum of eating, drinking, and music. The narrow laneways, barely wide enough for a car, are lined with restaurants and cafés, along with Quebec's beloved *boîte à chanson*. **Rue St-Paul**, **Rue St-Vincent** and, further west, **Rue St-Pierre** are good places to wander.

The rule of thumb is to watch the crowds, see where they are heading; then, having gained a sense of which spots are popular and which are not, decide either to follow the fashion or *set* it. Among the more popular restaurants these days are *Auberge le Vieux St Gabriel* on Rue St-Gabriele; *Le Muscadin*, *Le Grill* with its lovely courtyard in summer, *Chez Queux*, and *Brochetterie du Vieux-Port*, all on Rue St-Paul. A wonderful Vietnamese establishment, *Le Pavillion de l'Indochina*, is buried among these largely French restaurants.

Also on St-Paul, combining pub atmospheres with lighter fare, are *Le Keg* and *Chez Brandy*. *Zhivago* and *Bijou* further along on St Pierre should also be **Invitation in the Old Port.**

mentioned and offer reasonably-priced sandwiches and salads. For less expensive dining, *Giorgio* offers Italian food in a fortress-like building at the foot of Rue St-Laurent, as does the intriguingly named *Hyppo Resto* a block up the street. *L'Usine de Spaghetti*, near Rosco's Hotel, also has fair prices.

Finally, worthy of mention if only as an aside, is the *McDonald's* at the intersection of Rue Notre-Dame and St-Laurent. A plaque outside the restaurant informs the history buff that here once lived Antoine Laumet de Lamoníe (1658–1730), founder of Detroit *and* governor of the state of Louisiana. Lamoníe was certainly a busy man.

Visiting a *boîte à chanson* is virtually mandatory on any trip to Montreal. Literally a "music box," these beerhalls are boisterous, frothy, *joie-de-vivre* establishments where musicians, often solo guitarists, run through the current repertoire of Québécois folk songs, anthems, the latest chart hits, and the packed houses sing along, applaud, proffer requests that are variously adopted, deferred, even rejected out of hand – all depending on the tone and direction of the night.

Boîtes are authentically Québécois and impervious, by and large, to the encroachment of technology on music. A guitar, a microphone, pitchers of beer, a convivial audience: what more is needed? *Alexandre* and *Aux Vieux St-Paul* on Place Jacques Cartier both offer music. The quintessential *boîtes* in Old Montreal, however, remain *Le Pierrot* and its neighbour *Aux Deux Pierrot* on Rue St-Paul. Come early; the line-ups are long an hour before the music begins.

Finally, don't forget about the **Vieux-Port**. Though largely dysfunctional as a port facility, the park adjacent to the St Lawrence offers long summer evenings of music and dancing. With the Montreal skyline as a backdrop and the river, active with ships and sailboats, flowing gently past, the setting alone makes the park worth a visit.

The former Hôtel Viger, now a civic building.

Montreal's historic growth: Back to Place d'Armes. To stand in the square is to witness in visual terms the historic growth of Montreal as a city. The casual mingling of commerce with religion is, at first, disconcerting; Notre-Dame Basilica and the adjoining seminary appear lost in a sea of banks and, by modern standards, miniature office towers. After a while, though, the juxtaposition jars less, both because of the congruities between the buildings and, perhaps, a resigned acceptance of the "business of faith," and vice versa, in Quebec's history.

Maisonneuve, whose statue adorns the square, would certainly not have blessed this marriage of God and Mammon. As the founder of Montreal, Paul de Chomeday de Maisonneuve definitely deserved a memorial in a prominent location. Why Place d'Armes, however, with Admiral Nelson gazing so incongruously upon the city hall in Place Jacques Cartier, is anybody's guess. The statue depicts Maisonneuve holding the banner of France. He is surrounded by other pioneers, including Jeanne Mance, Louis Hébert and Lambert Closse.

All the figures are, in turn, surrounded by the likes of the Bank of Montreal, the New York Insurance Company, and the Bank Canadienne Nationale. Are Montreal's founding fathers (and mothers) at all uncomfortable with the company? Though Maisonneuve's expression is dour, the limestone otherwise reveals little.

Parked along the southern rim of the Green, rain or shine, snow or sand storm, is Montreal's venerable fleet *des calèches* – horse-drawn carriages. They are hard to miss. If the sound of wooden wheels rattling over cobblestones doesn't prick up the ears, the bellow of the drivers certainly will. "*Un calèche, Monsieur?*" they will shout across Place d'Armes. Or, sizing up the mark as a tourist: "Ride through old Montreal for you, Sir?" In high season the competition is fierce and drivers fan out across

A forest of flags on Rue St-Paul.

the square like angry bees. But in winter the men are more stoic and sit inside their vehicles watching funnels of their breath dissipate into the frigid air. Under these circumstances the invitation to visitors is more matter-of-fact, without conviction.

Touring Old Montreal in a carriage can be charming. Try it during the winter, with a bear skin protecting the lower body and, ideally, a flask of something warm tucked inside the pocket. During the busy months it is often best to wait until evening to hire a carriage. The streets are full of moving shadows; shafts of light seep between drawn curtains, water trapped between cobblestones glistening under the yellow streetlamps.

A few words of advice for the would-be rider. First, bargain. The price quoted for a tour is not necessarily the bottom line, especially in off-season. The carriages are restricted as to where they can travel, though, so be realistic. Finally, use a ride to experience the atmosphere of Old Montreal at different times of the day and year. *Don't* hire one to sightsee. Always do that on foot.

Place d'Armes is also home to the ubiquitous tour buses dropping visitors off for cursory tours of Notre-Dame and environs. The traveler aboard one of these buses who aspires to jump ship couldn't choose a better place to do it than the square, a launching point for for just about all the most interesting areas of Old Montreal. Mutinies of this kind are to be encouraged.

Notre-Dame Basilica on Rue Notre-Dame is Montreal's most famous church. The first chapel, built within the fort in 1642, was covered with bark. The current structure (1829) is a little more grand. A contemporary Montreal poet describes the church in winter:

In laden February, on Rue St-Jacques
we are dreaming the breeding of lilacs
and shuffling on ice toward Notre-Dame.

Notre-Dame Basilica.

Suddenly the cold bright square
the two arms of her towers and the
walk
into the blue sunrise of her altar.

The "twin arms of her towers" are magnificent, the mark of greatness in architect James O'Donnell's design. Each measures 227 feet (69 meters) and were completed only in the 1840s by John Ostell, who succeeded as architect after O'Donnell's death. The plainness of the exterior was both aesthetic and practical. Quebec lacked the stone-workers to do the work; the decision to leave the facade unadorned was, in the context, a wise one.

The west tower of Notre-Dame also houses a 12-ton bell that took a dozen men to ring it. Even today, powered by electricity, the bell is used sparingly. The basilica, still considered among the finest examples of the Gothic revival style in North America, was visited by architects from other cities to learn from O'Donnell's mastery.

The interior of the basilica is majes-tic. Designed by Victor Bourgeau, who also worked on the Mary Queen of the World Cathedral in Dominion Square, it is at once massive and welcoming, a feat achieved by the original use of woodworking and carpentry. Bourgeau encouraged local artists to apply tradi-tional methods and tastes in decorating the church. The result is a glittering, and at times overwhelming, use of paints – the aqua-blue nave, for example, is deli-cate and refined – and ornately carved wood statuary.

Note especially the main altar, which is perpetually bathed in flowers, and the figures of Jeremiah and Ezekial at the bottom of the pulpit. The wrap-around balconies are also splendid, and serve to narrow the distance between the wor-shipper and the sacristy. Also worth noting is the haunting presence of giant pipes in the organ loft. The effect, achieved by back-lighting the organ (also done with the "sunrise" behind the altar), is stunning: fingers of bluish light that arc upward into the nave.

Notre-Dame Basilica.

Notre-Dame keeps long hours to satisfy the flow of tourists, admirers, and worshippers who wander the aisles. Services are held several times daily, and, if lucky, one might hear the organ. The sound is sonorous and decidedly celestial.

Adjacent to the west wall of the basilica stands – miraculously, some say – Montreal's oldest building. The **Vieux Seminaire de Saint-Sulpice** dates from 1680. The Sulpicians, the order that founded the seminary, at one time wielded enormous power in New France. In 1663 the Société de St-Sulpice took over missionary duties from the Société de Notre-Dame, becoming, in effect, the landlords of *all* the island of Montreal. Even Maurice Duplessis would have envied such power. Today, more than 300 years after arriving, the Sulpicians – no longer *seigneurs*, no longer even the moral arbiters of life in Montreal – still own and operate the fieldstone seminary.

The seminary clock, by the way, was installed in 1701. It is considered the first public clock in Canada. Though the works were replaced by electronic movements in 1966, it still functions only periodically. Setting one's watch by it would be unwise.

If Notre-Dame was *French* Canada's assertion of values, the **Bank of Montreal building** across Place d'Armes provided *English* Canada's retort. Neoclassical in design, this 1847 structure offers an ornate facade that boasts six Corinthian columns with pediment sculptures – discernable only through lenses of some sort – of a sailor, colonialist, and two Amerindians, one a "noble savage" and the other a recalcitrant hell-bent on rejecting civilization. The facade was designed by a local architect, John Wells.

The interior of the bank is stunning. The lobby is spacious, the colors gentle and the light soft at all times of day. The atrium in particular, linking the older part of the building with a 1905 addition, is lovely, lined by eight Ionic col-

The Vieux Seminaire.

umns of Vermont granite with marble bases. The walls of the atrium are made of pink marble transported to Montreal from Tennessee. In the majestic front hall one discovers another 32 columns, also of granite, and counters of marble. Gold leaf covers everything and elaborate chandeliers hang from the ceiling.

What gives the interior its grace is both the simplicity of the design and the continuous presence of natural light streaming down from massive windows. The bank's architects worked directly from models of Italian churches; it is hard not to remark upon the "basilica" style of the structure. A provocative gesture? Artistic inspiration? Also worth a look is a fine statue of Patria in the atrium. The marble statue is a memorial to Canadians who died in World War I.

The Bank of Montreal offers visitors a small museum off the main lobby devoted to numismatics – money, to the layman. Displays of banknotes, coins, a collection of elaborate 19th-century

piggy banks, and other interesting memorabilia are to be found. Tours are also available in both official languages.

In tone and proportion the Bank of Montreal headquarters sent a message: on **Rue St-Jacques**, the street crossing the north end of the square, business would be calm, orderly and efficient. The result was the "Wall Street of Canada," an appellation applied to "St James Street" as anglo-Montrealers defiantly called it.

Until only 20 years ago, Rue St-Jacques was Canada's financial center, a street of busy Victorian buildings swathed to varying degrees in stucco, wrought-iron, columns, and elaborate porticos. A trolley, running down the middle of the road, serviced office workers.

Among the many stately edifices are the **Molson's Bank** at 228 St-Jacques, the **Bank of Commerce** across the street, an intriguing facade back at 230 that offers pillars and statues and, for the moment at least, little else – the building *behind* the facade has been demolished. The Molson's Bank, built in 1866 using brewery profits that today fuel, among other things, the Montreal Canadiens hockey team, is impressive, as are all the offices at the corner of St-Jacques and Rue St-Pierre. None, however, quite stack up to the **Royal Bank**.

Like it or not – and many Montrealers consider the building an exercise in ostentation – the former head office of the Royal Bank at 360 St-Jacques is a must-see on any tour of the business district. Constructed in 1928, the Royal Bank was for a brief period the tallest structure not only in Canada but the entire British Empire.

The exterior is grand but austere, even sober. Not so the interior. Architects who designed the building were said to have had in mind the Medici Palace in Florence, Italy. They certainly had ambitions. The main doors, framed in bronze replicas of coins, lead into a lobby noted for its coffered ceiling and

The Stock Exchange tower in Victoria Square.

the marble steps that climb to the main hall. Arches are covered with reddish limestone and walls are decorated with the coats of arms of Canada's provinces. Again the ceiling is ornately coffered; more marble on the walls, bronze screens, mosaic tiles covering the floor inlaid with Canada's royal coat of arms.

The effect is either dazzling or disheartening, depending on aesthetic tastes. Both in size and decoration, the Royal Bank begs comparison with the Bank of Montreal building. To the untrained eye, they are both formidable.

In the 1880s many commercial businesses followed the fashion and moved their offices further west to **Place Victoria** at Rue St-Jacques and Rue McGill. The square, now largely obscured by the construction of buildings on its green, was for a brief period a prestigious residential address and one of Montreal's prime shopping districts. Barely 20 years later, however, department stores, lured by the rapidly growing English community along Rue Sherbrooke, moved again to the current "mecca" of Rue Ste-Catherine. Place Victoria faded rapidly.

The historical demographics of commercial life in Montreal are a study in skitterishness and insecurity. Only the stalwarts, the banks and loan companies, had the presence of mind to stay along St-Jacques; until, that is, recent political developments precipitated a wholesale rethinking of location.

Place d'Armes features other prominent buildings. Dozens of offices and banks, many of them still functioning, line the streets on and around the square. But the area is also the focal point for Montreal's considerable newspaper industry. Within a few blocks can be found the offices of nearly all the major newspapers, and one significant ghost.

The *Montreal Star*, once the city's largest English paper, was located at 245 St-Jacques in the heart of the business district. Though the *Star* ceased publication in 1979, the *Montreal Ga-*

Old house, now a restaurant, in Côte du Beaver Hill.

zette, the current flagbearer, has its offices both on Rue St-Antoine and in the old *Star* building on St-Jacques. The *Gazette*, which began publishing in 1778, is the city's oldest newspaper. *La Presse*, North America's best-selling French daily, has both its original and modern home at the corner of St-Jacques and St-Laurent. The old *La Presse* building is quite stately.

Also in Old Montreal, appropriately isolated from the larger community, are the offices of the erudite and influential *Le Devoir*. If the other buildings *look* like the offices of large, busy, mass-appeal publications, then *Le Devoir*, groomed for a different class of reader, is appropriately solemn and demure. It is located at 211 Rue St-Sacrement.

Banks, business, newspapers: the markers of the new 19th-century industrial city as delineated by Dickens in England, Zola in France, James and Dreiser in the United States. Place d'Armes is the product of these modern realities – Second Empire Paris, Victorian London, the architectural landscape of reconstruction New York and Chicago. But, among the soaring edifices on the square, none are more impressive, more substantial, than the towers of Notre-Dame. The panorama is appropriately skewed. Peaceful co-existence has always been the unspoken motto in Montreal. Even the old warrior Maisonneuve, compromised by his location, appears resigned to the fact.

Origins, health, religion, death: Montreal began in **Place Royale** and **Place d'Youville**. These two squares intersect each other at the site of Pointe-à-Callière, where Samuel de Champlain landed in 1611 and declared the spot a "place royale." Thirty years later, Maisonneuve chose that same site to erect the fort that became Ville-Marie. An obelisk at the eastern end of Place d'Youville – Place Royale runs north to south, d'Youville east to west – commemorates the event. The inscription emphasizes that Maisonneuve ordered the simultaneous construction of a fort, **Café society.**

a chapel *and* a graveyard. Health, religion, and death: the basics.

It is difficult to imagine how Ville-Marie looked nearly 400 years ago. The St Lawrence has been pushed back for landfill, a small river that ran alongside the fort is now underground, and the dense forest that made reaching Mount Royal an arduous journey is today a forest of skyscrapers, the walk made tricky by rush-hour traffic. When Maisonneuve ordered the shifting of the village to Place d'Armes – 300 feet (100 meters) north – it was a move "inland," away from the dangers of the St Lawrence. The scale of things has changed dramatically.

But **Pointe-à-Callière** remains the literal birthplace of Montreal, and the surrounding streets its oldest neighborhood. A plaque in Place Royale calls the site the "first public square of Montreal," affixing the date 1657 to its creation. In a sense the "community" of Montreal also dates from that year. Before 1657 Ville-Marie was a wildly remote fort inhabited by a singular group of people: adventurers, traders, missionaries, soldiers and their officers.

Though it was where they lived, Ville-Marie was not their home. Instead the fort was variously a potential market, potential mission, potential conquest. The stake these pioneers had in the colony, while considerable, was not likely to produce citizens and samaritans. That required settlers, ordinary people devoted to simply establishing a life for themselves and their children. Communities are the sum of citizens, not conquistadors. In European society the traditional symbol of a community, a town, was a public square. So, too, in Montreal.

Despite its importance, this part of Old Montreal is the least known and least explored. From the mid-18th century, attention was drawn east to Place d'Armes and Place Jacques Cartier, never to return. All of which makes the area well worth a look. With a little imagination the derelict buildings are

Royal Bank of Montreal.

again bustling, the streets are jammed with carriages, and the squares throng with strollers, businessmen, and nuns from the nearby hospital crossing the green to tend to the sick.

Place Royale is disfigured by a building on its green. Surviving 19th-century photographs reveal a leafy park with a low fence to keep it neat; today the green is half concrete, half construction site. While several interesting buildings remain, the sense of the square has long been lost. At its southern end is a grandiose statue of **John Young** (1811-1879), the harbour commissioner credited with making the city a world-class port. Young's gaze still encompasses Rue de la Commune and the eastern docking facilities.

Keep in mind that the river, which today appears vaguely in the distance from Old Montreal, once flowed precariously near the shops and warehouses along the Commune. Photos from the period tell the story: floods, especially in late winter, submerging the lower streets in three feet of water. Though landfill curbed the St Lawrence's reckless power, stinging winds and sleet remind the visitor of the seaway's proximity.

Place d'Youville, Old Montreal's largest square, commences at the statue and runs west four blocks to Rue McGill. Besides Pointe-à-Callière, the square's other main attraction is the **Caserne Centrale des Pompiers**, a stylish 1915 fire station that combines Dutch and English architectural styles. The firehouse is now a museum of Montreal history and is worth a visit for anyone interested in studying the city's growth.

Place d'Youville was once the site of the parliament for both Upper and Lower Canada. The building, erected after the 1837 rebellion, lasted only a dozen years before rioters, protesting an unpopular British bill, burned it to the ground. Canada's pre-1867 legislature was housed briefly in the Marché Bonsecours, then resumed its quixotic search for a home: Kingston, Quebec City, and finally the current capital of Ottawa. There are a number of restored buildings on the square. The most famous, the **Hôpital des Soeurs Grises**, runs off Rue Normand. It traces its origins to 1693, the year François Charon de la Bare resolved to begin a "house of charity" for Montreal's sick, poor and handicapped.

In 1753 Maria d'Youville, who founded the Sisters of Charity, extended the project into a hospital under the care of the sisters, known locally – no one is quite sure why – as the gray nuns (*soeurs grises*). Though the hospital moved to Rue Dorchester in 1871, many of the original structures escaped demolition and were restored in the late 1970s. The job was superbly done, and the hospital's west wing, including the remains of the original chapel, are visible on Rue St-Pierre.

The courtyard facing the square is also charming. As well, a delicate stained-glass window along Rue St-

Tomorrow's customers.

Normand brightens an otherwise austere, functional exterior. Both Hôpital des Soeurs Grises and the adjoining **Écurie d'Youville** (d'Youville Stables) are currently finding use as multipurpose facilities. The courtyard of the stables, surrounded by 19th-century buildings, is a pleasant place for a cold drink in the summer.

The bottom of St-Pierre, also off the square, is a heartening example of successful urban renewal. Until recently empty, the block now houses luxury apartments, law offices, architectural firms, even a fancy cheese and chocolate shop. It is also the location of a small museum devoted to Marc-Aurèle Fortin (1888–1970), an important Québécois painter. Fortin's watercolours of the St Lawrence in all its seasonal variety are famous in Canada.

Further west, at the extreme edge of Old Montreal, are blocks of impressive 19th-century warehouses and customs houses. **Rue McGill** in particular has several fine buildings; the ornate former headquarters of the Grand Trunk Railway at 360, and the Wilson Chambers Building at 474, near Place Victoria. The third customs house at 400 Place de la Commune features a clock tower and a small cross above its turret. The building is designed from the Beaux-Arts classical style.

The streets north of Place d'Youville are still largely in limbo. Many buildings remain derelict, awaiting an entrepreneur to restore them to life. Wandering along Rue St-Pierre, Rue St-Nicolas and Rue St-Francois-Xavier, especially at night, can be an eerie but wonderful experience. Again, imagine a movie set once the crew has left for the day. Restaurants, antique and craft shops, the occasional apartment block, are sprinkled among the stone skeletons. The more willing the explorer, the more intriguing the explorations.

Beside the *Le Devoir* offices on St-Sacrement, the area also boasts the **Centaur Theater** at 453 St-François-Xavier. The theater, Montreal's leading

Elegance in Old Montreal.

English-language company, occupies a 1903 Beaux-Art structure that was home to the city's stock exchange until 1966. Before the Centaur building, the stock exchange was located in the *Le Devoir* offices around the corner. Before *that*, well, Montreal's 19th-century wheelers and dealers did their business in a coffee shop on Rue St-Paul!

Buildings in Old Montreal change functions far more quickly than they change facades.Why shouldn't they? Historic neighbourhoods often atrophy because they fail to make themselves useful to modern needs. A neighborhood needn't lose its soul to remain vital. Old Montreal has been struggling to retain its shape – or, better, to find a *new* shape – for nearly 30 years. Though the struggle is far from over, there is reason to be optimistic. Both the Vieux-Port and Old Montreal are slated for massive, ongoing restoration projects.

As part of the revitalization of the port, for example, in conjunction with the 350th anniversary celebrations in 1992, one suggestion involved removing some of the piers to "return" the shore of the St Lawrence *closer* to Rue de la Commune. Other plans, to whet the appetite, included the restoration of the Marché Bonsecours as a public building, the complete overhaul of Place Royale into an archaeology and history museum, the building of underground parking facilities on both Place d'Youville and Place Jacques Cartier to ease summer congestion.

The list was enormous and included both public projects and those funded by the private sector. Among the many private projects were plans for a hotel, a world trade center, and the systematic building by building restoration for modern use of the two main business streets, Rue St-Jacques and Rue McGill. All of this in the near future? Apparently. Old Montreal is already an integral part of any traveler's visit to the city. Soon it may be once again a comfortable and dynamic living space for its own citizens.

Pedal power.

Festival City

Montrealers start the summer months with a bang: the International Fireworks Festival features pyrotechnical wizardry with a twist: music! Try to imagine Tchaikovsky's *1812 Overture* to salvos of Roman candles and bombs, this by the inventor of the Roman candle and director of the Festival, Giovanni Panzera. Over the years, Montrealers have been treated to the very best in the field, with competitors from China, Japan, Spain, France, Italy and the US.

Then follows the International Jazz Festival, one of the main events of this type in the world. A small organization only 10 years ago, the Montreal Jazz Festival has become a 10-day extravaganza with over 500 musicians on outdoor stages and indoor concerts playing to throngs and throngs of onlookers. Jazz legends such as Oscar Peterson, a native Montrealer, team up with jazzmen the like of Pat Metheny, Dave Brubeck, Wynton Marsalis and Dizzy Gillespie, plus top players from Africa, South America and the Caribbean.

No sooner has the Jazz Festival come and gone than the Just for Laughs *(Juste pour rire)* comedy festival takes over, bringing together comedians from the US, Britain, France, Belgium and Canada. Comedy is a big ticket in Québécois culture: comedians have so pervaded everyday life that they often star in television commercials. Comedian André-Philippe Gagnon with his one-man rendition of the popular hit *We are the World* has even made it into the "inner sanctum" as a guest on American television's *Johnny Carson Show*. Just for Laughs organizer Gilbert Rochon has created a comedy school in Montreal in order to ensure the future success of the genre.

Montreal is also the home of the only circus school in North America, l'Ecole Nationale de Cirque, whose students are featured in the Cirque du Solcil, a one-of-a-kind circus (only one ring and no elephants or tigers) that has won acclaim for its high-flying theatrics in many an international competition. The Cirque du Soleil unfolds like a play, each act building on the other. In one popular act, a clown dons ski boots and, on a trampoline, conducts the *1812 Overture*.

Talent is definitely one of the city's major exports if one considers the MSO, the Montreal Symphony Orchestra, acclaimed as "the best French orchestra in the world today" under the baton of Swiss maestro Charles Dutoit. Montreal has also sent a great many names off the pop chart: Luba, Men Without Hats, The Box, singers Daniel Lavoie, Roch Voisine, Céline Dion and Ginette Reno. Montrealers Maureen Forrester, Louis and Gino Quilico and Joseph Rouleau have also made a name for themselves in the great opera halls of the world.

In dance, Montreal has produced many successes, among them La La La Human Steps, Ballets Eddy Toussaint, Marie Chouinard, Ginette Laurin and Margie Gillis. In theater, a new breed of directors, such as René-Daniel Dubois, René-Richard Cyr and Robert Lepage, have staged collective works in old firehouses, abandoned warehouses, train stations and chapels.

Many theatergoers have been enthralled by a six-hour play, *La Trilogie des dragons*, staged in an abandoned warehouse in the Old Port of Montreal. The performance is a rendition of a French play from the Middle Ages complete with period music and incorporates the technical wizardry of the *Théâtre sans fil* (producers of *The Lord of the Rings* with its giant puppets). This is a small sample of Montreal theater fare, yet one representative of its diversity.

Montreal has also taken improvisation to new heights: actors from France, Belgium and Switzerland now participate in improvisation "play-offs," a form of theater popularized by the *Lige nationale d'improvisation*, a takeoff from the National Hockey League, complete with teams, striped shirt referees, and organ background. Teams of actors are given a theme on which to improvise. The audience is responsible for the scoring and the critique. They show their disapproval in no uncertain terms by throwing galoshes on the "ice."

Summer finally winds down in Montreal with the International Film Festival, where bleary-eyed film buffs rush from one showing to the next in an effort to keep pace with 200-plus films.

DOWNTOWN

The St Lawrence River is a confluence of seas and lakes, a brackish bridge between the mighty Atlantic extending to Europe and the Great Lakes that form the watery heart of North America. Montreal's downtown is also a meeting place, a concourse of commercial enterprises, businesses, and residential neighborhoods. North America and Europe mingle freely in every district to produce a lively jumble of restaurants, shops, churches, architectural styles and ethnic communities. Together, they create a wonderfully vibrant picture that reflects the historical diversity of Montreal.

The first settlers built their homes snugly against the St Lawrence River in the area now referred to as "Old Montreal." Though the river was an important source of livelihood, it was also the very thing that eventually drove citizens to higher ground. Persistent flooding in the 19th century prompted city-dwellers to move north where the views from the mountain and the beauty of the surroundings assured the development of permanent settlements.

The downtown has undergone three eras of expansion. The first occurred during the late 19th century when English and Scottish fur traders accumulated fortunes and the city center shifted west from Place d'Armes to Dominion Square. During this period, waves of immigrants caused an expansion eastward, lengthening the parameters of the inner city. As a result, the area north of Rue Sherbrooke was transformed from farmland into affluent urban neighborhoods. The majority of Montreal's famous churches and illustrious buildings were constructed during this initial expansion.

Predictably, the subsequent period of growth began after World War II, extending through the building boom of the 1950s whose architectural aesthet-

ics have not worn well. This rapid development radically altered and in some cases destroyed certain downtown neighborhoods. Under the prolonged leadership of Montreal's mayor Jean Drapeau, the city underwent a third period of expansion during the 1960s and '70s, a period marked by bold and often dazzling architectural experimentation. Many "world-class" projects such as the Métro, Expo '67, and the facilities for the 1976 Olympics were constructed during Mayor Drapeau's mayoral reign.

The Underground: Montreal's urban development, however, has not only produced a vibrant surface life, but also an intriguing subterranean world. Begun in the 1960s and apparently based on an idea by Leonardo Da Vinci, Montreal's "Underground City" currently includes two railway stations, a bus terminal, six major hotels, 1,200 commercial businesses, 1,400 boutiques, 150 restaurants, 40 bank branches, two department stores, 30 cinemas and

Preceding pages: Place des Arts. Left, architectural contrasts. Right, image of the Underground City, home to countless boutiques.

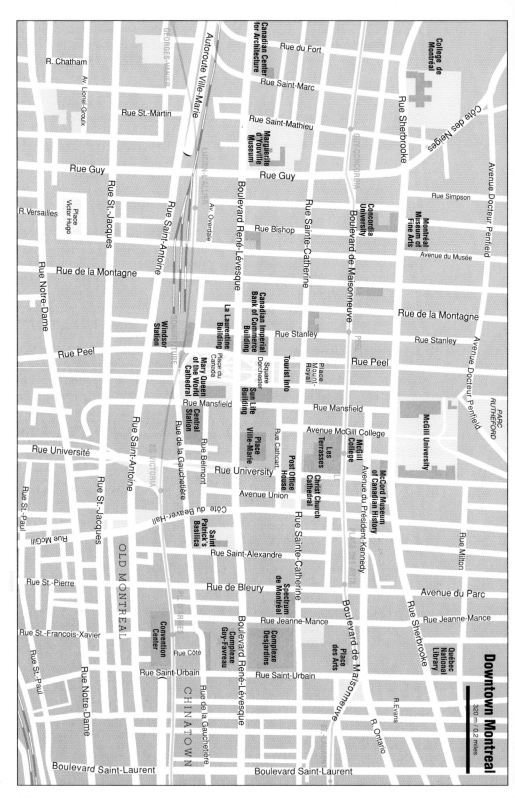

Downtown Montreal

320 m / 0.2 miles

Streets and labels on the map:

R. Chatham
Av. Lionel-Groulx
Rue St.-Martin
Rue Guy
R. Versailles
Place Victor Hugo
Rue St.-Jacques
Rue de la Montagne
Rue Notre-Dame
Rue Peel
Rue Université
Rue St.-Paul
Rue McGill
Rue St.-Pierre
Rue St.-François-Xavier
Rue St.-Paul
Rue Notre-Dame

GEORGES-VANIER
Autoroute Ville-Marie
LUCIEN-L'ALLIER
Rue du Fort
Rue Saint-Marc
Rue Saint-Mathieu
Marguerite d'Youville Museum
Rue Guy
Av. Overdale
Boulevard René-Lévesque
Rue Bishop
Canadian Imperial Bank of Commerce Building
La Laurentine Building
Place du Canada
Square Dorchester
Windsor Station
Rue Mansfield
Central Station
Sun Life Building
Place Ville-Marie
Rue Belmont
Rue de la Gauchetière
Rue University
Côte du Beaver-Hall
Saint Patrick's Basilica
Rue Saint-Alexandre
Rue de Bleury
Convention Center
Rue Côté
Rue Saint-Urbain
CHINATOWN
OLD MONTREAL
Rue Saint-Antoine
Rue St.-Jacques

Canadian Center for Architecture
Collège de Montréal
Rue Sherbrooke
Côte des Neiges
Concordia University
Boulevard de Maisonneuve
Montreal Museum of Fine Arts
Rue Simpson
Avenue du Musée
Avenue Docteur Penfield
Rue Sainte-Catherine
GUY-CONCORDIA
PEEL
Rue Stanley
Tourist Info
Place Mount-Royal
Rue Peel
Rue de la Montagne
Rue Stanley
Rue Mansfield
Avenue McGill College
McGill College
Les Terrasses
McCord Museum of Canadian History
McGill University
PARC RUTHEFORD
Avenue Docteur Penfield
Post Office House
Avenue Union
Christ Church Cathedral
Rue Cathcart
Rue Sainte-Catherine
Avenue du Président-Kennedy
Rue Milton
Spectrum de Montréal
Complexe Guy-Favreau
Boulevard René-Lévesque
Boulevard Saint-Laurent
Rue de la Gauchetière
Rue Jeanne-Mance
Rue Saint-Urbain
Complexe Desjardins
Place des Arts
Boulevard de Maisonneuve
Rue Sherbrooke
Avenue du Parc
Rue Jeanne-Mance
Québec National Library
R. Evans
R. Ontario
Boulevard Saint-Laurent

theaters, and sundry other outlets.

In a city where temperatures fluctuate dramatically, the underground downtown offers a warm (or cool), waterproof underworld that, glittering with chrome and smooth marble, resembles a labyrinthine but opulent ant colony. Shops, businesses and services are linked by Montreal's impressive and efficient transit system, the Métro – a network of 65 stations which were individually designed by prominent artists and architects. Entrances to Montreal's remarkable substratum are found throughout the downtown area, as well as in all subway stations.

The downtown core is large, bordered roughly by Avenue Atwater, Rue St-Denis, Rue St-Antoine, and Rue Sherbrooke (*see map*), but when divided into five main areas makes for a relatively easy tour. These areas are: Rue Sherbrooke and Golden Square Mile; Dominion Square; Rue Ste-Catherine; Chinatown; and St-Laurent and the Main. Even in fine weather,

you'll probably want to make use of Montreal's excellent *Métro* to access these areas. For the sake of this chapter, we'll begin our tour at the northern edge of the downtown – that is, at the foot of Mount Royal along Rue Sherbrooke.

Expansive era: The **Golden Square Mile** was the name bestowed upon the neighborhood enclosed by Boulevard René Lévesque, Rue Guy, Rue Université and Avenue des Pins. In 1900, the 25,000 residents of this square mile controlled 70 percent of the wealth of Canada. Those stunning figures and the buildings that remain from that period recall a grand and expansive era in Montreal's history. The most obvious symbol of this golden age is the **Ritz-Carlton Hotel**, located on Sherbrooke and Rues Drummond (*see page 156*).

Imagine Rue Sherbrooke nearly 100 years ago when the Ritz-Carlton towered over the three-storey mansions and stately elm trees that lined the boulevard. Today Rue Sherbrooke is lined with many modern hotels, including the

The Erskine and American United Church.

Four Seasons and the Shangri-La, office towers, art galleries in converted turn-of-the-century houses, and exclusive shops such as the famous **Cartier** and Canada's own **Holt-Renfrew**.

Perching gargoyles: There are also a few elegant apartment houses, including the imposing granite edifice just across the street from the hotel. The **Château Apartments** were built in 1925 for Senator Pamphile du Tremblay, a former owner of the powerful and influential *La Presse* newspaper. The building is intended to resemble a castle on the Loire River in France and has some amusing details. Gargoyles perch on window ledges holding coats of arms and side turrets, and stone-engraved crosses adorn the corners of the building. It also has a lovely interior courtyard.

This château-style design, with its decorative turrets, facades and porticos, can also be seen in many public and private buildings throughout Quebec. It represents the dominant architectural trend in the province during the first half of the 20th century.

Next door to the Château Apartments is the **Erskine and American United Church**. Built in 1863, the church and its neighbor share a moody, almost medieval ambience. The severity of the rusticated stone exterior contrasts the warm tones and circular floor plan of the church's interior. The exquisite stained-glass windows are from the Tiffany Studio in New York.

Along the north side of Rue Sherbrooke, next to the church, is the **Museum of Fine Arts**. Founded in 1860, it is Canada's oldest museum. The edifice has a classical design and is faced in Vermont marble, a theme carried through to the lobby which is dominated by an elegant marble staircase. The original building was quite small and the extension, completed in 1977, is unfortunately not well matched to the original and suffers from a lack of natural light.

The museum's permanent collection consists of a wide range of paintings, sculptures and drawings from North America and Europe. There is a good sampling of European art from the 17th century onwards, including works by El Greco, Rodin, Dalí and Picasso. Canadian Art is represented by Inuit woodcarvings, soapstone sculpture and paintings by the Group of Seven – a seminal group of Ontario landscape painters – and contemporary artists like Paul-Emile Boranas, Jean-Paul Riopelle and Betty Goodwin.

The museum also houses a fine collection of decorative arts from around the world. Regrettably, large portions of the permanent collection are often displaced because of lack of space and the demands of visiting exhibits. As a result, an extensive addition, located across the street, has recently been under construction.

Opposite the museum, to the west, is the noteworthy **Church of Saint Andrew and Saint Paul**. It is one of the many examples of Gothic revival archi-

Tiffany window in the Erskine and American Church.

154

tecture in Montreal and is best known for its stunning stained-glass windows. Two windows, located in the rear (left) and donated by the Allan family, are believed to have been done by Sir Edward Burne-Jones, the famous Pre-Raphaelite painter.

The Golden Square: Avenue du Musée, adjacent to the Museum of Fine Arts, is probably one of the best preserved streets in the area. It has little traffic and modern construction has made modest impact. The pleasures of residential architecture are subtle enough; and a stroll through this neighborhood can transport you back to a different, slower-paced age.

The status and wealth of these homes sets the imagination to wondering what life must have been like during the area's zenith in the first decades of the 20th century. A recent exhibit of paintings at the Museum of Fine Arts, borne out of a similar curiosity, discovered Monets, Sisleys, Renoirs, and Turners among the private collections of Mon-

Dali's Lobster at the Fine Arts Museum.

treal's former elite. Men who had expanded their wealth as rapidly and as haphazardly as Canada itself expanded – through railways, ship-building, natural resources – built extravagant homes for their families and furnished them expensively.

Remember that, at this time, the neighborhood would have been appropriately "out of the way" from the hustle and bustle of the downtown. With the slope of Mount Royal affording stunning vistas, with trees providing the requisite privacy, and with the Ritz-Carlton only minutes away on Rue Sherbrooke, and Ogilvy's Department Store three blocks further south on Rue Ste-Catherine, life would have been both tranquil and convenient.

The southern face of the mountain or the forests tucked into its plateau would have been ideal for a summer promenade. Hospitals and social clubs were close by, and excellent schools – such as Trafalgar Girls' School on Docteur Penfield and McGill University on Rue

THE GRANDE DAME OF SHERBROOKE STREET

Every major city deserves a Ritz-Carlton Hotel. Few, however, are lucky enough to have one. Montreal, however, is one of those "lucky" cities. Since its construction in 1911, Montreal's Ritz-Carlton has been a measuring stick for elegance and civility. The hotel is a symbol of old-world gentility in pleasant contrast to the sterile, hermetically-sealed towers that pass for gracious accommodation today. The fact that it hasn't changed much in its 80-year history is precisely why it is such a special place.

In the early 1900s, Charles Ritz was thought to be the owner of the best hotel in all of Europe. The Ritz in Paris, in fact, rivaled the equally splendid Carlton of London. It was Charles Hosmer, president of the Canadian Pacific Telegram, who thought Montreal could be well served by bringing the two great hotel traditions together.

Charles Ritz was finally convinced, but not without making stipulations unheard of at the time. He demanded that every room in the hotel have a private adjoining bathroom and a telephone. He also insisted that every floor be equipped with its own kitchen and that the concierge be available at all hours to fulfill the needs – no matter how ludicrous – of the guests. As if that wasn't enough, he also mandated certain changes in the hotel's interior design and decorations.

His instincts proved right; the Ritz-Carlton became synonymous with top-quality service and the hotel assumed the status of a North American landmark.

An illustrious moment in the hotel's early history came in 1916 when C.F. Sise, Bell Telephone's Chairman of the Board, made the country's first transcontinental telephone call from the Ritz-Carlton to Vancouver. It was also during those early years that the hotel played host to luminaries like the Prince of Wales, Queen Mary of Romania, and Hollywood stars Douglas Fairbanks and Mary Pickford.

While out-of-town guests were enjoying the Ritz-Carlton's fine service, the hotel established itself as an "unadvertised" private club for Montreal's anglophone business moguls. In the Ritz Bar, the Café Paris, or the courtyard garden, business and political decisions – big and small – were sealed. (The Café Paris now offers smokey, crowded but animated conversation against a piano backdrop.)

Though the hotel's bright lights were dimmed during the two world wars, its luminary status among the city's English speaking elite picked up again in the 1950s and early 1960s, and now rooms command more than $200 a night.

So equated was the Ritz-Carlton with Montreal's business community that Canadian novelist Mordecai Richler immortalized the hotel in his novel *Joshua Then and Now*. His characters, attracted to the cozy charm of the Ritz, mourn its passing as a covert private club in a humorous send-up: "The incomparable Ritz where once impeccably schooled brokers could conspire over malt whiskies and dishes of smoked almonds to send dubious mining stock soaring…"

Nowadays, just about anyone can work into the Café Paris, which, although no longer "private," is neverthless rather "elite." A shifting political atmosphere in the 1970s changed the business face of Montreal; still, the Ritz remained as solid as its granite facade.

In a way, one can admire the hotel as much for its stubborn self-confidence as for its elegance. The lobby is small, the bar is crowded, and both the number of rooms and functional facilities are modest. The Ritz-Carlton has no gym, no pool, not even the now mandatory disco. (If, however, you are of international fame, count on devoted service – two staff members to each guest!)

What was good enough for guests 60 years ago, the hotel believes, is, with few modifications, good enough today. Status is not measured in dimensions; excellence not commensurate with the varieties of gurgling fountains in a lobby. These qualities of status and excellence, elegance and charm, are, the Ritz-Carlton suggests, more subtle and elusive than we may care to believe. The line-up of Rolls-Royces and custom-built Lincolns indicates that the message continues to be communicated where it counts.

Sherbrooke – absorbed the progeny of the Montreal's affluent.

The business community centered around Dominion Square and Rue St-Jacques in Old Montreal always had a job for favored sons. And neighbors on the Golden Square Mile were, naturally, the "right people:" other business tycoons, bankers, various anglo-politicians, possibly foreign dignitaries from the consulates; even the rare wealthy French Montrealer who had been lured into the area by a beautiful home. Elegant living; propriety, social networks; along these steep narrow lanes life was, for a while "perfect," where all the newly gentrified Canadians wanted to live.

Dominion Square: A gradual shift of commercial enterprises from Old Montreal to areas further north allowed Dominion Square to assume a predominant position in the downtown plan by the late-19th century: the presence of corporate headquarters, a large hotel and a center of transportation helped to secure

One minute to catch the train at Windsor Station.

its place. Though today many large office towers line Boulevard René-Lévesque, Dominion Square retains a kind of symbolic importance.

It is one of the few green spaces left in a forest of brick and concrete and is always quite busy, especially during the summer. Office workers take their lunches under the tall elms while commuters stream across the square to Windsor Station. The stateliness of an older Dominion Square remains, redefined by the number of glass and concrete skyscrapers that vie for attention.

The square, once a Catholic cemetery, was officially made a public park in 1869. For years it was the site of Montreal's immense "ice palaces" and the center of the city's elaborate winter carnivals. Today there are a number of statues on the green including those of Robert Burns, the Scottish poet, Sir Wilfred Laurier, Prime Minister of Canada between 1896–1911, and a particularly well-executed monument commemorating the soldiers who fell in

the Boer War. There is also a fountain dedicated at the time of Queen Victoria's diamond jubilee.

The highlight of the square is the justly famous **Sun Life Building**. Begun in 1914, its present form did not fully emerge until the completion of the two wings in the late 1920s. Variously described as an immense "temple" or "wedding cake," the building was once Canada's largest and helped firmly establish Dominion Square as Montreal's new downtown center.

The **Windsor Hotel** deserves attention, albeit brief. Once among Montreal's finest hostelries, the Windsor spanned an entire city block and had a sumptuously decorated interior. A series of fires resulted in the hotel's demolition and today only a late addition to the original remains. Designed in a 19th-century Parisian style, the Windsor Building now houses offices. On the site of the old hotel is the **Bank of Commerce**, a tall 1962 glass tower with an extraordinary narrow base.

On the southeast side of the square stands **Mary Queen of the World Cathedral**. Its dome, once considered imposing, is now adrift in a sea of skyscrapers. If the cathedral's exterior looks familiar, that's because it was modeled after St Peter's in Rome – note the similar line of statues on the portico and the Greek columns. Mary Queen of the World Cathedral is only a quarter of the size of its Roman model and lacks, perhaps, a significant measure of grandeur. There was strong opposition to the plan to replicate St Peter's, particularly by the church's primary architect, Victor Bourgeau, the man also responsible for the interior of Notre-Dame Basilica. Bourgeau lost the argument and the aesthetic judgement of the church is still just a matter of opinion.

The cathedral, which took 20 years to build, was completed in 1884 and quickly became the center of worship for downtown Catholic residents. Its interior is bright and airy. The altar canopy, a reproduction of Bernini's *Baldacchino* in Rome, is probably the most notable aspect in an otherwise uninspired design.

At the far end of the square, at the corner of Rues Peel and de la Gauchetière, is the **Château Champlain Hotel**. A rather lifeless concrete tower, it was descibed by one travel writer as an "immense cheese grater."

Saved from the wrecking ball by a group of concerned Montreal citizens, **Windsor Station** dominates the southwest corner of Dominion Square. The site for the station was chosen for its elevation, away from the St Lawrence's menacing spring floods. From a distance, the station looks like a fortress, fitted out with arched windows and rusticated stone.

Designed by New York architect Bruce Price, the building is a celebration of strength and solidity. Its quasi-Gothic style and castle-like design are reminiscent of other structures built for the Canadian Pacific Railway by Price. A number of wings were added as the

Bath-time for Brother André, founder of St Joseph's Oratory.

railway company grew, with the final one completed in the 1950s.

Windsor Station's imposing exterior is not, however, matched by its interior. Recent renovations have left the waiting area cold and uninteresting.

Next is **St George's Anglican Church**. St George's was built to accommodate the city's west-end Protestant population. The church was completed in 1870 and is the square's oldest remaining building. It is certainly worth venturing inside simply to admire the carved woodwork that covers the interior. The entire ceiling is also exquisitely carved and has managed to survive the years gracefully.

St George's is evidence of the immense wealth of the Anglican community in Montreal and merits comparison with the lovely cathedral on Ste-Catherine. From its steps the view of Dominion Square is magnificent: the dome of the cathedral can be best appreciated from this angle – what, perhaps, the Catholic bishop had in mind!

One can also gain a fuller appreciation of the **Dominion Square Building** located to the north between Rues Metcalfe and Peel. Its distinctive design is actually Florentine. Though the facade has been renovated to match the commercial storefronts on Rue Ste-Catherine, from the steps of St George's, one can still appreciate the gracefully arched upper windows that look out over the green.

If Dominion Square serves as a symbol of 19th-century Montreal, **Place Ville-Marie** represents the city's modern face. The complex, located just east of the square on Boulevard René-Lévesque, looms up behind the Sun Life Building. Place Ville-Marie's cruciform shape – unabashedly symbolic in an overwhelmingly Catholic city – figures in many travel brochure photos. The project was one of the first by the now world famous I.M. Pei, who later caused a stir with his glass pyramid addition to the Louvre Museum in Paris.

What makes Place Ville-Marie par-

Mary Queen of the World Cathedral, with permanent sentinel.

ticularly distinctive is the vast underground city beneath it and, as conceived of by city planners in the 1960s, links the complex with other plazas and the subway system. Place Ville-Marie is, in a sense, the prototype for this radical urban development. (Ironically, the underground city concept has recently come under fire by critics who complain of the dehumanizing effects of too many sunless days!)

Place Ville-Marie is a complex of four buildings, dominated by the 45-floor **Banque Royale Tower**. These structures are connected by walkways and open-air plazas that host numerous outdoor cafés during the summer.

Rue Ste-Catherine: At any time of the day or night, it seems the heartbeat of Montreal originates from somewhere along Rue Ste-Catherine. Especially for Montreal anglophones, Ste-Catherine has been the main shopping district of the city since the latter years of the 19th century. The electric tram that formerly ran along the street enabled customers to shop in comfort from Ogilvy's all the way to the Bay.

Today, commercial businesses have spilled into the stately graystones and row houses – once private residences – on Rues Crescent, Bishop and de la Montagne. Even a brief walk will reveal noteworthy architecture, elegant shops, massive department stores, and, like it or not, some of the seedier aspects of downtown Montreal.

Most Montrealers would argue that Rue Ste-Catherine begins further east with Le Forum, the home of the beloved Montreal Canadiens. However, the street is relatively quiet until it intersects with Rue de la Montagne. Located at the corner is **Ogilvy and Sons**, one of the city's best known department stores.

The original granite structure still stands on the northeast corner, but, today, the store is housed in the 1910 building on the west side of de la Montagne. A plaque on the newer building states that Ogilvy and Sons was established in 1866, making it one year older than Canadian Confederation.

At the corner of Drummond and Ste-Catherine is the classically styled **Bank of Montreal**, built in 1921. Architecture buffs can walk north on Drummond where they will encounter a number of buildings that, though erected at the beginning of this century, are still in excellent condition.

The second famous department store along Ste-Catherine is **Simpsons**, located at Rue Metcalfe. Simpsons has always been a mainstay of Canadian commerce. It is a classic "family" department store selling everything from shoes to furs to Inuit sculptures, with cafés and restaurants for the weary but unsatiated shopper.

Next store is **Place Montreal Trust**, an example of the most recent thinking on urban architecture in the downtown. This shopping complex, an alternative to the labyrinthine underground city model of the 1960s, attempts to main-

Where would a modern city be without shopping malls like Montreal Trust?

tain a street presence – an active blend of shoppers, pedestrians, onlookers, commuters, even the proverbial "hanging out" crowd – and still allow for the ease of indoor shopping. Place Montreal Trust and other complexes like it represent the city's continuing struggle to temper its harsh climate through experimentation in "living spaces".

The intersection of Avenue McGill College is next. Take a moment to admire the view of **McGill University** as it ascends the steepening slope of Mount Royal. At the foot of Avenue McGill College is the underground entrance to **Place Ville-Marie**. This wide boulevard has recently been revitalized by a number of large building projects. New skyscrapers have helped shift the city's business district in a more easterly direction. Decorated with rows of lights in the winter, Avenue McGill College has an expansive, nearly grand feel. Watch for some amusing outdoor sculpture on the sidewalks and in the plazas.

Arbre de Noël, Place Ville-Marie.

Philips Square is the closest thing Ste-Catherine's has to a center. From the small green, Canada's two largest department stores are in plain view. The **Eatons** building is a two-block-long structure. Like its rival, Simpsons, Eatons is an all-purpose department store best known for its grand 9th-floor café, a lovely spot for afternoon tea. **The Bay** is housed in a smaller red sandstone building with a large modern addition attached.

Though a sense of proportion on Philips Square – befitting a classic downtown green – has been diminished by ungainly buildings and tacky billboards, the presence of older edifices and, in particular, **Christ Church Cathedral**, still offer a measure of grace and dignity. The church stands out prominently against the modern structures around it.

Designed by Frank Wills of Salisbury, England, in 1857, Christ Church is considered one of the finest examples of Gothic architecture in Canada. The

building is cross-shaped, like many 14th-century English churches, and its exterior design reflects a careful and graceful balance in design. The lovely narrow spire is made of treated aluminium, the original stone having been removed because of its weight. Grace and balance are also evident in the church's interior, primarily of stone except for the ceiling. There are carved heads of saints above the doors and the arcades of the nave are capped by leaves representing indigenous trees.

Maison des Coopérants, the elegant modern glass tower behind Christ Cathedral, ingenuously incorporates the lines of the church's apses and windows in its design. During the day the spire is reflected in its tinted glass; at night Christ Church is a shock of black outlined in the gray tones of the city.

Tucked between the church and Maison des Coopérants is the exclusive French restaurant **Le Parchemin**, a Parisian-style home done in the same speckled granite as Christ Church. One needs a thick wallet, or a slim credit card, to enjoy Le Parchemin's cuisine.

On Philips Square stands a rather large, even grandiloquent statue of **King Edward VII**. The proverbial Edwardian gentlemen is an appropriate spiritual mentor for the area. Sharing the square with The Bay (Canada's third partner in a department store trio that includes Eatons and Simpsons), is **Birks**, one of Canada's oldest jewelers, and the Canada Cement Company. Housed in well-preserved structures, they are, like the Anglican Cathedral, constant reminders of the old English money that built so much of the city.

As one continues east on Ste-Catherine, the shops become less interesting and certainly less grand. You might even notice a few unpleasant *parvenus* – pornographic movie houses and sex shops – that settled in the area during the boom of underground shopping in Montreal and haven't yet been driven away. These blocks are best walked through to reach **Place des Arts**.

McGill University: beauty behind bars.

162

A worthwhile stop, though, would be **St James United Church** at the corner of Rue St-Alexandre. Unfortunately the facade of St James was inauspiciously covered over in an attempt to "integrate" it into the commercial face of the street. The best view of the church, from St-Alexandre, reveals a modest sized Gothic edifice set in a quiet tree-lined green.

The architect, Alexandre Dunlop, decided on a rather unique design for the interior. He chose a horseshoe arrangement, a design known as "Akron" in honor of a city in Ohio where it was first used. The style is also very much like the 18th-century convocation halls at Oxford and Cambridge Universities in England. The curved wood balcony and central chandelier are striking and the general effect is very pleasing.

The final stopping point on Ste-Catherine is **Place des Arts**. The complex, famous for the sweeping curves of its design, is actually composed of two buildings that contain a total of three concert halls. The larger of the two, **Salle Wilfrid-Pelletier**, is home to the Montreal Symphony Orchestra. Completed in 1963, Place des Arts is an example of the innovative architectural atmosphere that ruled in Montreal under mayor Jean Drapeau. The hall has a permanent collection of works by modern Canadian artists, including two large tapestries designed by Robert La Palme and Micheline Beauchemin.

There are two more theaters in the smaller pyramid-shaped building, officially opened in 1966. Through an unusual design technique, the floors and ceilings of both theaters are suspended from thousands of springs, enabling the halls to be used simultaneously without fear of sound interference.

Adjacent to Place des Arts is a large hole that will, according to the sign, one day house the Montreal Contemporary Arts Museum. Though the project was due to be finished in 1987, it is yet at a nascent stage.

Directly across the street stands

The Montreal Symphony Orchestra.

Place Desjardins. Grouped around a central atrium, the complex contains three office towers, a hotel, along with the ubiquitous floors of shops and restaurants. A three-dimensional wood sculpture by the Québécois artist, Pierre Granche, serves as centerpiece in a brown concrete interior. The atmosphere is either serene or sterile, depending, perhaps, on your perspective.

Chinatown: Historical Chinatown differs dramatically from the present-day neighborhood. Rue de la Gauchetière, St-Laurent, and the small streets radiating from them were once home to the thousands of Chinese who began immigrating to Canada in the late 1800s. By law, the first wave of immigrants were men only. Social and economic discrimination forced the community to band tightly together, creating a self-reliant ghetto that, for obvious reasons, tended to attract some less than wholesome enterprises, including brothels and gambling dens.

The proximity of Chinatown to the downtown, combined with the ramshackle condition of many of the residential buildings, made it a prime target for development. In the past 15 years a number of the more interesting older edifices have been demolished. In their place today are large government office buildings, multi-use indoor complexes, and, quite frequently, barren parking lots. Old meets new in Chinatown, but not quite as harmoniously as in other parts of the city.

For the sake of our tour through the downtown, it is easiest to call this neighborhood Chinatown. Historically, however, the area belonged to another immigrant group, the Irish, and even once went by the name of "Little Dublin."

Interestingly enough, the two churches in "Little Dublin" have very different histories. **Église du Gésu** (Church of Jesus) on Rue Bluery between Ste-Catherine and René-Lévesque was an important site for Montreal's francophone community. For **Chinatown.**

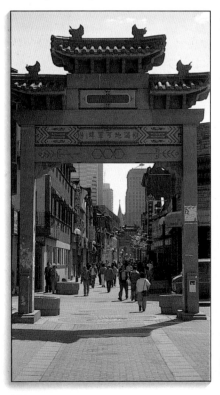

many years a Jesuit university, College Saint-Marie, was located just south of the church.

Its reputation as a center of rigorous intellectual activity, in the Jesuit tradition, was widely known throughout Canada. Many members of the French Canadian elite were educated there during the early part of the century, including poet Emilé Nelligan. The school, eventually taken over by University of Quebec at Montreal, was finally demolished in 1977.

Église du Gésu, modeled after its namesake in Rome, was built in the Italian baroque style. It was designed by an Irish architect, Patrick Keeley, and completed in 1865. The interior was renovated in 1983–84, including the murals and frescoes decorating the walls that were repainted and restored. The original parquet floor at the front of the church is striking, as are the imposing oil paintings of saints on either side of the altar, done by the Gagliardi brothers of Rome. The other church, **St Patrick's Basilica**, stands as a monument to the faith and building skills of the Irish community.

As in all Chinatowns, food looms large.

Across the street from St Patrick's at 454 de la Gauchetière, is the **Unity Building**, an excellent example of the Chicago School of architecture (typified by the designs of Louis Sullivan) and the only one of its kind in Montreal. Though the building is in a state of disrepair, its uniquely projecting cornice is quite distinguishable, despite layers of dirt.

To begin a tour of Chinatown proper let's begin at the corner of de la Gauchetière and Rue Bluery. Standing on the northwest corner is the lovely **Southam Building**. Constructed in 1912 by the Southam Company – owners of many of Canada's largest newspapers – it was sold in 1960 to a number of small businesses. Luckily, this delightful edifice remains intact.

There is a wealth of stone sculpture on the brick facade. Above the front entrance stand four women carrying

coats of arms, each figure with different features, each with a different coat of arms. Two of the women are supported by full-bodied cupids reclining in amusing positions. There are myriad naturalistic carvings elsewhere – animals, leaf motifs – that are certain to delight.

After another block, de la Gauchetiere turns into a bricked pedestrian walkway opening onto a large outdoor plaza between Guy-Favreau and Palais des Congrès. The massive buildings on either side of the plaza act as barriers: in the absence of any large trees or shrubs, the square looks rather barren, even in the summer. At one end stands the **Chinese Catholic Church**, saved from demolition because of its status as a historical monument. Though the original church dates from 1835, it had undergone many reincarnations.

At the other end of the plaza stands the **House of Wing**, believed to be the oldest building in Chinatown. It truly speaks of another era; erected in 1825, its exterior looks its age. House of Wing, once the British and Canadian School, is now a noodle and cookie factory.

De la Gauchetiere from Rue Côté to St-Laurent is adorned with two brightly colored ceremonial gates. Anyone familiar with traditional Chinese architecture will recognize the gates – vestiges of pre-Socialist China – as markers announcing the entrance to an important avenue, one that the emperor might travel. In China, the gates were meant to ward off evil spirits; in Montreal's Chinatown, however, they signal the beginning of the pedestrian mall lined with many restaurants and other commercial enterprises.

Try to come to Chinatown on the weekend. On Saturday and Sunday afternoons the streets teem with families. Chinese and non-Chinese alike eat sweets, gaze in display windows, search for those hard-to-find Chinese delicacies in shops and bakeries. The best way to explore this area is with chopsticks. Restaurants are in abundance and per-

For ethnic groups like the Chinese, bilingual living comes naturally.

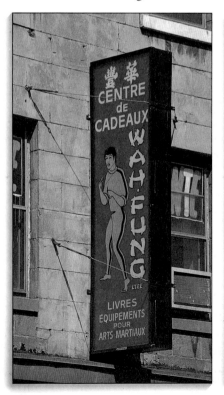

mit the curious epicurean to sample everything from Cantonese *dim sum* to spicy Szechuan beef. You can also snack on fried dough and mooncakes while shopping for Chinese herbs or inexpensive cotton clothes. Most restaurants hang their menus in the window and advertise various daily specials.

From the eastern gate of Chinatown on St-Laurent, you are just one block away from the **Monument National**, a building worth examining for its handsome facade. Since it was built in 1894, the Monument National has always functioned as a theater and was once the site of important cultural and political activity. This solid, gray granite edifice now houses the National Theater School which presents students performances, often of high quality and always free of charge. The interior, sadly, is in extremely poor condition.

A few blocks up St-Laurent brings the traveler to "The Main", the final leg of the downtown tour. If by this time you are also on *your* last leg, pay attention to the many signs advertising cafés, bars and smoked meat houses.

Microcosm of Montreal: The essence of what makes Montreal unique in North America is to be found on **Boulevard St-Laurent**. The street is a microcosm of the city itself, a neighborhood bursting with ethnicity, old-world charm, and the daily comings and goings of immigrants and their children. More and more, St-Laurent is also becoming the chic place to shop and eat; still, the street remains indomitably without pretense and with an energy all its own.

St-Laurent has always symbolized both division and unity in the downtown. It is still the east/west dividing line of the city's addresses while also being the central street of the St-Louis district. For many years, francophones lived primarily east of St-Laurent, anglophones to the west.

But succeeding waves of immigrants changed the nature of that division and expanded the street into a thriving com-

Montreal's Metro is an efficient way of getting around.

mercial district. The street became known as "The Main" when Russian Jews settled in droves during the 1920s. As much of the Jewish community moved out, Greeks, Hungarians, Portuguese, and, most recently, Latin Americans moved in.

In the winter, the boulevard is decorated with giant, red-striped candy canes. In the summer, however, crowds are its decor, especially during the annual food fairs and ethnic festivals. One reason why the street has managed to retain its charm is because many of the older facades have been utilized rather than torn down.

There is a mix of high and low, chic and oh-so-normal that keeps the area both unpretentious and unpredictable. Discount shoe stores stand next door to hip cafés while Greek bakeries and art galleries share old warehouse space. Come to St-Laurent to walk, browse, and, most importantly, to eat.

"The Main" is known for its smoked meat delis, and delis are known for lots of honest food at honest prices. Try **Schwartz's Delicatessen** (officially the *Charcuterie Hébraïque de Montréal*) at 3895. It was first opened in 1927 and is said to be the only restaurant that still makes its own smoked meat. Rubin Schwartz brought his curing recipe with him when he emigrated from Romania. **Moishe's Steakhouse** at 3961 opened in 1938 on the site of the restaurant where Moishe himself had been a busboy.

A good place to admire the old buildings of St-Laurent is between 3640 and 3712, once called the **Baxter Block**. The attached buildings have impressively large arched windows and still retain the original central heating system. Also worth checking out is **Cinéma Parallèle** at 3684 which houses a café and arts cinema. Further up, at 3950, are the **Shubert Baths**. Built in 1931, the baths were a necessity for the many people who didn't have bathrooms in their homes. Today, the swimming pool is still open.

Finally, one block over from St-Laurent on St-Urbain is one of the city's most beloved cafés, **Santrapol**. Its quirky interior, oversized sandwiches, and lovely summertime outdoor garden has secured it a place in the hearts of many Montrealers.

It is worth remembering that, unlike other neighborhoods in a city, a downtown is likely going to be a haphazard mixture of the residential, the commercial, the old and the new, the interesting and the mundane. Montreal is no exception. While Dominion Square, the Golden Square Mile, and The Main are by far the most vibrant areas, especially historically, along virtually every street, every alley, an inquisitive traveler will find something that surprises, astonishes, pleases.

These sorts of discoveries can be just as exciting as learning about famous monuments or exploring churches. Even in a sea of office towers, you never know what treasure may lie in their shadows.

Left, waterfront visitor. Right, spring comes to Christ Church.

BOHEMIAN MONTREAL

A few blocks east of the business district and north of Old Montreal, lies a street of Victorian townhouses with a mixture of businesses: cafés, croissanteries, boutiques, bookstores, a couple of theaters and cinemas. There are many streets in Montreal with a similar mix, but none have the easy charm of **Rue St-Denis**. It is the place where Montrealers seem to feel most at home, and casual observation gives the impression that the café crowd has indeed made a second home here.

One is tempted to say that nowhere else in Montreal has so "Parisian" or "European" a flavor, but the truth is that nowhere is more essentially "Montreal." It is the focal point of many of the festivals that now fill the summer months, and the area where, traditionally, Québécois separatists gather whenever nationalist feeling runs high. Recently the provincial government has begun to promote it as a place for visitors as well, but fortunately it has been saved from the dreadful fate of turning "touristy." With UQAM (the university) such a dominant presence in the area, and laws in place that restrict changes to the 19th century facades, it seems doubtful that it will become so in the near future.

"UQAM" (pronounced *Ooh-kwam*) stands for *l'Université de Québec à Montréal*, which occupies the striking building at the corner of Rue Ste-Catherine. The architect, Dimitri Dimakopoulos, incorporated the steeple and south transept of the old Eglise St-Jacques (1859) into his modernist design, to preserve something of the district's Victorian past in a building that otherwise embodies the hip atmosphere of the street.

UQAM enrolls about 22,000 students a year, and, as one of the five campuses of Quebec's youngest university (founded 1968), has never been a conservative influence. English-speaking scholars spill into the area from the McGill annex, which lies a few blocks west. With the constant patronage of academics, the local cafés, theaters, restaurants and bookstores flourish.

From UQAM come the intellectuals and the students, but the artistic crowd also make Rue St-Denis their turf. One of Canada's three major ballet companies, **Les Grands Ballets Canadiens**, and the Québécois dramatic company **Théâtre du Rideau Vert** (Green Curtain Theater) have their home here. The **Théâtre St-Denis**, just north of Rue Ste-Catherine, belies its ordinary exterior with a seating capacity of 2,500, making it the largest playhouse in the city after Salle Wilfrid-Pelletier at nearby Place des Arts.

Filmmakers have a permanent facility just off St-Denis at the **Cinémathèque Québécoise** at 335 Maisonneuve Ouest. Besides a repertory cinema and a large reference library, this building houses a museum following

Preceding pages: Rue St-Denis market. Left, and Right, shopping on St-Denis.

the history of filmmaking equipment.

Heaven knows where all the other people come from, but they all seem equally to belong here, whiling away hours in endless conversation over wine at a sidewalk café; sitting on the front steps of a duplex flat, watching the world go by on a warm summer evening; sifting through *La Presse* over coffee and croissants on a Saturday morning. The natives are obviously comfortable here.

Guidebooks still refer to the Rue St-Denis district – roughly the section that runs from Rue Ste-Catherine to Rue Sherbrooke – as the "Latin Quarter," after the *Quartier Latin* in Paris between the Sorbonne and the Seine, a district renowned for its bohemian edge. Montrealers don't use the old nickname much these days, but it evokes the right connotations: Rue St-Denis has a gallic flair, and a youthful, gently bohemian personality that attracts personalities – or just anyone who loves café society and *la dolce vita*.

The cafés are, of course, not cafés at all, in a strict sense, as they pour out far greater quantities of beer and wine than coffee. Tables are usually placed close together, decors are attractive but secondary, prices are reasonable. A few offer a complete menu. At the corner of Rue Emery, **Le Faubourg St-Denis**, perhaps the largest bistro on the street, serves full meals in a dining area behind the sidewalk café. **Le Grand Café** and **Les Beaux Esprits** are two locations with a reputation for live blues or jazz, but for the most part conversation and people-watching constitute the entertainment along St-Denis.

As pleasant as it is to simply stroll the sidewalks, it's often rewarding to explore further. If the weather is fine, the garden terrace at the rear of the **Café St-Sulpice** can be magical, when furry white flakes of pollen from some hidden source swirl about in drifts so thick that it seems to be snowing. Water splashes into a rock pool from a fountain at the far end of the terrace. Empty in the late afternoon, after the lunch crowd leaves, the vacant chairs await a crowd that will arrive late in the evening and stay until 2 or 3 a.m.

There are those who prefer the raucous oom-pah-pah down at the **Vieux Munich** to the more contemporary sounds up the street. This cavernous beer hall, where Rue St-Denis meets Dorchester-René Lévesque, has a gallery around three sides that overlooks a revolving stage where a Bavarian band *oomps* and *pahs* for the crowd. The atmosphere here may be a corny imitation of the true German beer garden, but the revellers polka down the aisles and the waitresses splash pitchers of beer onto the tables every weekend, year in and year out. Whatever your intentions when you walk in here, don't plan on driving home.

The making of St-Denis: The particular spirit of the St-Denis district is the product of a fate that drove the street from riches to rags and then back towards riches. The street was originally carved **Wall art.**

out of the estates of two leaders of the 1837 rebellion against British rule, Denis-Benjamin Viger and Louis-Joseph Papineau. St-Denis became the main street of a posh residential district named the "Faubourg St-Laurent," one of Montreal's first suburbs as the city overflowed its old walls. Once home to the premier of the province and the elite of the business class, most of the original buildings were destroyed by the Great Fire that devastated Montreal in 1852.

Some of the wealthy moved north and west, but it remained fashionable until this century. The Victorian elegance of some of the townhouses can be discerned in neoclassical and art nouveau embellishments on some upper storeys (particularly the Mendelson Apartments at Boulevard Maisonneuve.)

In 1897, the **Université Laval** opened a center next to the Eglise St-Jacques, which was then Montreal's cathedral, and so first drew academic life to the area. The **Bibliothèque Nationale du**

Québec, which holds the official archives of the province, was erected in 1915, and still resides behind its stately Beaux-Arts facade on the west side of St-Denis, now sandwiched between busy cafés. The Laval center gained independence as the **Université de Montréal**, but abandoned the area in the 1940s for its opulent new campus in Outremont.

Meanwhile, many large residences had been converted into rooming houses, and the clergy had opened homes for the growing numbers of the sick and destitute. Lacking the academy, St-Denis fell victim to the same urban decay that most of east Montreal suffered as the folks with money settled down in the suburbs.

In the 1960s, city planners made brave attempts to revitalize the area by making it a transportation crossroads. But the construction of the Voyageur bus terminus on Rue Berri only congested the roads. In 1966, the Berri-de-Montigny Métro station opened (now

A beer in bohemia.

Berri-UQAM) at the corner of Rue Ste-Catherine. It was the main transfer point on the slick new subway system, but for the most part easy access to underground shops left commuters without any special reason to venture up to the streets to patronize local business.

Money, if not respectability, returned to the district during the later 1960s and '70s, as St-Denis cafés gained notoriety as the hotbed of separatism and radicalism. Enterprising restaurateurs began to move in and renovate; among the first was the **Faubourg St-Denis**.

There was no lack of vitality, as the street would explode with celebrations and demonstrations every year on the Québécois feast day: **Fête Jean-Baptiste** (June 24, now the *Fête Nationale*). The scene looked much the same whenever the Montreal Canadiens hockey club won the Stanley Cup, a pretty regular event in the 1970s. Among the intellectual and artistic community that gathered here, the youth of Montreal defined themselves

no longer as "French Canadians" but as "Québécois."

The opening of UQAM in 1979, and a slow but steady effort to push the heart of downtown east toward St-Laurent has had a positive effect: today the area flourishes, with a steady influx of visitors from far and near to add to the local clientele. All summer long, one international arts festival after another keeps the street busy and interesting.

Still, the traces of a less prosperous past are visible in the less savoury flavor of some businesses along "la Catherine": strip clubs and off-color bookstores still pepper the busy central artery. The clubs seem to be able to resist the perennial efforts of politicians to get rid of them. Legislators are eager to clear away at least the more lurid street signs, but ironically, the very laws that so carefully guard freedom of expression under Canada's new charter of rights also make it difficult to draft legislation that would eradicate smutty language on storefronts.

Fortunately, the pleasant atmosphere of Rue St-Denis is in sharp contrast to that of some of the neighbors. In fact, the sector north of Rue Sherbrooke to Mount Royal Avenue is increasingly becoming a fashionable, up-scale shopping area. Antique stores and boutiques sell fine Québécois tapestries and woodcarvings or handicrafts in pewter and pottery, as well as pricey European imports, such as tiffany lamps and art deco furniture.

Other boutiques specialize in contemporary and futuristic designs in furnishings. Trendy clothing stores, and some excellent new and rare bookstores (mostly but not exclusively French) are sprinkled along the whole length of the street.

Rue St-Denis is most alive during the summer festivals, of which there seem to be no end. Among these events, the most important is the **Montreal International Jazz Festival** (*see feature on page 179*), but St-Denis is also a focus for the **Just for Laughs** comedy festi-

Braces for sale.

176

val, the **Festival International de Nouvelle Danse**, the **Montreal International Mime Festival**, and the annual **World Film Festival**. Each of these is among the largest in its medium and draws performers and fans from around the globe.

Tens of thousands mill along the street during the Jazz Festival, held every year in the first two weeks of July. For much of the festival, the street is closed to traffic and becomes a carnival arcade. It seems the whole city comes out to hear the free concerts at temporary stages set up at the intersections, and to watch unofficial street performers juggle, mime and eat fire. With 1,000 musicians from five continents, and up to 50 concerts daily, the festival has helped to make avid jazz enthusiasts out of Montrealers.

Prince Arthur and Duluth: Festivals brighten up a city wonderfully, of course, but on **Rue Prince-Arthur** there is an on-going celebration of basic human pleasures: people and food. Citizens of Montreal claim to excel at enjoying life together, and have tried to resist the tendency of modern cities to bury the human scale under megaliths and speedways. The restaurant district on Prince-Arthur, though a bit more contrived than St-Denis, represents a small triumph for the pursuit of simple pleasures in the heart of the big city.

Just north of the bistros of St-Denis, the restaurant mall runs west from **Square St-Louis** to **Boulevard St-Laurent**. In 1981, the city closed these five short blocks to vehicles, paved them with brick, and spruced them up with trees and poster-pillars and a small fountain. It encouraged new restaurants to forgo a liquor license and allowed customers to bring their own bottle of wine with them. The opportunity to dine well for less money held obvious appeal for this city of epicures, and the street has flourished.

Restaurants offering a wide range of ethnic menus, especially Greek, Vietnamese and Italian, now line the mall,

St-Denis' splendid architecture.

interspersed by a few small boutiques. Québécois cuisine is harder to find. Most of the big Greek restaurants that dominate the area have a similar atmosphere, price and menu, serving kebabs, stuffed grape leaves, grilled chicken, swordfish, and shellfish from the Maritime provinces or the tiny Îles-de-la-Madeleine.

On weekend nights the mall fills up with a meandering crowd of diners, often distracted by jugglers, musicians and sketchers who find here an ideal forum to show off their skills. Diners at second-storey windows get a view of the whole parade of life below. Tables arranged out on the mall itself let customers eat under the sun or the stars, or in the shade of a parasol.

Many restaurants here and elsewhere in Montreal no longer bother to display a sign that says "*Apportez votre vin*" (Bring your own wine). It is nevertheless worthwhile to check with the staff, since most Greek restaurants – and many others – encourage patrons to run into a liquor store or the local *depanneur* (a corner grocery) and pick up a bottle of something to bring inside. There the waiter will gladly uncork and serve it as though the wine had been ordered from the menu. (There is a *depanneur* on the north side of Prince-Arthur, and around the corner on the main street, St-Laurent, there is a well-stocked provincial liquor store.)

Access to the mall from St-Denis is through **Square St-Louis**, a block north of Rue Sherbrooke. This small, pretty park with lots of benches around a broad Victorian fountain provides a treasured spot for locals to idle away the summer hours, or in winter to skate on the paths that the city floods over. Well-preserved, sometimes ornate 19th-century townhouses border three sides of the square.

The easy charm of Rues St-Denis and Prince-Arthur give the impression that Montrealers are "at home" in these wandering streets, bohemian retreats and quiet, beguiling cafés.

Rue St-Denis market.

THE JAZZ SCENE

For 10 days in early July, the Montreal International Jazz Festival books 1,000 performers from around the globe into venues all over the city. What makes this festival extraordinary is that these venues include not only pricey clubs and concert halls but also whole streets, blocked off to let thousands hear free concerts at stages erected at major intersections on Rue St-Denis and Rue Ste-Catherine. These nightly block parties lend the city a euphoric jazz atmosphere that makes the festival the highlight of Montreal's summer – and one of the best jazz events anywhere. With an attendance exceeding 650,000, the festival now rivals Montreux and Monterey.

In Montreal, the term "jazz" is defined fairly loosely, so that performers like Joan Baez and Van Morrison have made the bill. But most acts belong much more obviously within the jazz orbit.

Ever since the days when Montreal was the only major city on the continent not subject to Prohibition, nightlife has flourished here. But jazz has held an insecure foothold in a town that has generally preferred dance music like swing or rock'n'roll. Still, great jazz was heard in a handful of clubs throughout the 1930s and '40s. The heart of the jazz scene throbbed away at "the Corner" where St-Antoine crosses Mountain Street, the home of the Café St-Michel and Rockhead's Paradise.

The most renowned performer to emerge from this era is the pianist Oscar Peterson, who began his career at 17 playing swing in the Johnny Holmes Orchestra at Victoria Hall in Westmount. He created his own sound in a trio that performed in the Alberta Lounge opposite Windsor Station, and later found fame in the US. Trumpet player Maynard Ferguson also started with Johnny Holmes, and likewise found success in the States after forming his own band.

Sixty years ago, in the days of gang wars and rampant vice, there were hundreds of nightclubs open 24 hours a day; jazz prospered with a small audience and the passionate devotion of its performers. They sustained the energy of Montreal's jazz until about 1954 when Mayor Jean Drapeau started to clean up the city. The heavy pressure on nightlife and the competition of television and rock'n'roll finally smothered the jazz scene. (The whole story has been lovingly told by critic John Gilmore in a recent history of jazz in Montreal called *Swinging in Paradise.*)

Within the context of the cultural revival that accompanied the "Quiet Revolution" of the 1960s, the Jazz Libre quartet pushed free jazz to its limits. Their style was related to John Coltrane's, but even further radicalized by a heavily separatist-socialist ideology. On the other hand, Vic Vogel's Big Band began to play much more mainstream jazz in 1968, and the group remains a popular staple of today's scene. A fusion band named UZEB has been gaining a following in Quebec for the last decade, and in France their record sales rival Miles Davis.

The jazz audience in Montreal has been expanding ever since Alain Simard, then aged 29, presented the first jazz festival in 1979. The vibrancy of the festival does not represent the state of things during the other 11 months of the year, but unmistakably there is new life in today's jazz picture. Charlie Biddle, who came from Philadelphia in 1949, plays bass with some of the best talent around at his own Biddle's Bar and Restaurant (2060 Aylmer). Club Jazz 2080 (2080 Clark) offers excellent live jazz on its tiny premises, and visitors to Old Montreal can enjoy jazz acts at L'Air du Temps, Claudio's or Le Bijou. On St-Denis, Le Grand Café presents a performance four or five nights a week.

Other testimonies to the new enthusiasm: a local jazz label called Justin Time Records and a degree program in jazz studies at McGill University. Even the son of the Provincial premier, François Bourassa, heads a prize-winning trio.

Finally, Les Ballets Jazz de Montréal add another dimension altogether to the portrait of jazz in the city. To music ranging from Gershwin to Pat Metheny, sometimes exploring social themes such as gender relations and nuclear holocaust, they have presented exuberant and accessible ballets to audiences worldwide, and rank among the three major ballet companies in Canada.

WESTMOUNT AND OUTREMONT

A Montrealer would probably scoff at the idea that Outremont and Westmount share any physical or, worse, historical affinities. They might point out that Westmount is where well-to-do anglophones (English Canadians) have always lived as the majority voice in the community. Outremont, on the other hand, has been home to French Canadians (francophones). These neighborhoods, in many ways, are considered to be the "two solitudes" of Canada.

On the surface, it appears that Westmount and Outremont are worlds apart. And yet, a look into the origins of these cities within the city reveals common ground. Both communities were borne out of the impulse to escape from the more crowded and sometimes dirty conditions of 19th-century city living. Both began as farming communities which developed at a slow pace around the sloping inclines of the mountain. Leaders of each community defended their power to control construction, landscaping, architectural styles, and zoning. Most of all, they sought to preserve the privileged relationship each had with the mountain and the unique landscape they lived in.

Westmount is built on both the western slope of Mount Royal, known as the *petit montagne*. Though the area is surrounded on all sides by the city of Montreal, it is a significant parcel of land, covering nearly 1,000 acres (405 hectares). **Outremont** on the other side of Mount Royal, is the incorporated city to the north. Though smaller in area, to the eye it shares much in common with Westmount: gracious residences, leafy parks and lively commercial districts.

In the 1670s, the Sulpician Order established an outpost on what is now Rue Sherbrooke Est, today considered the dividing line between the city of Montreal and Westmount. Two circular defense towers stand on the north side

of the street in front of the Grand Seminaire as reminders of this early settlement. Eventually, the order began to cede lands on the *petit montagne* to farmers. Old Indian trails and horse tracks connected these farmers to the city but, by any standard, they were isolated and it wasn't until the mid-1800s that the community on the *petit montagne* grew in size.

As transportation gradually became more efficient, Scottish and English fur traders, much taken with the splendid views, clean air, and lower rates of taxation, began to settle in the area. In 1869 the first English school was established in what was then called the village of Côte St-Antoine.

As more people settled in and around the village, a movement developed to preserve the residential, non-industrial character of the community. In 1890, the Côte St-Antoine Improvement Committee was formed and, composed of mainly anglophone residents, created a city plan for municipal buildings

Preceding pages: on the slopes of Mount Royal Park. Left, wrapped up for winter. Right, Outremont Park.

and parks. The committee was successful at regulating commercial development and for many years banned the "gathering of families under one roof" in apartment houses.

Their enthusiasm was fueled by both a desire for a peaceful residential community and by a deep distrust of the Montreal city government. In a vote that was very nearly defeated, the city council changed the name of the village to Westmount in 1895 and the city of Westmount received its charter in 1908. As the population became more homogeneous, a distinct enclave of middle-class anglophone Montrealers was established.

While Westmount residents appear to have been strict teetotalers at the turn of the century, they were also avid sportsmen. In fact, they seem to have been absolutely wild about sport: Westmount established a golf course, a Toboggan and Snow Shoe Club, a Cricket Club in North America was established in Westmount in 1913 and the town hosted the 1894 Canadian Speed Skating Championships.

Significantly, it was the site of what is thought to be the first lacrosse match ever played under lights and, as every Canadian nationalist knows, lacrosse, not hockey, is Canada's national sport. Today, the city is renowned for its parks; a reflection, no doubt, of this long tradition of outdoor pursuits.

It was also the Sulpician Order who were the original owners of much of the land which is today the city of Outremont. The Order began to yield large portions of it in the early 1700s but population growth was very slow owing to its distance from Montreal, the crowded fortress by the St Lawrence River. For many years the farms of the Outremont produced "Montreal melons" and prospered by the sale of them to hotels in New York.

In the mid-1800s the two largest landowners, besides the St Viateur religious order, were farmers by the name of Bouthillier and Beaubien. The Beaubien family's power, in fact, quickly translated into political influence when a son went on the become an important mayor of Outremont.

Outremont's population quadrupled between 1900 and 1911. While the first settlers were primarily Scottish and English, newcomers included French Canadians attracted to the less expensive homes as well as the proximity of Catholic churches. Jews also moved in and set up shops along Rue Van Horne.

Like Westmount citizens, Outremont residents, fueled by the fears of over-development, formed a "beautification committee." They were successful in obtaining more park land and regulating the size of apartment buildings. In its greatest coup, the committee persuaded the utility companies in 1914 to bury their telephone and electrical wires underground, thus eliminating unsightly poles and wires on the streets.

Today, Westmount and Outremont are exceedingly homogeneous. Approximately 6 percent of Outremont's

Traditional Westmount staircase.

population is anglophone and the percentage of francophones in Westmount roughly the same. For inner city neighborhoods, they are both exceptionally lovely, full of green spaces, elegant architecture and plenty of personality. Their cultural identities have not been compromised and, for the residents of each, a wonderful balance has been struck between urban living and an appreciation of nature's beauty.

The Municipal Center: Westmount cuts a large swathe from north to south. Of its two districts, the central portion shares more in common with the general atmosphere of Montreal's downtown, while upper Westmount hangs precipitously, hugging the sides of the *petit montagne*. In a recent survey by the city designed to track historical buildings, it was revealed that a remarkable number of 19th-century structures have survived in Westmount. Very little demolition has taken place except at the most southerly edge of the city around Rue Maisonneuve.

The municipal center of Westmount is loosely arranged on the English "green" model. The City Hall sits on a triangular site at the apex of two streets: Chemin de la Côté St-Antoine and Rue Sherbrooke. Across the street is the beautifully landscaped **Westmount Park**, the municipal Library, Conservatory and Meeting Hall.

Westmount City Hall, at 4333 Côté St-Antoine, is an imposing Tudor-style structure surrounded by colorful beds of flowers. One of its architects, Robert Findley, was also responsible for the design of Westmount's other municipal buildings.

Nearby is the **Library** which opened in 1899 and was Canada's first free library. It is distinguished by an unusual Romanesque style, leaded-glass windows, and delightful bas-reliefs which glorify "knowledge." Despite its 19th-century construction, the attached **Conservatory** still functions and beautifies Westmount's parks and streets with its winter-grown plants. **Victoria Jubilee**

Hall, although echoing the design of the city hall, is intended to resemble English medieval buildings and is used for a variety of public functions.

Going up the mountain: West of the municipal area is the oldest building in Westmount, located at 563 Côte St-Antoine. Because this street cuts across the lower half of the mountain, it made early construction on the steeper inclines extremely difficult.

Maison Hurtubise was built in 1688 by Pierre Hurtubise on land granted to his father by Maisonneuve. The house, the last remaining farmhouse from the 17th century in Westmount, reflects the style typical of residential architecture of the time, recognizable by its steeply gabled roof, fieldstone walls, small panes of glass and dormer windows. Because the house built was so far from Montreal (Ville-Marie), early inhabitants named it *la haute folie*.

The Boulevard is a particularly lovely street, lined with imposing homes of every shape and size. These homes mir-

Coming home from Penfield Avenue School.

PARK MOUNT ROYAL

You can see it from just about anywhere in Montreal: buying a newspaper at the local stand, gazing idly out from a kitchen window, taking the dog for its nightly walk. *Mont Réal* – or, as Montrealers call it, *la montagne* (the mountain) – looms up in the middle of the city like a natural obelisk emphatically proclaiming Montreal's presence. The mountain lends a poise and dignity to Montreal by drawing the city, like a billowing skirt, close to its stalwart legs.

For Montrealers, the mountain embodies a kind of grandeur, a place where nature's sublime and wild moods play freely across a landscape untouched by the heavy hand of urban development. Mount Royal is more than a park. It is like an unmistakable family trait – the mountain is a cherished feature of a rich and vibrant history.

It was here in 1535 that explorer Jacques Cartier was led by Indians through wooded hills and up rocky crests to the summit. It was to here that the 17th-century *habitant,* one mile away, turned his gaze each morning as he walked through the dawn toward his fields. And it is here, today, that all of Montreal's ethnic groups can be found sunning, sledding, strolling, folk-dancing and picnicking.

That Mount Royal is not covered by roads, walks, cafés, electric cable cars and vast amphitheaters is largely owing to the aesthetic sensibilities of Frederick Law Olmstead, the man hired by the City of Montreal in 1874 to design the park. Olmstead, who also designed Manhattan's charming Riverside Drive, and the elegant Morningside and Central parks, firmly believed that nature was a source of spiritual sustenance and that parks, if properly designed, could provide urban dwellers with relief from the oppressive routines of metropolitan life. He urged Montreal to preserve its gracious mountain and warned voracious developers that if they dealt with Mount Royal "as if it had the impregnable majesty of an alpine monarch, you only [will] make it ridiculous." So far, his words have been heeded, although developers still harbor hopes.

Most of Mount Royal's pleasures can be taken advantage of in any season: a stroll through its 500 acres (200 hectares) along winding trails, a walk to the summit for a look at the 100-ft (30-meter) cross. (It is now electrified; the original was raised in 1643 by Paul Chomedy de Maisonneuve when the fledging colony of Ville-Marie was saved from a flood.) You can also take a jaunt to one of the park's two lookouts (at the chalet or along Camillien Houde Parkway) for a spectacular view of central Montreal, the St Lawrence River and the Montérégian mountains.

Near the chalet are monuments to the explorer Jacques Cartier and to King George VI, as well as carvings entitled *La Sentinelle* and *Les Sans-Abris* (to the homeless). Visit the *Musée de la Chasse et de la Nature* for exhibits on local fauna and flora. In warmer months, horse-drawn carriages *(calèches)* are a relaxing way to traverse the park, and free nature walks *(randonnées)* are conducted in French and English. In winter, skaters take to Beaver Lake (an artificially made pond) and cross-country skiers travel along tranquil tracks. Tobogganing attracts shoals of enthusiastic children.

Like Highgate and Brompton, London's grand cemeteries, the Mount Royal cemeteries contain ornate mausoleums, sinuous trails and almost suffocatingly lush vegetation. Covering half the mountain, these resting places are eloquent, in a rambling way, on the subject of French-Canadian genealogy.

Beneath the soils of Mount Royal Cemetery (Protestant) are the remains of some remarkable Montrealers: Sir John C. Abbot, prime minister of Canada; Sir Allan Hugh, a shipping magnate and political wheeler-dealer, Anna Leonowens, governess to the king of Siam, and Sir George Simpson, fur trade financier.

Located next door in the Catholic cemetery, Notre-Dame-des-Neiges, are other illustrious and interesting Canadians: Calixta Lavallée, the composer of the national anthem *O Canada*; Wolfred Nelson, a leader in the 1837 rebellion; Sir Georges-Etienne Cartier and D'Arcy McGee, fathers of Canadian Confederation; and Pierre Laporte, the minister tragically murdered by terrorists in the 1970 FLQ crisis.

ror not only the eclectic tastes of their original owners, but also recent technical advancements in construction. Wreathing the top of the mountain are **Sunny Avenue** and **Summit Circle**. No. 14 Sunnyside Avenue, built in 1911 for Charles A. Smart, a member of the Quebec Parliament, is thought to be one of the most impressive residences in all of Westmount.

On Summit Circle is the **Westmount Lookout**, a small park and viewing area. It affords a breathtaking panorama to the west, the flat plain and volcanic hiccups of the area's mountains. The houses around the lookout seem precariously sturdy at best; the dramatic views from their living rooms could certainly never appeal to anyone with a fear of heights.

Above is the wooded peak of the *petit montagne*. In 1928 McGill University sold the land, once site of a botany lab, to Westmount, stipulating that it could never be developed. It is now a sanctuary for hundreds of species of birds.

Greene Avenue and Lower Westmount: Commercial enterprises in Westmount are clustered along **Greene Avenue** as well as **Rue Sherbrooke**. Here there is a mixture of convenience stores, banks and restaurants, all catering to the needs of the community. There are a few upscale antique and clothing shops, but Westmount residents seem to prefer to spend "big money" downtown. Greene Avenue was refurbished with brick sidewalks and flower pots in the early 1970s and retains an unpretentious charm. **The Double Hook** bookshop, located at 1235a Greene Avenue, was the first shop in Canada to sell exclusively "Canadian" books.

Sometimes referred to as Lower Westmount, the streets below Sherbrooke are full of interesting rowhouses. While obviously less grand than the residences on the mountain, these display everything from the fortress style to mansard roofs, with numerous examples of stone and wood designs. Of particular note are the **Tow-**

Westmount mansion.

ers at 4130–40 Dorchester (Westmount's first terrace), and those at 47–41 Holton (which show the classic Montreal pattern of alternating units).

In the direction of Montreal's downtown via Rue Sherbrooke, is **The Mother House of the Sisters of Notre-Dame**. Now the campus of **Dawson College**, Quebec's largest *anglophone cejep* (junior college), it is impossible to miss. An awe-inspiring edifice designed by J. Omer Marchand in 1904, its distinctiveness is derived, in part, from the well-judged use of pale-colored stone and a flamboyant Beaux-Arts style. At one time the building was used simultaneously as a hospital, retirement home, school and headquarters for the religious order.

Outremont: Outremont's boundaries are roughly defined by the commercial Rues Van Horne and Laurier, and the residential Chemin de la Côte Ste-Catherine and Rue Hutchinson. These boundaries are not strict, however, and the neighborhoods which stretch beyond them are deemed, at least in the classifieds, to be "adjacent" or "outer" Outremont. Today, being on the edges of this chic section of Montreal is good enough to secure a higher rent from prospective tenants or better sale of a home. An address in Outremont tells people a lot about you: it means that you are most likely a francophone, most likely a dyed-in-the-wool urbanite, and well-enough-off to be able to afford this great in-town location.

But it wasn't always this way. Before the gentrification that took place in the 1960s and 1970s, Outremont's streets, such as Rues Laurier and Bernard, and especially **Rue Van Horne**, were common, ordinary car lanes, even considered to be on the shabby side. The area around Van Horne was once semi-industrial and is still referred to as "lower" Outremont. Older residents remark that Rue Van Horne, the district's northern boundary, still retains the original character of the neighborhood. There you will find a modest array of shops and

Waiting for the mailman.

restaurants, row houses built more closely together, fewer parks and smaller yards.

Outremont's attractions: Now, with a good pair of walking shoes on, you can journey into the French version of "the elite." The following sights represent merely a taste of Outremont and will lead you into some of its more interesting neighborhoods.

Outremont's municipal center is rather understated. The **City Hall** and **Public Library** are located off Côté Ste-Catherine. Ironically, the city hall is housed in a stately private residence thought to have once been a Hudson's Bay (a British company) trading post. It is one of the oldest buildings in Outremont, constructed around 1800. The library is also located in an old private home behind city hall, but is a rather inadequate facility for such an established community.

The finest architecture in Outremont is found in its public buildings: schools, cinemas and churches. One of the most striking buildings is **Académie Querbes** at 215 Rue Bloomfield. Designed by J.A. Godin in the Beaux-Arts style and completed in 1915, the building lends a distinctly European atmosphere to the otherwise typical North American residential architecture which surrounds it. Today, it houses a pre-school.

Residents had to fight hard to save the **Outremont Cinema** on Rue Bernard. Plans to convert it into a multi-use complex were blocked by a public awareness campaign and petition drive. The bas-reliefs on the outside of the building are remarkable, despite the considerable damage they've suffered because of harsh weather. The interior is abundantly grand, reminiscent of Montreal's old theaters including the Strand, Loews and the Capitol.

At the corner of Rues Laurier and Bloomfield is the imposing **Eglise Saint-Viateur** completed in 1913. Its Gothic-Revival style is strongly represented in the church's facade which

Leafy Outremont.

towers above the modest apartment buildings surrounding it. Interestingly, the sides of the church aren't as well constructed as the front – a frequent feature of buildings where the architect concentrated on the facade.

At Côte-Ste-Catherine and Avenue D'Indy are two other interesting public buildings, **Eglise Saint-Germain**, which stands at the intersection of these two roads, was built in 1931 and has a magnificently large bell tower as its centerpiece. The other building, facing out on Côté Ste-Catherine, was once the Pensionnat du Saint-Nom-de-Marie. Designed in 1903, its most striking feature is the classically designed portico which incorporates a remarkable number of other architectural styles.

The residential areas of Outremont are generally organized around a number of parks. The houses are beautiful simply for the fine construction techniques and the regularity of their design. The unique detailing makes them interesting to look at; one can see a variety of stained-glass designs, wood and iron trims, and stone bas-reliefs inserted into the brick facades.

The houses around Outremont Park have the best vantage point to view the changing seasons on the mountain. **Parc Joyce** and **Parc Pratt**, which take their names from the farmers who once owned the land, also afford views of the mountain, the campus of the **University of Montreal**, and **St Joseph's Oratory** which rest on its northern face.

In these rather idyllic settings, a myriad of famous French Canadians have lived, and still live. The leader of the Parti Québécois, Jacques Parizeau, lives in Outremont and former Prime Minister Pierre Trudeau grew up on Rue McCullough. The much-loved Québécois writer Maurice Tremblay also lived in Outremont.

Finally there is quite a lively contrast between the quiet, tree-lined residential streets of Outremont and its commercial areas which hum day and night with activity. All along **Rue Laurier** and **Rue Bernard** one finds a treasure trove of clothes shops, cafés and mouth-watering bakeries.

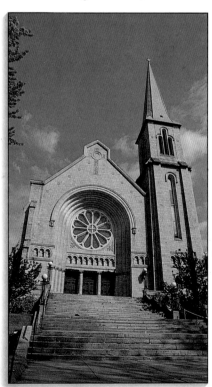

Many buildings on these two streets have been successfully recycled from parking facilities into multi-use centers or from garages into galleries. Here you can take your cat to a "post-modern" veterinary clinic or buy the latest in light fixtures or kitchen utensils. On Rue Laurier in particular, one will also find a slew of very fine French-language bookshops.

Westmount and Outremont as two solitudes? Perhaps. But polar opposites? Hardly. Both communities possess an abundant sense of pride and independence, considering themselves unique and indivisible. They *are* desirable places in which to live. They are not, however, the unchanging bastions of the "civilized." The age of insular living spaces has passed. Modern Montreal is a diverse, multi-racial city and Westmount and Outremont increasingly reflect this bounty.

St-Germaine, Outremont.

OUTREMONT CAFÉS

When the word "café" is mentioned, images of smoky brasseries, sun-dappled terraces, or brooding artists bent over manuscripts come to mind. This tableau is enmeshed in the cafés along Rues Bernard and Laurier in Outremont. For a taste of Europe, step into one of these cultural enclaves, most of which hum day and night. Experience the "café culture" of Outremont and savor a café-au-lait with a delectable pastry.

The cafés on the busy thoroughfares of Rues Bernard and Laurier range from the refined to the humble. From the exquisitely decorated to the unadorned, each has a distinctive ambience and a devoted clientele. What they all share, besides delicious coffee, is their neighborhood role as meeting places.

Café Romolo, located at Jeanne-Mance and Bernard, is just outside the official limits of Outremont. Its unique character and fine coffee draw a steady crowd, many of whom live in Outremont or, perhaps, simply frequent the Rialto Cinema which is just around the corner.

The Romolo is recognized by its long picture windows and pool tables that dominate one of the two rooms. At small tables with plain wooden chairs people read newspapers or converse in small groups, their heads ringed in a haze of smoke, the smell of which mingles with the potent fragrance of fresh coffee. Smooth, frothy café-au-lait is served in tall glasses as in Italy and Spain; sugar and cinnamon sit on each table. The café also serves expresso, alcoholic beverages, and pastries which the owner "imports" from the Greek bakery next door. Café Romolo is open all day, every day. Students, artists, and a host of "nine to fivers" come in for a quick coffee, a game of pool, or just a quiet break in which to read the newspapers or write a letter.

Further down Bernard, near the Outremont Theater, is the Café du Cinema. A Charlie Chaplin sign board invites you into a cozy basement-level bistro. The café is intimate, with seating for no more than 30. Pictures of film stars decorate the walls and the black-and-white tile floor completes the movie decor. Café du Cinema serves an array of full meals, emphasizing continental cuisine. It is frequented by the after-theater crowd.

Le Bilboquet, at 1309 Bernard, is renown for its ice cream, sorbet and frozen yogurt. The café is closed for a portion of the winter, but is kept busy all summer long. Its breezy interior is accentuated by an art-deco green-pink-and-black tile floor.

La Croissanterie D'Opale is located on Rue Hutchinson, one block east of Rue Laurier. Nestled within a residential area, the café's daytime customers are generally neighborhood regulars. They stop in for a sandwich, homemade pastry or a cappuccino made strong with a frothy mound of hot milk and a generous dash of cinnamon on top. The café's interior is an eclectic mix: a full-sized African statue stands alongside plants, fondu pots, and the well-hidden remnants of a previous restaurant's interior. Large ceiling lamps and fans, together with large picture windows, give D'Opale a pleasant, airy feel.

While there are a few cafés located on Rue Laurier, La Petite Ardoise appears to be many people's favorite. Its wood-paneled interior emits a cozy glow that warms the spirit while the café's imposing bowls of café-au-lait warm the body. The rich coffee-milk medley is a little more expensive here but it's worth the extra cost. Homemade pastries are also featured, though a variety of sandwiches and full meals are also served. Along the stretch of exposed brick, local artists display paintings and collages for sale, while a bulletin board at the back announces gallery openings and other cultural events. In the summer, a small back garden is transformed into an outdoor terrace and patrons are encouraged to eat and drink at a leisurely pace. The café's refined atmosphere is softened by the relaxed pace and neighborhood familiarity.

Cafés in Montreal play an important role in promoting social cohesion because, while they are an essential part of a francophone's cultural identity, many of the city's newer immigrants – Greeks, Italians, Africans – are increasingly drawn to them. For anglophones, cafés are a special treat, serving as reminders of how "un-American" this North American city truly is.

ST JOSEPH'S ORATORY

The word "oratory" means house of prayer – and St Joseph's Oratory is just that, albeit a very big one. St Joe's cupola, rising 790 feet (263 meters) above sea level, is a vast, imposing, but familiar sight towering high above Montreal's rooftops. Celebrated as "one of Christendom's outstanding monuments of faith," this is the Grand Central Station of devotional Catholicism in Montreal. Built in honor of Canada's patron saint, the shrine hails over 3 million visitors a year and rivals devotions to the Lourdes and Fatima shrines.

From the foot of the 278 stairs which lead up to the entrance, St Joseph's Oratory is an overpowering presence. The gigantic oratory exudes a unselfconscious resignation to its own monumentality – much like a whale placidly accepting its behemoth dimensions. An architectural arrogance characterizes this oratory, whose cumbersome haunches make other edifices in Montreal seem like sidedishes.

The oratory of Mount Royal is (as the famous Canadian cleric, Cardinal Tisserant, noted) "the world's capital of devotion to Saint Joseph." While this proclamation alone draws several million pilgrims to St Joseph's stately doors, simple curiosity also propels several thousand pairs of feet toward the shrine. For the devotional Catholic, St Joseph's is a religious event, a holy place, a sacred duty; for the mere visitor the shrine offers an intriguing glimpse into a Catholic culture that, at one time, permeated almost every aspect of French-Canadian life.

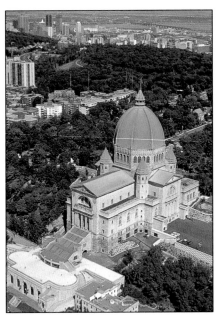

Whether religious inspiration or anthropological curiosity propels you to this site, a visit to this oratory inevitably means an encounter with stairs – plenty of them: 99 from street level to the entrance of the crypt-church and 179 more up to the basilica proper. Pilgrimage groups usually gather around the bronze and granite monument to St Joseph located inside the main gate and, drawing a few deep breaths, prepare a steep ascent toward the celestial structure. Some pilgrims, as act of penance and reverence, will make an edifying and excruciating climb on their knees up to the church-crypt. The stairs at St Joseph's are not properly *scalae santae* or holy stairs which, when ascended on the knees, are a way in which Catholics can obtain indulgences (divine pardon) for past, present or future sins. This rather painful practice, however, currently remains a devotional act intended to purify the soul for an encounter with the saintly patriarch.

The crypt-church, the first stop on the way up, was completed in 1917 and derives its name from its vault-like appearance and, one could add, vault-like feel since the ponderous stone walls create the sensation of being sealed underground. The stained-glass windows depict gospel episodes in which St Joseph factors prominently: the Flight into Egypt, the Birth of Christ, the Circumcision, Life at Nazareth, and so on.

Adjoining the crypt-church is what is called a votive chapel designed for private devotions. St Joseph's importance for the Catholic church is reflected in the eight plaques which display the saint's titles: Guardian of Virgins, Terror of Demons, Protector of the Church, Hope of the Sick, Patron of the Dying, Comfort of the Afflicted, Mainstay of Families and Model of Workmen. (A busy saint!) In addition to preserving virgins and deflecting devils, St Joseph heals through miracles. The crutches and braces scattered throughout the chapel are "testimonies" left by pilgrims cured by the oil found in a basin beneath the statue of St Joseph. (The oil is also on sale in the gift shop.)

In the center of the votive chapel is the flickering of over 3,500 vigil lights, candles lit either in memory of the dead or as a request for blessing. The wrought-iron railing contains a "holy relic" a tiny particle of St Joseph's clothing, allegedly authenticated and venerated for its miraculous healing powers. Behind the main lamp rack is the resting place of Brother André, the founder of the oratory who died at the age of 91 and who was finally beatified by Rome – one step below Roman Catholic sainthood or canonization.

Brother André was the innocuous door keeper at Notre-Dame College, a boys' school, located across the street from the Oratory, before he became the celebrated founder of St Joseph's. A museum displaying artifacts related to his origins, childhood and service in the oratory is located two stories below the basilica. The exhibits include a peculiar "exact" replica of the austere cell Brother André occupied while a doorkeeper and a "thoroughly authentic" reproduction of the hospital room in which he died on January 6, 1937.

Heading upwards again, visitors climb toward solid Canadian granite, staunchly defending the oratory against time and the elements. A brief pause here under the Renaissance-style facade affords not only a bird's-eye view of Montreal but also a chance to catch your breath before advancing into the real caverns of the behemoth.

Aesthetic sensibility has always been one of the great human mysteries and exactly what was running through the minds of the Basilica's designers will indeed mystify many. Although almost grotesquely huge, St Joseph's exterior is nevertheless stately, and its Romanesque-Renaissance style is also curiously appropriate for a religious monument. St Joseph's bowels, however, are strangely barren, and exude about as much charm as an airplane hangar. Inside, "awful" 1960s art combines with an alienating "functionalist" modern design to create an understatement so overwhelming that the step from the outside to the inside can be quite jarring to the senses.

A closer look at the sanctuary (if you're up to it) can tell you much about the Catholic liturgical innovations inspired by Vatican II (1962–65), the second international meeting of Catholic bishops and clergy to discuss the church's role in the modern world. (The first meeting was in 1870.) Unlike the altars in some of the older churches in Montreal, where the priest celebrated Mass with his back to the congregation, St Joseph's altar is placed forward on its platform and the rituals of the Mass are performed by a priest who faces the people. This new altar arrangement was intended to establish not only a closer tie, but also a greater accountability, between clergy and laity. Yet the incredible size of the basilica is hardly conducive to intimacy. Seventh in floor space among the world's temples, St Joseph's is able to accommodate up to 12,000 people at one time. (Standing room only, of course!)

Back outside, there's still plenty to see of the oratory. Secluded gardens ranging beyond the basilica and out into the mountainside encourage meditative meanderings. Many visitors choose to follow Louis Parent's famous Way of the Cross, a series of prayers performed in front of 15 stone tableaux representing the stages of Christ's death and resurrection.

Each station's foliage was carefully chosen to reflect a mood: at the third tableau, where Christ is shown falling on the way to crucifixion, the predominant color is red to connote the flow of blood; where Veronica wipes the face of Christ, the colors are delicate pastels to suggest tenderness, and at the 13th station, where Christ is taken down from the cross, the colors are bland and austere, conveying grief and desolation.

By far the most endearing and interesting of St Joseph's offerings, however, is the tiny shrine to Brother André, dwarfed beside the looming Oratory. Inside, cracked walls stand behind the faded paint of once garish religious statues, and the floors groan as bended knees approach them. Simple, humble, worn out, the chapel is endearing in a dusty sort of way and is a welcome contrast to the pomposity of its grandiose cousin next door. Here too are weathered plaques thanking St Joseph for his intercessions, some dating from the chapel's earliest days.

Finally, a trip to St Joe's wouldn't be complete without a visit to the "gift shop," located back at the bottom of the hill. Here almost every kind of Catholic religious paraphernalia can be found, from four-foot statues of St Joseph, whose heart (once the statue is plugged in) will glow an ethereal rose, to miniature versions of the saint specially designed for the dashboard or refrigerator. There are almost 100 varieties of rosary to choose from: expensive red crystal ones where the beads are shaped like hearts to the lightweight, plastic, economy model.

Here, with people pawing through bins of plastic medallions, glow-in-the-dark rosaries, and laminated holy cards, St Joseph's commercial side is brazenly exposed. While celebrating the transcendent human soul, the shrine is also a monument to a culture capable of commoditizing even its most "immaterial" aspects.

STADIUMS AND GARDENS

As one travels east along Rue Sherbrooke, the **Olympic Stadium** looms up suddenly amid rows of unassuming duplexes, as though a mollusc-shaped starship from another galaxy had settled down uneasily in the suburbs. Futuristic, majestic, impractical and incredibly expensive, controversy still surrounds the "Big O" long after the memory of the 1976 Olympic Games has begun to fade.

Roger Taillibert, the French architect who designed the futuristic stadium, claimed that sports arenas are the cathedrals of our age. The metaphor appealed to a city with a history of building magnificent churches: St Joseph's Oratory on Mount Royal, for example, boasts a dome larger than any except St Peter's in the Vatican in Rome.

But the plan for the new sports dome – designed to assert the city's modern, cosmopolitan flair rather than its Roman Catholic history – was far more ambitious and ultimately demanded even more financial sacrifice. And just as the slow construction of St Joseph's depended upon the personal charisma of Brother André, so the sudden realization of the Big O was only possible through the force of one personality: the irrepressible Jean Drapeau, Montreal's mayor from 1954 to 1986.

Drapeau gets credit for sheer visionary ambition. The Olympic Stadium's revolutionary design boasts a leaning tower 55 stories high from which a flexible Kevlar roof descends along cables over the playing field. (Kevlar is the stuff used to make bullet-proof vests.) Tower and stadium alike are imaginatively modeled in fluent curves that soar at beautiful and seemingly impossible angles.

But Drapeau must also shoulder a large part of the blame for the Big O's other unofficial nickname: "the Big Owe." Montreal's stadium just may be the most spectacular sports arena in the world – but there is no question that it is the most expensive. The price tag of $1.2 *billion* gives it the distinction of being the world's most costly building. That means that each of its 70,000 seats cost more than $17,000. In 1984, an accounting firm determined that the Big O had cost only slightly less than all the other domed stadiums in North America put together – and that was before it had a roof.

Yet Mayor Drapeau had promised Montreal "modest games" that would pay for themselves through revenues from tickets and souvenirs. He remains notorious for his assurance that the Olympics could no more run a deficit than a man could have a baby. Predictably, local cartoonists enjoyed depicting the former mayor heavy with child.

The reasons for the exorbitant price-tag are easy enough to find in hindsight. The concept of a retractable canopy roof suspended from a tower leaning at 45° had never before been attempted on

Preceding pages: Botanical Gardens; fun at La Ronde. Left, picnic on Ile St-Hélène. Right, Olympic Park Tower.

this scale. Since the top of the tower had to be centered over the stadium's roof, the circular opening in the center of the stadium slants slightly toward the tower, so that the end of the ellipse near the tower's base is lower than the far end. The pleasing asymmetry of this design made the task of casting the huge, irregular concrete ribs of the stadium extremely tricky and delicate – and, of course, expensive.

But the real construction headaches were caused by the rigid deadline that Olympic Games always impose upon the host city. The clock ticked away as the builders waited for detailed plans from the architect; in the end, they built most of the complex in just two years, between 1974 and 1976. At the opening ceremonies, Montreal had a magnificent stadium, but still no tower and no roof. Nevertheless, in the giddy flush (and relief) of the moment, the city gave Drapeau a standing ovation. The tower would not be completed, in fact, until 1987.

Does the city's professional baseball team, the Montreal Expos, need so extravagant a home? Those who defend the Olympic Stadium ask another question: does anybody worry about how much the Pyramids cost? Or the Roman Coliseum (which, as it happens, would fit onto the Big O's playing field)? Drapeau once reminded his critics that the ancient Athenians had rebuked Pericles for building the Parthenon instead of warships.

Only one other professional baseball team plays under a retractable roof: the Toronto Blue Jays. Montrealers acknowledge that Toronto's "Skydome" is tidy and efficient – like the city around it – but Montreal's stadium makes an impression that few monuments can match.

A visitor need only ride the funicular cable car that runs up the spine of the tower to the observatory deck to appreciate the architect's imagination. One might say that the tower combines the grace of the Eiffel Tower with the ec-

Waiting for the game to begin.

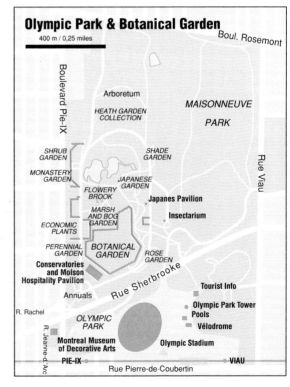

Olympic Park & Botanical Garden

400 m / 0,25 miles

Boul. Rosemont

Boulevard Pie-IX

Arboretum

HEATH GARDEN COLLECTION

MAISONNEUVE PARK

Rue Viau

SHRUB GARDEN

SHADE GARDEN

MONASTERY GARDEN

JAPANESE GARDEN

FLOWERY BROOK

Japanes Pavilion

MARSH AND BOG GARDEN

Insectarium

ECONOMIC PLANTS

PERENNIAL GARDEN

BOTANICAL GARDEN

ROSE GARDEN

Conservatories and Molson Hospitality Pavilion

Rue Sherbrooke

R. Rachel

Annuals

Tourist Info

R. Jeanne-d'Arc

OLYMPIC PARK

Olympic Park Tower

Pools

Vélodrome

Montreal Museum of Decorative Arts

Olympic Stadium

PIE-IX

Rue Pierre-de-Coubertin

VIAU

centricity of the Leaning Tower of Pisa. While the top of this concrete tripod overhangs the roof of the stadium, the hollow base forms the roof of the Olympic Pools, with wing-like lobes that spread out on either side. (Come equipped for a dip, as the spacious pools are open to the public year-round.)

Thirteen stories of office space fill up about two-thirds of the tower's neck, with a three-floor observatory at the summit where the tower broadens as its three corners begin to sweep apart. The exterior double-decker cable-car carries up to 90 passengers and, as it emerges into the open air about a third of the way along its path, it offers an increasingly spectacular view of the eastern horizon.

From the observation deck at the summit, the view extends about 50 miles (80 km) in each direction along the other three points of the compass, and includes an unobstructed westward view of Mount Royal and the city skyline, with the St Lawrence River winding around from the left. There is also a vertiginous view straight down into the stadium.

The cables that suspend the roof pass down from a niche (where the roof is stored) only a few feet below the deck, affording a unique perspective on the operations that raise and lower the 65 tonnes of fabric. Forty-six winches must operate in precise synchronicity in order to unfurl the roof over an area that measures more than 200,000 sq. feet (18,500 sq. meters). When lowered, the canopy stretches over the playing field into a tent-like cupola.

For all this nifty engineering, the retractable roof still does not entirely eliminate rain delays. If an unexpected shower occurs in high winds, the game has to wait until the winds let up before the roof can be unfurled. In fact, the roof cannot be lowered in winds stronger than 15 mph (25 kph), while the roof of Toronto's Skydome can operate in winds up to 40 mph (65 kph). As it takes almost 45 minutes to drop the roof into

The Olympic Stadium.

place, the stadium officials normally rely on a meteorologist to predict whether the roof should be lowered for an event, rather than leaving the decision for the last minute.

Some baseball fans criticize the sight-lines at the Big O, which was designed more with track and field in mind. In any case, the stadium plays host for all kinds of events now that the roof allows the stadium to be used year-round. Trade shows, rock concerts, and Canadian football attract crowds to the stadium's stands. Special events, like the visit of Pope John Paul II, and a spectacular production of Verdi's *Aida* (complete with a 40-foot sphinx, live elephants, and over 1,000 singers) can have an unforgettable impact in this setting – one that sometimes converts even die-hard pragmatists to Drapeau's grand ambitions.

The **Vélodrome**, which spreads out from the base of the Olympic Pools, was built to accommodate the cycling events at the Olympic Games, but in recent years has often been used to house exhibitions. The Quebec government has announced plans to convert the space into a life-sciences museum called the **Biodôme**, which will incorporate four ecosystems under the structure's one vast, nearly transparent roof. The project will bring together plants and animals in environments that reproduce a tropical forest, a northern (boreal) forest, a polar region and the saltwater gulf of St Lawrence.

The Botanical Gardens: The Biodôme will complement the glories of nature already on display across Rue Sherbrooke. As sports fans roar inside their concrete cathedral, 26,000 species of plants repose in tranquility at the **Jardin Botanique**. If Montreal, with its harsh winters, seems an unlikely setting for one of the world's largest botanical gardens, consider the pleasure of sitting inside the tropical greenhouse, among the pineapple trees and the orchids, during a December blizzard. But most of the 2 million people who visit every year are more interested in the houseplants and exotic gardens than they are in a chance to come in from the cold.

Located on a 180-acre (73-hectare) rectangle across the street from the Olympic Park, the gardens have been steadily evolving since Brother Marie-Victorin founded the project in 1931. (A modest statue of him stands to the right just beyond the main gate.) Although a total of nine greenhouses protect the tropical flora from the elements, spring and fall are still the best seasons for a visit, since the vast majority of plants are divided among the various outdoor gardens. Different groups bloom each month between April and October.

Even visitors who can't tell a begonia from a rhododendron can enjoy a stroll among the blooms, but those who prefer a chauffeur can take a guided tour on the mini-train. With about 30 plots in which the plants are grouped according to particular themes, a trip through the gardens is a little like moving through a series of stage or films sets. Some gar-

Botanical Gardens.

dens are as much an educational experience as a sensual one.

The monastery garden displays medicinal herbs in an arrangement that recreates the quiet enclaves of medieval monks in the age of Charlemagne. Information panels offer useful trivia about such topics as the aphrodisiac power of absinthe, and the laxative properties of licorice. The poisonous plant section is only a few feet away. (These plots are located just beyond the neatly arranged perennials and test gardens, to the left after the entrance.)

Winding paths, ponds thick with lilies, rock gardens, and a "flowery brook" make a poetic setting at the center of the gardens. An assortment of birds live among the aquatic plants in the ponds. In the Alpinum, flora from the world's mountain ranges are gathered together beside a quaint waterfall. When the flowers bloom, choruses from *The Sound of Music* pop into mind. Beyond the ponds that lie behind the Alpinum, the Arboretum is more like an open park, with trim heaths, dwarf spruces, shade trees and chestnuts. In fall, of course, the maples begin to turn splendid colours, and the dense assembly here provides a convenient way to go "foliage peeking."

The greenhouses recreate the climates of the warmer parts of the globe: an equatorial rain forest, with the musty bouquet of orchids; then a hot, dry desert with human-sized cacti, and a Mexican Villa with a popular collection of carnivorous plants (the famous Venus fly-traps are just one of many "meat-eaters").

The bonsais and the penjing collection, in which the caretakers take special pride, have an oriental setting in a cooler greenhouse with the whimsical name "The Garden of Weedlessness." Several other permanent and temporary exhibitions are housed under glass here as well. A computer controls the climate of each of the ecosystems in the exhibition areas. There are also trivia-quiz computer games for the kids to play, and

Tea House at Botanical Gardens.

audio-guides in French and English.

The rhododendrons, by the way, are in a specialized garden (where they bloom in June), while the 100-plus species of begonias are gathered with the gesneriads in the tropical greenhouse.

A recent addition to the Botanical Gardens is the small but intriguing **Insectarium**, first opened in 1990 following the initiative of an enthusiastic collector named Georges Brossard. Part museum, part zoo, the project has been designed to educate children and adults about creatures that usually get the attention of humans only when they want to swat them dead. Inside this pavilion, itself shaped like an insect, kids and grown-ups peer into display cases and absorb their minds in games and puzzles that shed a whole new light on the world of bugs.

An extraordinary variety of safely dead, perfectly preserved insects, from butterflies to golden scarab beetles, are mounted on the walls, while an assortment of living insects inhabit worlds behind glass walls. Some of these creatures seem to be a little shy of the spotlight, but they are easy enough to find with a little patience. All together, there are about 130,000 specimens here.

Île Ste-Hélène and Île Notre-Dame: Opposite Old Montreal, two islands in the St Lawrence River function as the city's fairgrounds. Until the 1960s, there was only one island here, **Île Ste-Hélène**, which was about half its present size. But the earth excavated from the Métro tunnels was used to expand the island and to create a whole new one beside it: **Île Notre-Dame**. This park became the site of Expo '67, the great exposition that drew 50 million visitors during the summer of Canada's centennial year, 1967.

More than any other single event in Montreal's history, Expo changed the way the city felt about itself, and awakened Montreal to its potential as a center for international gatherings of all kinds. Perhaps the notion that Montreal had at last entered "the big league" was what **The Insectarium.**

prompted the naming of Canada's first pro baseball team after Expo.

The original plans envisioned temporary structures that would stand for just the one summer, but many of the 83 pavilions were so sturdy and impressive that it made no sense to demolish them, so Expo survived for 14 years as *Terre Des Hommes* (Man and His World).

Today, the site is an eerie remnant of its former self, like a tarnished, deserted metropolis from another galaxy. But not completely deserted: the old French pavilion remains in use as the **Palais de la civilisation**, a striking and intricate space that nicely accommodates the major exhibitions that pass through town, like shows on China and the Pharaoh Rameses II. There are also plans to transform the famous geodesic dome designed by Buckminster Fuller into a science museum. A fire burned away its outer skin in 1978, but the former American pavilion still stands 20 storeys high.

With St Joseph's Oratory and the Olympic Stadium, the "biosphere," as some call it, is the third of Montreal's remarkable domes. With no internal supports, it encloses 7 million cubic feet (198,240 cubic meters) of air, and yet the weight on its foundations is less than the weight of the materials that compose it. It has been said that, if the structure were a mile wide, it would float away.

La Ronde, the amusement park built for Expo, is still going strong on Île Ste-Hélène. The original Mini-Rail and cable-car SkyRide still seem refreshingly novel ways to get around the park. But there are new attractions too, such as Le Monstre, the world's second tallest roller coaster at 132 feet (46.2 meters), and a popular complex of water slides called Aqua-Parc, with a water-slide for everyone from toddlers to daredevils.

During two weeks in the early summer, admission to La Ronde includes a ring-side seat from which to view the annual International Fireworks Competition. Each night for two weeks a differ-

Roller-coasting at La Ronde.

ent national team attempts to put on the most spectacular pyrotechnics display over the river and the city skyline. The La Ronde ticket also includes admission to the **Aquarium de Montréal**, with its penguin tank, performing seals, sharks and hundreds of other more or less exotic marine creatures.

In mid-June the roar of Formula One racing cars can be heard at the Molson Grand Prix at the **Gilles Villeneuve Race Track** on Île Notre-Dame. A refuge from all this noisy excitement is not far away: a good chunk of Île Ste-Hélène is still green, wooded and quiet, except for the traffic on the Jacques Cartier Bridge.

The simpler past can be visited at the 1822 Fort near the bridge, now the **David M. Stewart Museum of Discoveries**. As well as naval and military paraphernalia, visitors can see the Compagnie Franche de la Marine and the 78th Fraser Highlanders re-enact parades here in 18th-century costume throughout the summer.

Chapelle
Saint
Bernard
1942

Montreal is ideally situated for quick get-aways to an astonishing variety of four-season adventures: river rafting on the Rouge, ice-fishing on Île Perrot, climbing frozen waterfalls in Estrie, hiking, skiing, mountain biking; crafts fairs and pleasure boat cruises, gondola rides and aqua slides, historic forts and ports, maple sugar feasting and sleigh rides at *cabanes à sucres* (sugar shacks); manors and museums, bush-whacking and moose tracking. Disappear with a tent into the wilds of a *réserve faunique* (wildlife reserve), rent a chalet, or sleep in a log castle with room service.

Points of the compass: *To the north –* the deep silent woods, glacial lakes and alpine villages of the Laurentians, resting on the oldest rock formation on the planet – is the Canadian Shield. *To the south* lie the rolling pastures, brightly painted barns and white-steepled towns of Estrie, a French version of New England. *To the east* are five of the Montérégian hills carved by the ancient Champlain Sea that arc across the St Lawrence plain, and the historic Richelieu Valley, battleground of the Iroquois, French, English and Americans, and scene of the 1837 Patriots Rebellion against the British regime. *To the west* lies the Outaouais, land of big logging lakes and rivers and the great fighting muskie.

The **Laurentians**, Quebec's *pays d'en haut,* and **Estrie** (the Eastern Townships) are the two main play-grounds for Montrealers. North America's first alpine ski rope tows were erected at Prévost in 1930, and at St-Sauveur-des-Monts in 1934. Montrealers soon flocked to the Laurentians to try the new-fangled sport, and the glamour of ski and après-ski began to saturate the region.

Today acrobatic skiing, torch-light parades, luging, and tobogganing are all popular on Quebec slopes. The Laurentians have the largest concentration of alpine ski centers and lighted runs in North America, and Estrie runs a close second. But summer brings another medley of pleasures – canoeing, sailing, horseback riding, camping, fishing, swimming, water-skiing, or capuccino-sipping on a well-situated café-terrace; antiquing, boutiquing, gallery browsing, summer theater and *bôites à chansons* which keep going till dawn.

Like the Laurentians, Estrie (from *est* for east and *patrie*) is ski and sailboat country, sprinkled with chic auberges and inns, artisan boutiques and impeccable restaurants. But the farm culture tempers the elegance of resort towns like Lac Brome, Eastman, North Hatley, Sutton and Magog with an earthy charm. The milder microclimate and proximity to the US border give the region an adventurous spirit.

The following day trip destinations are divided into four categories: Laurentians, Estrie, Montérégie, and

Preceding pages: autumn leaves. <u>Left</u>, Eglise Mont-Tremblant Lodge. <u>Right</u>, Ile St-Hélène.

Coeur-du-Québec. They provide a focus for day or weekend trips, but taking the historic and scenic routes – #117 through the Laurentians, #138, known as the Chemin du Roy, #132, #342, #344 and #223; and exploring the back roads, called "rangs," will lead you to chance encounters, odd little museums, roadside curiosities and other unmapped treasures of Quebec.

Laurentians: *Route: Laurentians Autoroute 15 North, exit 21 to 640 West, which leads to the park's eastern reception center; from Paul Sauvé Park, Route 344 West to* **Oka**; *ferry to* **Hudson**; *342 west to* **Rigaud**.

Colorful sailboards float like confetti off the silvery 4½-mile (7-km) long beach of the **Parc de Récréation Paul-Sauvé**, on the **Lac-des-Deux-Montagnes**. The lake's shallow waters are ideal for trying out the sport, and rental facilities are close by. But the most exotic recreation here is a canoe excursion through the marsh around Grand Bay. You'll paddle through a floating garden walled by rushes and cattails, carpeted with flowering lily pads and delicate duckweed, with marsh ducks, muskrats and Great Blue Herons in your wake, and possibly arouse the curiosity of beavers at work. For information on excursions led by park naturalists, call (514) 479-8337.

Parc de Récréation Paul-Sauvé's summer activities feature geological excursions, forest nature walks, bicycle trips to explore the dunes and effects of glaciation, and evening talks on Oka's native American legends. The park's flat wooded terrain is popular with cyclists and cross-country skiers.

Oka and **Hudson** are charming lakeshore villages linked by an old-fashioned ferry across Lac-des-Deux-Montagnes. French-Canadian Sunday school songs describe pilgrimages to Oka to buy cheese made by monks at **l'Abbaye Cistercienne d'Oka**, one of the oldest monasteries in North America. Oka's Trappist monks came from the Bellefontaine Abbey in France

Taking a break.

and you can see the humble miller's home where they first settled, stroll the gardens surrounding the monastery, and buy the world-famous Oka cheese made here since 1893.

A climb to top of the **Oka Calvary**, east of village and across from Parc Paul-Sauvé, is loveliest in autumn. The stations of the cross up here were built between 1739 and 1742 to inspire the local Amerindians, and three of the seven original chapels have been preserved. Since 1870, Amerindians and pilgrims from over Quebec come to Oka to celebrate the Feast of the Holy Cross on September 14, and to enjoy the magnificent view of the Lac-des-Deux-Montagnes from the summit.

From Oka you can take the tiny car ferry across to **Hudson** to go antique hunting. The seasonal ferry leaves from the dock on Rue des Anges next to the Argenteuil Manor. From Hudson, you can drive on to **Rigaud**, a charming spot, and between mid-March and late April, gorge yourself on maple syrup

dishes at the **Sucrerie de la Montagne** (300 Rang St Georges [514] 451-5204; 451-0383).

Rouge River rafting: *Route: Hwy 15 north to 148 west; from April–September only.*

The Rouge River has some of the best whitewater rafting in North America on the 15-mile (25-km) course between Harrington and Calumet, Quebec.

"Steep Throat," a ledge drop of 12 feet (3.7 meters), has been called "the Everest of rafting in Canada," and other Rouge River rapids are known by such names as Confusion, Turbo in the Morning, Avalanche, Washing Machine, Slice 'n' Dice, and The Monster.

Don't be daunted. Experienced river guides will brief you on "body surfing," "hydraulic action" and "ledge drops" and be there to yank you back into the raft in less than 30 seconds should you inadvertently bail out. Most day packages provides 5–6 hours of rafting (about 11 miles/18 km) and include a lunch break, along with all equipment,

Lac des Sables, Ste-Agathe, Laurentines.

one experienced river guide per raft, shuttle service from the base camp, and a post-dinner video show of the day's adventures.

Ste-Adèle/Val David/Ste-Agathe-des-Monts:

Route: Laurentians Autoroute 15 North to Ste-Adèle, or take more scenic local 117 North. From Ste-Adèle, take 117 North to Val David and Ste-Agathe-des-Monts.

Ste-Adèle is a lively ski resort and a thriving writers' and artisans' colony by the shores of Lac Rond and the slopes of Mont Ste-Adèle. At local studios artists make enamel plates and vases, jewelry and ornamental belt buckles, and do traditional wood sculpture and cabinet-making. Visit the **Village de Séraphin**, an historical reconstruction of a mid-1800s Laurentian settlement, inspired by Québécois Claude-Henri Grignon's popular 1933 novel *Un homme et son péché* (A Man and His Sin). Each house in the village is based on a Grignon character or illustrates an episode in the life of Séraphin Poudrier, the novel's

miser. The village of 20 buildings includes post office, general store, doctor's office and school, with a miniature train running through the grounds.

Val David is known for its abundance of traditional Québécois houses with mansard roofs, charming inns and fine cuisine and its talented painters and artisans – engravers, ceramicists, and basketweavers. Quebec's first *boite à chanson* (folksong club) was built here in 1959, and now the rustic structure houses the **Théâtre La Butte**, a summer café-theater featuring French-Canadian plays.

Rock climbers flock to Val David to scale **Mont Condor**, a devilish rock 125-ft (38 meters) high (halfway between Val-Morin and Val-David), and the awesome 75-ft (22 meters) high **Condor Needle**, one of the few rock needles in Eastern Canada.

Ste-Agathe-des-Monts is the metropolis of the Laurentians, and a hot spot for Québécois and international celebrities, especially during the 10-day *Le Nord en fête* festival of popular music and song held every summer. With three public beaches and a gorgeous lake, the traffic of bikinis and sailboats and sailboarders is something fierce.

To get an idea of the Laurentians' old-guard wealth, take a quick cruise around **Lac des Sables** on the Bâteau Alouette. You'll see such baubles as the estate built by Twentieth Century Fox tycoon William B. Fox and the 42-room "summer cottage" built by a millionaire who kept his own orchestra to play for him day and night, and a greenhouse in which he cultivated only roses.

St-Faustin/Parc Récréational du Mont Tremblant:

Route: Laurentians Autoroute 15 North, exit 83; to 117 North to Ste-Agathe-des-Monts; Chemin Tour du Lac to Chemin du Lac-Caribou to St-Faustin Educational Centers; from St-Faustin exit on 117, toward Lake Superior and Mont Tremblant park entrance.

St-Faustin's Forest Education

Village of Knowlton, Ville de Lac Brome.

Centers of the Laurentians exhibit a fiery blaze in autumn. Two hiking trails and six interpretation trails wind around Lac du Cordon, over rustic boardwalks and footbridges. Quebec's eight Forest Education Centers are dedicated to informing the public on the anatomy and ecology of a forest, and this center has animations and videos, and free pamphlets on autumn coloration, conifers, and Quebec forests, richly illustrated and written.

Naturalists will gladly show you the insides of a Jack Pine cone or let you whiff some oil extract of white pine, and exhibits at the Interpretation Pavilion will tell you everything you always wanted to know about trees. (Chemin du Lac-Caribou, St-Faustin, [819] 326-1606.)

Algonquin sorcerers called their mountain *Manitonga Soutana* (Devil's Mountain) because it roared and rumbled whenever the tranquility of its forested slopes was disturbed. To protect the peace of this wilderness, **Mont Tremblant**, the highest of the Laurentian peaks (3,150 ft/960 meters) was established as the first of Quebec's provincial parks in 1894. The mountain is thick with maple and pine forests, and shelters black bears and Virginia stags, beavers, lynx, and hundreds of bird species. The park's 500 lakes and three major rivers – the Rivière Rouge, Rivière Matawin and Rivière du Diable – all provide great swimming, canoe camping, and fishing for trout or jumping landlocked salmon.

You can take a cruise on Lac Tremblant, go hiking and horseback riding, or take the chair lift up to the top of the mountain from the Station Mont Tremblant Lodge, and camp here in winter as well as summer.

As for skiing, Mont Tremblant is the highest skiable peak in Eastern Canada, with a vertical drop of 2,132 ft (650 meters), and the longest trail in Quebec 3.2 miles (5 km) long. (For park information, call [819] 688-2281, 424-2954, 883-1291.)

Ekwantshit woman from Mingan.

Estrie: *Route: Eastern Townships Autoroute 10 (east) to exit 90, to 243 South to **Lac Brome**; 104 West to 215 South to **Sutton**; 139 North to **West Brome**; 139 North to Eastern Townships Autoroute (west).*

Lac Brome (Knowlton): A mill pond cuts through the heart of this Victorian village, and colorful boutiques in 19th-century homes give it a festive air. Lac Brome is a charming spot for lunch, brunch, coffee with wickedly rich desserts, antiquing and strolling beside the pond and lake. Flocks of wild ducks are omnipresent: they are Lac Brome's gastronomic specialty, and Lac Brome is surrounded by splendid (not necessarily flat) cycling country.

In stagecoach days Lac Brome (Knowlton) was a stop on the Boston-Montreal run and this story is told in the **Pettes Memorial Library**, established in 1894 as the first free library in Quebec and in the **Brome County Historical Museum** on 130 Lakeside Road ([514] 243-6782).

The museum's nine buildings house Abenaki artifacts, pioneer bric-a-brac (foot-warmers and pill-making machines), a local history archive (survey maps, old letters) a military collection, general store, blacksmith shop, fire tower and county courthouse. The white brick building that was the village's original school (1844) contains a World War I Fokker biplane with the camouflage covering still intact – sent to Canada in 1919 as part of the war reparations act. For hiking and bicycling maps and news of local happenings, contact the Lac Brome Chamber of Commerce, (514) 243-6033.

Sutton bustles with hikers and skiers bound for the long winding wooded trails of Mont Sutton, and shoppers bent for quilts and woven rugs, ceramics and pewter in the local artists' cooperatives. The main street of this ski resort at the base of Mont Sutton is flanked with graceful old houses, auberges, crafts shops, art galleries and tempting restaurants and outdoor cafés.

Paddling in the Grand Bay marshlands of Parc Paul-Sauvé.

In summer the Saturday flea market on Curley Street is a lively meeting place, and on Sundays the local tradition is brunch followed by a hike up Mont Sutton. Star-gazing soirées are popular, as is summer mountain biking on ski-doo trails. Local topographical and cycling maps give the best routes for excursions on 10-speed or *toute-terrain* mountain bikes. Vélotours de l'Estrie (Townships Bicycle Touring) organizes day and weekend trips. ([514] 538-2361.)

The **Sutton Heritage Museum** (at the corner of Rue Principale and Rue Montagne) tells the history of communications in a collection of antique switchboard and telephones, phonographs, and radios housed in an early post office, telegraph office, printing shop, fire alarm center, telephone exchange and radio station. (Open May 1–Sept 1, [514] 538-2544.)

F.G. Edwards Country Store, West Brome (just off Route 139) is worth a detour to visit, even if you don't buy a thing. A wheelbarrow and feed sacks deck the front porch, and locals hover around boxes of candy-colored seeds ready to sprout into Sugar Snap peas, pencil pod black wax beans and Kentucky Wonder green pole beans. F.G. Edwards & Co. Ltd is a hallowed institution founded in 1857 to serve the farmers of West Brome.

As in horse and buggy days, it's still the place to swap yarns, post local news and buy everything from pitchforks, work socks and boots, horse bridles, yoyos and udder wash, to baby chicks, penny candy, ant traps and bird feeders. A browse through this aromatic shop will give you a feeling for rural life in Estrie.

Orford Arts Centre/Magog/Abbaye St-Benoît-du-Lac: *Route: Eastern Townships Autoroute 10 to exit 115, to 141 North, to **Parc Récréational du Mont-Orford**; 141 South to **Magog**; from Magog, follow signs to rural road to **St-Benoît-du-Lac** along west side of **Lac Memphrémagog**.*

Mont-Orford: Classical music rings into the woodland air from studios scattered throughout Mont Orford **Arts Center**'s 222 sylvan acres (90 hectares). From May to September this thriving arts center in the heart of Estrie's Appalachians offers a festival of art exhibitions and daily concerts.

The Arts Center, in the **Parc de Récréation du Mont-Orford**, is popular in all seasons, with skiing, skating and snowshoeing in winter, and swimming in the two lakes, hiking, golf, chairlifts to the summit, and hang-gliding over a panorama embracing the Sutton Mountains and Lac Brome, the Monteregian hills, and St Lawrence plain.

Magog (Lac Memphrémagog): Magog isn't a spectacularly pretty resort town, but its location at the northern tip of Lac Memphrémagog, the 30-mile (48-km) long narrow lake linking Quebec with Vermont, makes it handy for boating activities.

Magog has a variety of restaurants, shops, art galleries, a public beach and

Lac Magog.

federal quay. You can take a cruise, or rent a sailboat with a private skipper, fish for *ouananiche* (landlocked salmon), test your balance on a sailboard, see Lac Memphrémagog from a snorkeling mask, or while dangling from a parachute 150 feet (46 meters) in the air.

As an exhilarating, effortless and rather goofy way to see the lake, parasailing has caught on. Your harness is attached to a parachute, which is attached to a rope towed by a motor boat. (For information on waterskiing and parasailing on Lac Memphrémagog, contact Ski Lac Memphrémagog, 268 Rue Orford [819] 843-1114.)

Abbaye St-Benoît-du-Lac: Gregorian chants echo over Lac Memphrémagog from the pink granite towers of the Benedictine abbey of St-Benoît-du-Lac. Commanding the lake like a fairy castle, this monastery with its octagonal towers, triangular gables and narrow pointed windows, was designed by Dom Paul Bellot (1876–1944), a French monk who settled here in 1937 and became one of Quebec's major ecclesiastical architects.

The monks of the Benedictine order of Solesmes, France, are the only inhabitants of this independent municipality. You can tour the abbey's rich mosaic interior, participate in the chanting of vespers in Gregorian, (Sunday mass and daily at 5 p.m. and 7 p.m. on Thursdays), pick apples in the abbey's orchard, and buy cider and delicious cheeses (St-Benoît, Ricotta and L'Ermite), made by the monks. You can even stay here as a guest and wake up to dawn over Mont Orford. The abbey reserves 40 rooms for men and 15 for women.

Stanstead Plain/Rock Island-Derby Line/ Beebe Plain: *Route: Eastern Townships Autoroute 10 to exit 121 to Highway 55 South to the **Stanstead Plain** Exit; from **Rock Island**, Route 247 West to **Beebe Plain**, and 247 North to Magog.*

Estrie's border towns, hotbeds of international gossip and smuggler's tales, give the region its spice. This pocket of townships, although it is run-down and neglected by North Hatley standards, is nevertheless intriguing.

Stanstead Plain has a number of buildings of architectural interest – Stanstead College (1872), the Ursuline School (1884), the Christ Church Anglican Church (1858) and Butter House (1866), and the Colby Curtis Museum on Dufferin Street features antiquarian dolls, toys, military artifacts and mementos of 19th-century life.

Stanstead Plain's main street leads directly into **Rock Island** which straddles the Quebec–Vermont border. In some houses here a meal is cooked in Canada and eaten in the US; the bathtub is in Canada and the toilet is in the US – which makes for endless local jokes.

Dilapidated factories, mills and river buildings give Rock Island an air of decay, but there are architectural gems among them, notably the Romanesque revival **Haskell Free Library** and **Opera House**, built on the boundary line in

Horse trekking has become a big business.

1904 (Route 143 and Rue Church). The ground floor is a feast of lustrous wood, marble and granite, lit by stained-glass windows and chandeliers. The international boundary line puts the circulation desk and stacks in Canada and the reading room in the US.

Upstairs the 450-seat opera house is a delightful scale-model of the Boston Opera House. During the Festival d'Art Lyrique in August, the performers sing arias on the stage in Quebec, while the audience applauds in the US.

The white line down **Beebe Plain**'s main street, Canusa Avenue, divides the US from Canada. According to international law, Mrs Brown is not permitted to cross the street to borrow a cup of sugar from Madame Blanche without first reporting the matter to customs. But in a spirit of community goodwill, local immigration officers ignore the small print.

Montérégie: *Route: 132 west to Melocheville. Follow Hébert Blvd (Route 132) past the Beauharnois Hy-dro-Québec power station and **Melocheville** Locks to **Emond Street**; 132 west to **St-Timothée**.*

Archaeologists at **Pointe-du-Buisson Archaeological Park** say it will take decades to interpret the tons of material unearthed on this 66-acre (27-hectare) woodland site by the St Lawrence River rapids. A remarkable Iroquois complex and 7,965 objects, four fireplaces and the traces of 42 poles of long house were discovered in the month of April 1967 alone.

Tomahawks, stone utensils, pipes and harpoons dating as far back as 5,000 years indicate that this site was once the hunting, fishing and burial grounds of several Amerindian peoples, and a stopping point for explorers, missionaries, soldiers and merchants en route to the Great Lakes.

Hundred of artifacts are displayed in the two exposition centers. You can take a guided archaeological tour of five digging sites, and on special days take part in activities related to Amerindian

The black line on Haskell Free Library's floor on Rock Island is the international border with the US.

music and dance, Iroquois medicine, carving arrowheads, and making cornmasks and dolls.

In the small farming village of **St-Timothée**, the **Musée Maurice Gendreau**, the eponymous gentleman's home-spun museum of 10,000 objects, is wonderfully eccentric and *très* Québécois. M. Gendreau has filled his house and barn and sheds and a few old school buses with antique sewing and washing machines, auto parts, door knobs, eye glasses, tractor seats, cigar boxes, butter churns, license plates, school desks, wind-up Victrolas, dentist's drills, barber's chairs, shoe forms, and a pair of alligator shoes that his aunt bought in the 1930s, still wrapped in their packing tissue.

Gendreau has arranged nine rooms of his house to portray life at the turn of the century, and his hand-typed descriptions guide the visitor through the dining room, music room, parent's room, children's room, smoking room and attic. You'll wonder where his collecting

madness will end. (530 Boulevard Edgar-Hébert, St Timothée, [514] 377-2100. May 1–Oct 31.)

The Canadian Railway Museum/Côte Ste-Catherine Locks: *Route: 15 South to exit 42; 132 West to 209 South to St-Constant; from St-Constant, 209 North to 132 West to Côte Ste-Catherine-Locks.*

Depending on how enamoured you are with trains, you can spend a few hours or a day exploring the 118 pieces of rolling stock standing like old soldiers at the Canadian Railway Museum at St-Constant – the largest railway museum in Canada.

Assembled here are antique locomotives, trolleys and trams, sleepers and street sweepers, snowplows, boxcars and cabooses, parlor cars, diners and diesels, a one-car traveling schoolhouse and even some horse-drawn sleighs, spread over 15 acres (6 hectares) and housed in two giant hangars. An elaborate model electric train whistles through papier-mâché mountains and **All biked out.**

steams past tiny cows, using a variety of more than 200 locomotives and cars. It's the liveliest attraction in the Hayes Building which houses Canadian Railway Historical Association's archives, artifacts and memorabilia.

There is an authentic 19th-century railway station, and you can hop a ride on a diesel locomotive, or a vintage Montreal street car for a short but dramatic mile.

Just down the road from St-Constant, another transport adventure takes place as deep-sea oil tankers, long lakers and grainers, make their way through the **Côte-Ste-Catherine-Locks** into the St Lawrence Seaway. The bridge lifts, the ship edges through the narrow canal; valves open and the water drains to lower the ship to seaway level, and a horn blast signals the ship to pass through.

Cross the lifting-bridge to the far side of the lock for an eye-level view of the captain's deck and crew's quarters of ships from as far away as Panama and the Soviet Union. The bridge serves as the entrance to **Côte-Ste-Catherine Park**, which affords stunning perspective of the thunderous Lachine Rapids, the Montreal cityscape and the Monteregian hills. The park has a swimming pond, camping area, and bicycle path along the whitewater's edge, and closeby is an island colony of herons.

Fort Chambly/St-Jean-sur-Richelieu/ Fort Lennox: *Route*: *Autoroute 20 or highway 112 East to 223 South to Chambly*; *223 South to **St-Jean-sur-Richelieu** and **St-Paul-de-l'Île-aux-Noix**.*

Fort-Chambly's castle-like walls have been licked by the treacherous rapids of the "River of the Iroquois" for nearly three centuries, but Fort Chambly stands by the edge of the Richelieu Rapids, the names of the heroes of New France carved in stone at its gates. The first fort on this site was built of wood in 1665 by Captain Jacques Chambly and the soldiers of le Régiment de Carignan-Salières, to de-

fend against Iroquois attack. And the first European settlement on the Richelieu grew up around its borders, becoming the town of Chambly. In 1709–11, the wooden fort was replaced by the massive structure with five-sided corner bastions that stands today. It was occupied by the French until 1760, by the English until 1775, and by the Americans under General Montgomery until 1776. It later held American prisoners during the War of 1812, and Canadian patriots during the Patriot Rebellion of 1837–38.

After exploring Fort Chambly and its museum of weapons and artifacts, take a look at the **St Hubert House** (1760), **Maigneault House**, and the **Laureau House** (1775). You can see the operation of the Chambly canal's three locks, or go canoeing in the Chambly basin, just below the Richelieu Rapids. (Fort Chambly is open mid-May to Labor Day. 2 Rue Richelieu, Chambly. [514] 658-1585.)

On the way to Fort Lennox, stop at **St-**

Lac des Sables at Ste-Agathe.

Jean-sur-Richelieu to stroll through the old part of this historic military town, along Jacques-Cartier, St-Charles, Longueuil and St-Georges Streets and on the promenade along the Chambly Canal. St-Jean has a lively public market on Wednesdays and Saturdays, and in August, during its 10-day Festival des Montgofières, outrageously colorful hot-air balloons float over its rooftops and steeples. Cruises on the Richelieu leave from the wharf at foot of St Georges Street.

At its northern end, l'Île-aux-Noix is an idyllic spot for picnic and hikes along the marshy riverbank to observe painted turtles, muskrats, bullfrogs and diving kingfishers. And at the southern tip of this island, which is only 15 miles (24 km) from the US border, is the impressive star-shaped **Fort Lennox**, with a moat 60 feet wide and 15 feet deep (18 by 4.5 meters).

The French built the fort in 1759 to defend against British advance, but they evacuated it the following year under British seige. In 1775, Americans captured the l'Île-aux-Noix to use as a base for attacks on Montreal and Quebec City, but a year later a smallpox epidemic forced them to abandon the fort.

Lively animated tours of Fort Lennox take you through the guardhouse (1824), gunpowder magazine, officer's quarters, guardhouse, prison, barracks and commisary, and a museum exhibiting military equipment and documents. On special days actors perform re-enactments of 18th-century skirmishes, using replicas of period uniforms and weapons. (Fort Lennox, open late May to early October, is accessible by the Crosières Richelieu ferry from St-Paul-de-l'Île-aux-Noix, at the Reception Center on 61st Avenue. [514] 291-5700.)

Mont St-Hilaire/Vieux Beloeil: *Route: Autoroute 20 East to exit 113; 133 South to* **Mont St-Hilaire**; *bridge over to* **Beloeil**.

When the wind is calm, and the air balmy, you can lie for hours on "Sugar Loaf," the flat rocky summit of **Mont St-Hilaire**, feasting on the contours of the land below. The Monteregian hill is only 1,350 ft (410 meters) above sea level, but it rises abruptly from the St Lawrence plain, affording a dreamy view of its sister peak, Mount Royal, in the heart of the metropolis, the Richelieu River and the sinewy St Lawrence, and Monts St-Bruno, St-Grégoire, Rougemont and Yamaska.

Mont St-Hilaire is an ecological marvel thriving only 22 miles (35 km) from Montreal – an environment so unspoiled that UNESCO designated it as the first Biosphere Reserve in Canada. This highest of the eight Monteregian hills shelters the last vestige of the dense woodland that once covered the St Lawrence Valley. In a lush hardwood forest with canopies of 100-ft (30-meter) red oaks and 250-year old white pines, there are hundreds of mosses and ferns, 600 species of flowering plants, 32 of flowering trees and 187 of birds.

Mont St-Hilaire's hiking trails wind

Orchards along the Richelieu.

through an aquatic zone, a wildflower meadow, lush ferny areas, along Lac Hertel, a lake once humming with seven mills, and up to an exposed windy summit with Arctic vegetation. Mont St-Hilaire's habitat is ideal for bird watching, crosscountry skiing and snowshoeing.

Just across the Richelieu River from Mont St-Hilaire's apple orchards lies **Vieux Beloeil**, established in 1694. Its yacht harbor, boutiques, art galleries, artisan shops, restaurants and cultural center attract Montrealers in all seasons. Vieux Beloeil's magnificent old buildings include a presbytery built in 1772, the Près-Vert and Lanctôt houses, and the Rouville-Campbell Manor, now an art gallery. The Quebec painter Ozias Leduc was born in the Correlieu House, and the local church contains one of his frescos.

Sorel/Ste-Anne-de-Sorel: *Route: Eastern Townships Autoroute 10 to 30 North to* **Sorel**; *132 East to* **Ste-Anne-de-Sorel**.

Canada's fourth oldest city, **Sorel**, is known for its busy shipyards and its lively marina – the focus of nautical tourism in Quebec. The **Place du Marché** at the end of Rue Roi near the port is a bustling marketplace, and the **Carré Royal** is a magnificent 18th-century park curiously shaped like a Union Jack. Sorel makes a really convenient base from which to explore the bewitching archipelago of islands off its shore.

Ste-Anne-de-Sorel has come to be known as *Pays du Survenant* (Land of the Unexpected Visitor) because of Germaine Guèvremont's novel of that name. The **Musée de l'Ecriture et Maison de Germaine Guèvremont**, across a hanging bridge on the tiny islet **l'Îlette au Pée**, is devoted to the lives and works of Quebec writers (3139 Chemin Chenal-du-Moine, [514] 743-8605).

The Chemin Chenal-du-Moine leads across a steel bridge to **Île aux Fantômes**, whose dwellings are set up high

Autumn on the Iles de Sorel.

on pilings as a protection against flooding. From a dead-end road you can cross over to the **Île d'Embarras** and its tiny fishing village strung with drying fish nets. Two old ice houses on the tip of the island are now restaurants featuring traditional regional cuisine – notably *gibelotte*, fish stew made from the locals' daily catches.

Les excursions et expéditions de canots des Îles de Sorel, Inc. run from mid-April to mid-October, and leave from the quay at 2786 Chemin Chenal-du-Moine, Ste-Anne-de-Sorel (514) 742-3080.

Village d'Antan/Odanak Abenaki Reserve: *Route: Autoroute 20, exit 181 to Le Village Québécois d'Antan; from Drummondville, Route 143 to Route 132 northwest to Pierreville/Odanak.*

Le Village Québécois d'Antan (the Quebec Village of Yesteryear) in Drummondville, is not as corny as it sounds. The 18th-century village recreated on this pastoral site attracts serious historians, cultivated museum-goers,

filmmakers, and Québécois looking for their roots, as well as those eager for nostalgia.

The village's 50 historic buildings and 30 historic reproductions constructed by regional artisans portray the days of colonization between 1810 and 1910. Guides in period costume animate 25 traditional houses in nine different architectural styles, and 18 artisan workshops, including a saddlery, tinsmith, shoe-maker and broom-maker, and cabinet maker – *à la Québécois*.

The list goes on... an oddly stocked general store, apothecary, old post office, blacksmith forge, a sawmill, a telephone museum, an old style *caisse-populaire* (savings bank), one-room schoolhouse, a *cabane à sucre*, garage and gas station with antique cars, and even a covered bridge (*circa* 1878) transported from Stanbridge. Farm animals have a cattle shed, henhouse, and pighouse, a safe distance from restaurant and picnic tables. (Village Québéc-

Competing by kayak.

ois d'Antan, June 1–Labor Day; R.R. 3, Rue Montplaisir, [819] 478-1441.)

Around the corner from Pierreville, the small town that is Canada's biggest producer of fire engines, is the **Odanak Abenaki Reserve** on the shores of the St Francis River. In the 17th century the Abenakis came from New England to settle in Odanak, and the Jesuits established a mission here to educate them.

In the heart of the reserve is a riverfront park graced with rustic gazebos, tepees, carved totem poles and contemporary Abenaki sculpture. The stone chapel built in 1828 is filled with Amerindian woodcarvings, and the red brick convent across from it has been transformed into a museum of Abenaki history and culture. On the rambling porch stand massive wooden sculptures of mythological figures, and inside are 14 rooms filled with Abenaki history, culture and crafts.

The **Musée des Abenakis** contains displays on constructing birch-bark canoes, Abenaki cornhusk masks, ash-

splint basket-weaving, and a model of a 17th-century Abenaki fort. Local shops sell sweetgrass baskets, buckskin jackets, native crafts, and smoked sturgeon, a local specialty. (108 Rue Waban-Aki, Odanak [514] 568-2600. Hwy 20, exits 175–185; May 1–Oct. 31.)

Village du Bûcheron/Parc Nationale de la Mauricie: *Route: 40 East to 55 North (at Trois Rivières); 55 North to 155 North to Grand-Piles; park entrance at St-Jean-des-Piles.*

On a cliff overlooking the St-Maurice River is the lovely village of **Grand-Piles**, once a transfer harbor for lumber boats, and the **Village du Bûcheron** (Lumberjack Village). The heyday of Mauricie's logging industry and lumberjack days (1850–1950) is celebrated in 25 log buildings containing hundreds of photos and over 5,000 artifacts. The Village has an art gallery and craft boutique, and on weekends you can see the sawmill in operation and have a typical lumberjack meal at the Cookerie. (Open mid-May to mid-October; 780 Fifth Avenue, Grand-Piles, [819] 538-7895.)

Mauricie National Park is a paradise for would-be Robinson Crusoes. This watery wilderness speckled with tree-covered islets has 34 lakes which are off-limits to motor boats. From the Île-aux-Pins lookout over **Lake Wapizagonke**, a peek through field glasses reveals a jaunty red canoe beside a camper dozing in blissful solitude on a white sandy islet beach.

The national park is a canoe-camping, trout fishing heaven. All lakes are accessible by well-bridged portage trails, but the most popular route is the 7-mile (11-km) stretch up Lake Wapizagonke's shoreline of cliffs and densely forested hills.

The park is wild enough for moose, black bear and coyote, wolf and lynx, yet tame enough for picnicking, swimming, camping (summer and winter), bicycling, hiking and birdwatching. More than 193 species of birds have been sighted here, and 116 of them nest in the region.

Below, into the wind. Overpage: fiery welcome at La Ronde Park.

TRAVEL TIPS

Getting There

226	By Air
226	By Rail
226	By Land

Travel Essentials

226	Visas & Passports
226	Money Matters
227	Health
227	What to Wear
227	Animal Quarantine
227	Customs
227	Extension of Stay

Getting Acquainted

227	Government & Economy
228	Geography & Population
228	Time Zones
228	Climate
228	Etiquette
228	Language
229	Business Hours
229	Holidays
229	Festivals & Events

Communications

230	Postal Services
230	Telegram & Fax
230	Telephone
231	News Media

Emergencies

231	Security & Crime
231	Medical Services
232	Pharmacies
232	Other Services

Getting Around

232	Maps
232	From the Airport
232	Public Transport
232	Taxis
232	Private Transport
233	By Foot
233	Bicycle Rental

Where to Stay

233	Hotels
236	Bed & Breakfasts

Food Digest

237	Where to Eat
242	Drinking Notes

Things to Do

242	City
244	Tours & Attractions

Culture Plus

245	Museums
246	Art Galleries
246	Concerts & Operas
247	Ballet & Theaters
247	Public Libraries

Nightlife

248	Cabarets & Dinner Theater
248	Jazz & Dancing

Shopping

250	What to Buy
251	Department Stores

Sports

251	Participant
253	Spectator

Special Information

253	Children
254	Disabled

Further Reading

255	Booklist

Useful Addresses

255	Tourist Information
255	Embassies & Consulates

GETTING THERE

Note: Unless otherwise stated, the area code for telephone numbers in Montreal and the surrounding areas is 514.

BY AIR

There are two airports serving Montreal: Dorval International is 14 miles (22 km) west of the city and handles domestic and most US flights; Mirabel International, 34 miles (55 km) northwest, handles all flights from outside of North America.

BY RAIL

Amtrak has daily service from the US. Complete information about fares can be obtained by calling 1-800-426-8725.

Montreal is connected to most major cities of Canada through VIA Rail (tel: 1-800-361-5390). The terminus for both companies is located at 935 Rue de la Gauchetière Ouest, Bonaventure.

BY CAR

A number of highways lead into Montreal. At the Canadian border be prepared to show proof of citizenship and your vehicle's ownership papers. On holidays and weekends, traffic can back up and travelers can expect a wait of a half hour or more at the crossing. From New York, take I-87 (the New York State Throughway) which becomes Highway 15 at the border 30 miles (47 km) from the outskirts of Montreal. From New England, take Route I-89 to Route 133 which becomes a two-lane road at the border. From Vermont, take I-91 which becomes Highway 55 in Canada; follow this route to Highway 10 to Montreal. From Toronto take Highway 401 directly to Montreal.

In Quebec, the roadsigns are in French but are easy to decipher. The speed limit and distances are posted in kilometers. The official speed limit is 100 kph (62 mph) and the highways are well patrolled. Quebec has a seat-belt law.

BY BUS

Greyhound/Trailways connects Montreal with various cities in North America. Vermont Transit connects Boston, New York and other cities in New England with Montreal. Both lines use the Voyageur Terminal located at 505 Maissonneuve Blvd Est, tel: (514) 842-2281.

TRAVEL ESSENTIALS

VISAS & PASSPORTS

US citizens and citizens of the United Kingdom do not need either a visa or a passport to enter Canada, though some proof of citizenship (driver's license, birth certificate or passport) is required. All other visitors are required to present passports. Resident aliens should carry their US alien registration or green card. Visitors wishing to stay over three months may need a visa.

MONEY MATTERS

Traveler's checks and major credit cards are readily accepted in Montreal. Cash may be needed for small restaurants and stores, though many establishments accept US currency. Buying some Canadian dollars before you leave home will help you to avoid long lines at the airports. Traveler's checks can also be purchased in Canadian dollars. At the current exchange rate, one Canadian dollar is worth somewhere between 80 and 90 US cents. Banking hours in Montreal are 10 a.m.–3 or 4 p.m. Suggested banks for currency exchange include: Bank of America Canada, 1250 Rue Peel, tel: (514) 393-1855, open daily 9.30 a.m.–5 p.m; Guardian Trust

Co., Dorval Airport, tel: (514) 636-3582, open daily 6 a.m.–9.30 p.m. for all currencies and 6 a.m.–11 p.m. for US dollars; National Commercial – Foreign Currency, 1240 Rue Peel, tel: (514) 879-1300, open Monday–Friday 8 a.m.–5 p.m., Saturday 8 a.m.–3 p.m.

A 9 percent sales tax is applied to all goods and services except hotel rooms, books, home furnishings and shoes costing less than $125 and clothes less than $500. In addition, there is a 10 percent meal tax on all orders over $3.25. For further information about the tax laws call Revenue Quebec, (514) 873-2611, local 296.

HEALTH

To obtain a list of English-speaking physicians in Montreal contact the International Association for Medical Assistance to Travelers (IAMAT), 736 Rue Center, Lewiston, NY 14092. In Canada: 188 Nicklin Road, Guelph, Ontario, N1H 7L5 and in Europe: Gotthardstrasse 17, 6300 Zug, Switzerland.

If your health insurance does not cover medical problems while traveling, the following companies may be of assistance: Health Care Abroad, International Underwriters Group, 243 Rue Church Ouest, Vienna, VA 22180, tel: 1-800-237-6615; Travel Guard International, 1100 Centerpoint Drive, Stevens Point, WI 54481, tel: 1-800-782-5151. Hospital and medical services are excellent. Rates for care vary by hospital. Adult in-patient care starts at $900 a day.

WHAT TO WEAR

During the cold winter months, travelers should come equipped with warm layers of clothing as well as hats, gloves and boots. Even in the summer, bringing a sweater for the cool evenings is advisable. Be sure to bring athletic clothes, shoes and a bathing suit as many of Montreal's hotels have health clubs and indoor pools.

ANIMAL QUARANTINE

Canada allows unrestricted entry of cats. Dogs, however, must have proof of veterinary inspection to show that they are free from various communicable diseases such as rabies. Livestock, horses, and fowl are subject to veterinary health inspection upon arrival in Canada.

CUSTOMS

There are no restrictions on clothing or professional tools and equipment. American and British visitors aged 16 and over can bring in duty-free up to 200 cigarettes, 50 cigars, two pounds of tobacco, personal cars (up to six months), boats, canoes, rifles and shotguns (but no handguns or automatic weapons), 200 rounds of ammunition, cameras, recreational equipment and radios. If you are driving a rental car keep the contract with you. If you have any questions before you leave, phone Canadian Customs at (514) 283-9900.

EXTENSION OF STAY

If you plan to extend your stay over the standard three-month limit, contact the Department of Employment and Immigration in Ottawa, Ontario.

GETTING ACQUAINTED

GOVERNMENT & ECONOMY

A mayor and a 56-member council elected for four years and a six-member executive committee selected by the council govern the city of Montreal. As in all Canadian municipalities, the city government is controlled by the provincial legislature. In 1969, the Montreal Metropolitan Corporation replaced the Montreal Urban Community in administering the affairs of metropolitan area.

Montreal is the headquarters for Canada's largest banks, railroad lines and insurance companies. The city is also an important center for shipping and industry.

GEOGRAPHY & POPULATION

Located in the province of Quebec, Montreal is built on an island that is roughly 32 miles (40 km) long and 10 miles (16 km) wide, situated at the confluence of the Ottawa River and the St Lawrence Seaway. Prominent in the middle of the island is Mont-Royal. Montreal is the second largest city in Canada after Toronto. Approximately two-thirds of the population is French and it is claimed that Montreal is the largest French-speaking city apart from Paris.

TIME ZONES

Montreal is within the Eastern Time Zone, which is the same as New York City and Boston, one hour ahead of Chicago, and three hours ahead of San Francisco. On the last Sunday in April, the clock is moved ahead one hour for Daylight Savings Time. On the last Sunday in October, the clock is moved back one hour to return to Standard Time ("Spring forward, Fall back"). Using Eastern Time, when it is 12 noon in Montreal (depending on Daylight Savings Time) it is:

11 a.m. in Chicago
9 a.m. in San Francisco
8 a.m. in Hawaii
5 p.m. in London
6 p.m. in Bonn, Madrid, Paris and Rome.
7 p.m. in Athens and Cairo.
8 p.m. in Moscow
9.30 p.m. in Bombay
11 p.m. in Bangkok
12 a.m. (the next day) in Singapore and Hong Kong
1 a.m. (the next day) in Tokyo
2 a.m. (the next day) in Sydney

CLIMATE

Montreal has nearly five months of cold and snow. Montrealers, however, rarely hibernate. Skating, skiing and sledding are very popular pastimes. The subway system, known as the Metro, is well heated and the Underground City provides a haven from the cold. In summer, the city becomes alive with the warm weather and outdoor cafés and festivals bring people out on the streets. In July temperature can reach as high as 90°F, yet average temperatures hover around 70° during the day. The average daily highs in Montreal are:

Month	(C)	(F)
January	−10.2	14
February	−09.0	15
March	−02.5	27
April	05.7	42
May	13.0	55
June	18.3	64
July	20.9	69
August	19.6	68
September	14.8	58
October	08.7	47
November	02.0	35
December	−06.9	20

ETIQUETTE

It is customary to tip waiters and taxi drivers between 10 and 15 percent of the bill or fare. Some restaurants add the tip to the bill but this will be identified on the check. For porters, $1 per suitcase is expected. For hotel doormen who hail a cab or give other assistance, $1 should be given. Checkrooms usually have a fixed rate of 75 cents.

LANGUAGE

Most Montrealers are fluent in both English and French. Québécois French has a more nasal quality and singsong tone than Parisian French. Some useful phrases to know are:

Yes/No	*Oui/non*
Please	*S'il vous plaît*
Thank you	*Merci*
(very much)	*(beaucoup)*
You're welcome	*De rien*
That's all right	*Il n'y a pas de quoi*
Excuse me, sorry	*Pardon*
Sorry!	*Désolé*
Good morning/ afternoon	*Bonjour*
Good evening	*Bonsoir*
Goodbye	*Au revoir*
Mr (Sir)	*Monsieur*
Mrs (Ma'am)	*Madame*
Miss	*Mademoiselle*
Pleased to meet you	*Enchanté*
How are you?	*Comment allez-vous?*
Very well, thanks	*Très bien, merci*

And you?	*Et vous?*
Do you speak English?	*Parlez-vous anglais?*
I don't speak French	*Je ne parle pas français*
I don't understand	*Je ne comprends pas*
I understand	*Je comprends*
I don't know	*Je ne sais pas*
I'm American/English	*Je suis américan/ anglais*
What's your name?	*Comment vous appelez-vous?*
My name is…	*Je m'appelle…*
What time is it?	*Quelle heure est-il?*
How?	*Comment?*

BUSINESS HOURS

The standard business hours for most businesses are 9 a.m.–5 p.m. Banks are usually open weekdays 10 a.m.–3 p.m. Museums follow regular business hours and shops are generally open Monday–Wednesday 10 a.m.–6 p.m., Thursday and Friday 10 a.m.–9 p.m., Saturday 10 a.m.–5 p.m. Most stores are closed on Sunday.

HOLIDAYS

Government agencies and many banks, businesses and schools close on the following holidays:

New Year's Day: January 1
Good Friday
Easter Monday
Fête de Dollard/Victoria Day: May 21 (or closest Monday).
Fête Nationale (Saint Jean Baptiste Day, Quebec Holiday): June 24.
Canada Day: July 1.
Labor Day: 1st Monday in September.
Thanksgiving: 2nd Monday in October.
Christmas Day: December 25.
Boxing Day: December 26.

FESTIVALS & EVENTS

Festivals of all kind abound in Montreal, including art, music, film, theater, sports, and folk dancing. These celebrations demonstrate Montreal's truly international character. The main season for these celebrations is from May to September. For a complete and detailed list of all festivals and celebrations, consult the Calender of Events published twice yearly and available at information centers in the city. The main information office is located at 1010 Ste-Catherine Ouest, tel: 871-1595.

JANUARY – FEBRUARY

La Fête des Neiges (from mid-January until early February, snow sculptures, cross-country skiing competitions, barrel-jumping, dog sled races, ice canoe races, folk dancing, strolling makeup artists and clowns).

APRIL

International Art Festival, Convention Center.

MAY

International Festival of Young Cinema.
La Super Enfant-Fête.
Montreal International Chinese Film Festival.
International Benson & Hedges Fireworks Competition (held on Ile Ste-Hélène, best views from La Ronde park).
Montreal International Mime Festival (held at Complexe Desjardins and along Rue St-Denis).
Museum Day (Open House at 16 of the city's museums).
Sun Carnival.
Super Motorcross Laurentide.
Theater Festival of the Americas.

JUNE

Montreal International Music Competition (various concert halls in summer).
Festival de Créations Jeunesse.
La Classique Cycliste de Montréal.
International Children's Theater Festival of Quebec.
Le Tour de L'Ile de Montréal.
Molson Grand Prix (part of world circuit of Formula One racing).
Lanaudière Summer Festival of Classical and Jazz Music.
Montreal International Puppet Festival (first week in June).
Jour de St-Jean-Baptiste (Quebec's national holiday, June 24).
Antiques Bonaventure (the dealers descend).

JULY

Carifête (a festival of Dance and Music from the Caribbean).

Festival Juste Pour Rire/Just for Laughs Festival.

Drummondville World Folklore Festival.

Montreal International Jazz Festival (by names in concert halls plus free outdoor concerts and carnival atmosphere in streets).

AUGUST

Le Grand Prix Cycliste des Amériques (224-km professional race in streets and on Mount Royal).

Haut-Richelieu Hot Air Balloon Festival and North American Championship.

Montreal World Film Festival (500 screening at various tournament).

Player's Challenge (major international tennis tournament).

SEPTEMBER

Montreal International Marathon (42-km run for professionals and amateurs).

Montreal International Rock Festival.

Montreal International Music Festival (classical music gets its turn).

Festival Internationale de Nouvelle Dance (in odd-numbered years only).

OCTOBER

Autumn Moon Festival (Chinatown, at beginning of month).

International Festival of New Cinema and Video.

Montreal New Music Festival.

Canadiens ice hockey games resume at the Forum.

COMMUNICATIONS

POSTAL SERVICES

The main post office (general delivery) is located at 1025 Rue St-Jacques, tel: (514) 283-2567. Open: Monday–Friday 8 a.m.–5.45 p.m., Saturday 8 a.m.–12 noon.

Other stations are located at:

1250 Rue University, tel: (514) 283-2576. Open: Monday–Friday 8 a.m.–5.45 p.m.

1250 Rue Ste-Catherine Est, tel: (514) 522-3220. Open: Monday–Friday 8 a.m.–5.45 p.m.

In addition to the post offices, stamps can be bought at coin machines in airports, bus terminals, and hotel lobbies.

You can have mail addressed to you at Poste Restante, or general delivery at the Post Office at 1025 Rue St-Jacques. The American Express office will also hold mail for its customers at its office at 1141 Blvd de Maissoneuve Ouest.

TELEGRAM & TELEX

Telegrams and cablegrams are handled by CNCP Telecommunications at 740 Rue Notre-Dame Ouest, tel: (514) 861-7311. The office is open by phone: daily, 8 a.m.–11.30 p.m. or at the counter: Monday–Friday 8 a.m.–4.30 p.m.

TELEPHONE

Public pay phones require 25¢. Long-distance calls may be dialed directly to all points in North America and most countries in Europe. Bell Canada provides immediate billing service which you must handle in person at 700 de La Gauchetière Ouest, Monday–Friday 9 a.m.–5 p.m. Tel: (514) 870-8883 for more information about this service. The area code in Montreal and surrounding areas is 514.

Both French and English language newspapers, radio and television stations are available in Montreal. For listing of television stations check the daily newspapers. Radio stations are listed in the *Yellow Pages* of the telephone book.

NEWSPAPERS

The two major daily newspapers in Montreal are *La Presse* (French) and *The Gazette* (English). Many other smaller newspapers, journals and special interest publications are also found in the city.

EMERGENCIES

Dialing 911 will connect you to the police or other emergency assistance. No coins are needed in telephone booths.

SECURITY & CRIME

As a rule, it is safe to walk around downtown Montreal during both the day and evening. Areas to avoid at night include the X-rated movie houses along Rue Ste-Catherine Est. Whenever possible, travel with another person while sightseeing or shopping, particularly at night. Do not walk in deserted or rundown areas alone. If driving, lock your car and never leave luggage, cameras or other valuables in view. Put them in the glove compartment or trunk to avoid a break-in. Park under a street light.

In regard to your personal belongings, never leave your luggage unattended. While waiting for a room reservation, for example, keep your property in view. Never leave money or jewelry in your hotel room, even for a short time.

Carry only the cash you need. Use credit cards and traveler's checks whenever possible and avoid showing large amounts of cash.

Although health care is excellent in Montreal it can also be quite expensive, especially for non-residents. Most hospitals have emergency rooms with doctors on hand round the clock. For information on clinics and other health services consult the *Yellow Pages* of the telephone book.

HOSPITALS

Catherine Booth Hospital
4375 Montclair
Tel: 481-0431

Centre Hospitalier de St-Laurent
1275 Côte Vertu
Tel: 747-4771

Centre Hospitalier J. Henri Charbonneau
3095 Sherbrooke Est
Tel: 523-1173

Centre Hospitalier Jacques Viger
1051 St-Hubert
Tel: 842-7181

Centre Hospitalier Saint Charles Borromée
66 Blvd René Lévesque Est
Tel: 861-9331

Maissoneuve-Rosemont Hospital
5415 de l'Assumption
Tel: 252-3400

Montreal General Hospital
1650 Avenue du Cédar
Tel: 937-6011

Saint-Luc Hospital
1058 St-Denis
Tel: 281-2121

St Mary's Hospital Center
3830 Lacombe
Tel: 344-3511

Villa Medica Hospital
225 Sherbrooke Est
Tel: 288-8201

PHARMACIES

There are many full-service pharmacies throughout the city. One store which provides 24-hour service is the Jean Coutu Drug Store located at 1370 Avenue Mont-Royal Est, tel: (514) 527-8827.

OTHER SERVICES

The **Dental Clinic** at 3546 Rue Van Home, tel: (514) 342-4444, offers 24-hour service. **Weather Information**: 636-3026. **Consumer Aid Services**: 1-800-567-8552. **Handicapped Consumers**: 287-1083 **Quebec Poison Control Center**: 1-800-463-5060. **Travel Information**: 871-1595.

GETTING AROUND

MAPS

Excellent maps of the city are available at any of the tourist information offices. Street signs with a large question mark point the direction to office locations around the city. The main office is located at 1010 Ste-Catherine Ouest, tel: 871-1595.

FROM THE AIRPORT

Aerocar bus service, tel: (514) 397-9999, is available from both Dorval ($7) and Mirabel ($9) airports. Several major taxi companies also provide service from the airports for roughly $19 from Dorval and $45 from Mirabel.

Limousine service can be arranged through Contact Limousine Service, tel: (514) 631-5466, or Murray Hill Limousine Service, tel: (514) 937-5311. The trip will cost about $30 from Dorval and $60 from Mirabel.

PUBLIC TRANSPORT

Public transportation in Montreal is very efficient, clean and comfortable. The Société de Transport de la Communauté de Montréal (STCUM) administers both the bus and Metro, and the tickets and transfers are good on either service. Exact change is required on the buses.

The rubber-wheeled Metro trains operate from 5.30 a.m. to 1 a.m. and run as often as every three minutes on crowded lines. Directions of the Metro trains are indicated by the name of the last station on the line and are also distinguished by different colors.

The single fare for adults is $1.50. Monthly passes cost $38 and a strip of six tickets can be bought for $6. Free maps of the Metro and bus system may be obtained at the ticket booths. For additional information, tel: (514) 288-6287.

TAXIS

The rate for all taxis in Montreal is 70¢ per kilometer and all require a $2 minimum. Each has an orange or white plastic sign on its roof which is lit when available. Some of the major taxi companies include: Champlain, tel: 273-2435; Co-op, tel: 725-9885; La Salle, tel: 277-2552; Veterans, tel: 273-6351.

PRIVATE TRANSPORT

CAR RENTALS

Most car rental companies have branches at the airport and at major hotels in addition to their central offices. Car rental rates vary by firm and by model and size of the car. Most companies offer unlimited mileage and special weekend rates as well as liability insurance. Gas and collision insurance are extra and there is a 10 percent sales tax. Some of the rental companies include:

Ansa International Rent-A-Car
10975 Côte-de-Liesse
Tel: (514) 631-1355
Open: seven days a week.

Avis
1225 Rue Metcalf
Tel: (514) 866-7906 or 1-800-268-0303
Open: Monday–Wednesday 7 a.m.–10 p.m.,

GREAT EXPLORATIONS

IT IS A PLACE LIKE THIS, THAT, AT THE END OF THE NINE-TEENTH CENTURY, GREAT CANADIAN STATESMEN BUILT OUR COUNTRY.

OPEN YEAR
ROUND
SUMMER HOURS:
May to September. Free
admission every day.

458, Notre Dame Street East
Old Montreal
Tel.: (514) 283-2282
🌐 Champs-de-Mars

SIR GEORGE-ÉTIENNE CARTIER

NATIONAL HISTORIC
SITE

 Environment Canada
Parks Service

Environnement Canada
Service des parcs

Canada

*Experience the diversity of the United States with **Crossing America**, a guidebook that is colourful, informative and fun. Or explore the Sunshine State of Florida, check out the Californian lifestyle or the spirit of aloha in Hawaii, see the unforgettable scenery of the Rocky Mountains, visit the large metropolises of New York and Chicago. Canada is also a land of many images, mirrored vividly in the **Insight Guide**. From the beaches of the Atlantic to Ontario's stunningly beautiful parks to the cobblestone streets of romantic Montreal.*

DUNGEK CHE CUM CAN CHULLY!

Alaska
American Southwest
Boston
California
Canada
Crossing America
Florida
Hawaii
Los Angeles
Miami

New England
New York City
New York State
Northern California
Pacific Northwest USA
Rockies
San Francisco
Southern California
Texas

A P A
INSIGHT
GUIDES

Thursday and Friday 7 a.m.–11 p.m., Saturday and Sunday 8 a.m.–10 p.m.

Budget
Central Station
895 Rue de La Gauchetière Ouest
Tel: 1-800-268-8970 (French) or 1-800-268-8900 (English).
Open: Monday–Friday 7 a.m.–9 p.m., weekends 7 a.m.–7 p.m.

Thrifty/Viabec
1600 Rue Berri, Suite 9
Tel: (514) 845-5954
Open: Monday–Friday 8 a.m.–8 p.m., Saturday 9 a.m.–5 p.m., Sunday 9 a.m.–3 p.m.

Hertz
1475 Rue Aylmer
Tel: (514) 842-8537 or 1-800-263-0678
Open: Monday–Friday 7 a.m.–9 p.m., weekends 7 a.m.–7 p.m.

Tilden
1200 Rue Stanley
Tel: (514) 878-2771 or 1-800-361-5334
Open: daily 7 a.m.–11 p.m.

Via Route
1444 Blvd René-Lévesque Ouest
Tel: (514) 871-1166
Open: Monday–Friday 8 a.m.–7 p.m., Saturday 8 a.m.–5 p.m., Sunday 9 a.m.–5 p.m.

BY FOOT

Walking in Montreal is very enjoyable and finding your way around is quite easy. Street names and directions are in French. If you get lost or need directions ask someone passing by. Montrealers love to help out and will be more than willing to assist you.

BICYCLE RENTAL

Bicycling is popular in Montreal, especially in the city's many scenic parks. A few of the companies which rent bikes are:

Maison Saint-Jacques
Old Port: Blvd St-Laurent at Rue de la Commune, tel: 526-4132.
Open: mid-May to Labor Day, Monday 12 noon–8.30 p.m., Tuesday–Sunday 11 a.m.–8.30 p.m.

Quadricycle International Inc.
Old Port: tel: 398-0634.
Open: September–October 30, Saturday and Sunday 10 a.m.–12 midnight; June–September, daily 10 a.m.–12 midnight.
Ile Notre-Dame: Open: June–September, daily 11 a.m.–6 p.m.

La Cordée
2159 Rue Ste-Catherine Est, tel: 524-1515.

Cycle Peel
6665 Rue St-Jacques, tel: 486-1148.

WHERE TO STAY

HOTELS

Most hotels in Montreal fall in the Expensive to Deluxe range, especially downtown. Large hotels often offer weekend or family discounts. Prices can range from $300 a night for a double room in a deluxe hotel to $55–$75 a night in a moderate hotel.

DELUXE

Ritz-Carlton
1228 Rue Sherbrooke Ouest
Montreal, Quebec H3G 1H6
Tel: 842-4212 or 1-800-327-0200
Caters to an elite clientele.

Le Meridien
4 Complexe Desjardins
Montreal H5B 1E5
Tel: 285-1450

Le Quatre Saisons
1050 Rue Sherbrooke Ouest
Montreal H3A 2R6
Tel: 284-1110
Multilingual concierge, complete fitness center, good food and 24-hour room service in an excellent location.

La Reine Elizabeth
900 Blvd Réne-Lévesque Ouest
Montreal H3B 4A5
Tel: 861-3511
Dependable comfort in good location.

EXPENSIVE

Auberge Ramada Inn
5500 Rue Sherbrooke Est
Montreal H1N 1A1
Tel: 246-9011
Located at Olympic Park. Offers Olympic-size pool, nightclub and full-service conference facilities.

Le Pavillion
7700 Côte de Liesse, Rue St-Laurent
Montreal H4T 1E7
Tel: 731-7821 or 1-800-361-6243
Minutes away from Dorval International Airport. Meeting and banquet facilities to accommodate 250 people.

Hôtel La Barre
2019 Blvd Taschereau Est
Longueuil, Quebec J4K 2Y1
Tel: 677-9101, 1-800-361-2091
Concierge service, outdoor swimming pool and gardens.

Hôtel Ruby Foo's
7655 Blvd Decarie
Montreal H4P 2H2
Tel: 731-7701 or 1-800-361-5419
Oriental decor, outdoor swimming pool, health club and spa, and beauty salon.

Hôtel Arcade
50 Blvd René-Lévesque Ouest
Montreal H2Z 1A2
Tel: 874-9090 or 1-800-363-6535
Game room for children.

Hôtel le Baccarat
475 Rue Sherbrooke Ouest
Montreal H3A 2L9
Tel: 514-842-3961 or 1-800-361-4973

Hôtel Shagrila
3407 Rue Peel
Montreal H3A 1W7
Tel: 288-4141 or 1-800-648-7200
Oriental atmosphere with a Szechuan-style restaurant, Dynastie de Ming.

Le Grand Hôtel
777 Rue University
Montreal H3C 3Z7
Tel: 878-1370 or 1-800-361-8155
Revolving rooftop restaurant, complete spa facilities with heated pool and aerobics classes.

Hôtel de Gouverneurs Place Dupuis
1415 Rue St-Hubert
Montreal H2L 3Y9
Tel: 842-4881 or 1-800-463-2820
All rooms have views of Montreal, Mount Royal or the St Lawrence river.

Hôtel La Citadelle
410 Rue Sherbrooke Ouest
Montreal H3A 1B3
Tel: 844-8851 or 1-800-458-6262
Piano bar, health spa, roof-top indoor pool and European-style atmosphere.

Bonaventure Hilton International
1 Place Bonaventure
Montreal H5A 1E4
Tel: 878-2332
Surrounding 2½ acres of gardens atop Montreal's "underground city", this hotel offers three restaurants, nightclub, health club, 24-hour room service and a black-and-white TV in the bathrooms!

Le Centre Sheraton
1201 Blvd René-Lévesque Ouest
Montreal H3B 2L7
Tel: 878-2000 or 1-800-325-3535
Gourmet restaurant, indoor pool, health club and specialty boutiques all situated in a convenient location.

Holiday Inn Crowne Plaza
420 Rue Sherbrooke Ouest
Montreal H3A 1B4
Tel: 842-6111 or 1-800-HOLIDAY
Basic Holiday Inn style equipped with two bars, café-restaurant, health club and indoor pool. Package rates available.

Ramada Inn
1005 Rue Guy
Montreal H3H 2K4
Tel: 866-4611
Recently renovated hotel offers two restaurants, bar and meeting facilities.

Ramada Renaissance du Parc
3625 Avenue du Parc
Montreal H2X 3P8
Tel: 288-6666
Located in the Mont Royal Park district, this hotel offers squash and tennis courts, Nautilus equipment and all-season indoor/outdoor pool.

Ramada Airport
6600 Côte-de-Liesse
Montreal H4T 1E3
Tel: 342-2262

MODERATE

L'Hôtel Montreal-Crescent
1366 Blvd René-Lévesque
Montreal H3G 1T4
Tel: 878-9797
Small, intimate hotel in the heart of downtown Montreal.

Château De L'Argoat
524 Rue Sherbrooke Est
Montreal H2L 1K1
Tel: 842-2046

Hôtel Manoir des Alpes
1245 Rue St-André
Montreal H2L 3T1
Tel: 845-0373
Transformed Victorian building.

Auberge des Glycines Inc.
819 Blvd de Maisonneuve Est
Montreal H2L 1Y7
Tel: 526-5511 or 1-800-361-6896

Hôtel Le St-André
1285 Rue St-André
Montreal H2L 3T1
Tel: 849-7070
Recently renovated. Complementary in-room continental breakfast.

Hôtel de L'Institut
3535 Rue St-Denis
Montreal H2X 3P1
Tel: 282-5120
Owned and operated by the Quebec Institute of Tourism and Hotels, this hotel is the training ground for future hotel and restaurant managers. Institutional exterior but the service is excellent.

Auberge de la Fontaine
1301 Rue Rachel Est
Montreal H2J 2K1
Tel: 597-0166
Relaxed atmosphere. Some rooms have terraces or balconies.

Hôtel de Paris
901 Rue Sherbrooke Est
Montreal H2L 1L3
Tel: 522-6861
Near the heart of the French quarter. Reasonably priced.

Hôtel Maritime
1155 Rue Guy
Montreal H3H 2K5
Tel: 932-1411 or 1-800-363-6255
Designed for budget-conscious corporate traveler and private guests. Has special hockey packages.

Roussillon Royal
1600 Rue St-Hubert
Montreal H2L 3Z3
Tel: 849-3214
Recently renovated.

Hôtel Atlantian du Parc
4544 Avenue du Parc
Montreal H2V 4E3
Tel: 274-5000 or 1-800-363-9803
"No-frills" budget hotel. Complementary limousine transportation to business districts. Some rooms have in-room kitchenettes.

Hôtel Château Napoleon
1030 Rue Mackay
Montreal H3G 2H1
Tel: 861-1500

Hôtel Lord Berri
1199 Rue Berri
Montreal H2L 4C6
Tel: 845-9236 or 1-800-363-0363
In the center of the Latin Quarter.

Château Versailles Hotel
1659 Rue Sherbrooke Ouest
Montreal H3H 1E3
Tel: 933-7102 or 1-800-361-3664
Converted from four Edwardian mansions in downtown Montreal. Special weekend rates from October–May.

YWCA
1355 Rue Dorchester Ouest
Montreal H3G 1T3
Tel: 866-9941
Single and double rooms available to women at reasonable rates. Longer-term residence (minimum of eight weeks) also available. Convenient cafeteria, pool, sauna and whirlpool offered.

YMCA
1450 Rue Stanley
Montreal H3G 1W3
Tel: 849-5331
Conveniently located and reasonably priced, this hostel offers a wide range of sports facilities and cafeteria for men, women and families.

La Residence du Voyager
847 Rue Sherbrooke Est
Montreal H2L 1K6
Tel: 527-9515

Hôtel Viger Centre-Ville
1001 Rue St-Hubert
Montreal H2L 3Y3
Tel: 845-6058
A wide variety of rooms offered at low rates.

LONGER-TERM RESIDENCES

La Tour Belvedere
2175 Blvd de Maisonneuve Ouest
Montreal H3H 1L5
Tel: 935-9052
Full facility parlor and one-bedroom suites available by the week or month.

Le Montfort
1975 Blvd de Maissoneuve Ouest
Montreal H3H 1K4
Tel: 934-0916
Studios, alcove suites, one- and two-bedroom suites offered in good location.

Manoir Le Moyne
2100 Blvd de Maisonneuve Ouest
Montreal H3H IK6
Tel: 931-8861
Split-level rooms and suites provided with fully equipped kitchens, an indoor swimming pool, restaurant and bar and summer garden terrace.

BED & BREAKFASTS

Bed and breakfast offer affordability with residential lodging.

La Maison de Grand-Pré
4660 Rue Grand-Pré
Montreal H2T 2H7
Tel: 843-6458
Cozy and quiet, 19th-century house near St-Denis area.

Bed and Breakfast Network
P.O. Box 575, Snowdon Station
Montreal H3X 3T8
Tel: 738-9410
Offers accommodation in French or English-speaking homes in downtown locations at reasonable prices. Also offers sightseeing tours, restaurant discounts and short-term apartment rentals.

Hospitality Montreal Relay
33977 Rue Laval Street
Montreal H2W 2H9
Tel: 287-9635
Arranges accommodation in private homes with complete breakfasts included. Contact Mathe Pearson.

Bed and Breakfast Chez-Nous
3713 St-Famille
Montreal H2X 2L7
Tel: 485-1252
Arranges overnight and longer-term accommodations. Contact Jacqueline Boulanger.

**A Bed and Breakfast
– A Downtown Network**
3458 Avenue Laval
Montreal H2X 3C8
Tel: 289-9749
Discounts on tours available and family and extended rates are available. Contact Bob Finkelstein.

RESIDENCES & STUDENT HOUSING

Auberge Internationale de Montréal
3541 Rue Aylmer
Montreal H2X 2B9
Tel: 843-3317

Collège Français
5155 Rue De Gaspe
Montreal H2T 3B3
Tel: 495-2581

Concordia University Residences
7141 Rue Sherbrooke Ouest
Montreal H4B 1R6
Tel: 848-4756

Résidence de L'Université de Montréal
2350 Rue Edouard Montpetit
Montreal H3T 1J4
Tel: 343-6531.

Résidence des étudiants de L'Université McGill
3935 Rue University
Montreal H3A 2B4
Tel: 398-6367

FOOD DIGEST

WHAT TO EAT

Due to the French passion for fine cuisine, dining out is a pleasure in Montreal. There is no shortage of restaurants (5,000) or varieties of cuisine. Although wine with the meal can be expensive, the food is often a great value.

WHERE TO EAT

EXPENSIVE

(Over $30 per person)

Auberge Le Vieux St-Gabriel (Québécois)
426 Rue St-Gabriel
Tel: 878-3562

Beaver Club (French)
Hôtel Reine-Elizabeth, 900 Blvd René-Lévesque Ouest
Tel: 861-3511

Café de Paris (French)
Hôtel Ritz-Carlton
1228 Rue Sherbrooke Ouest
Tel: 842-4212

C'est La Vie (French)
Hôtel La Citadelle
410 Rue Sherbrooke Ouest
Tel: 844-8851

Chez La Mère Michel (French)
1209 Rue Guy
Tel: 934-0473

Chez Pauze (Seafood)
1657 Rue Ste-Catherine Ouest
Tel: 932-6118

Daberto (Italian)
1177 Rue de la Montagne
Tel: 866-2191

La Marée (French)
404 Place Jacques Cartier
Tel: 861-8126

Le Festin du Gouverneur (Québécois)
Ile Ste-Hélène
Tel: 879-1141

La Lutetia (French)
Hôtel de la Montagne
1430 Rue de la Montagne
Tel: 288-5656

Le Parchemin (French)
1333 Rue University
Tel: 844-1619

Le Royer (French)
2 Rue Le Royer Est
Tel: 876-1386

Le Saint-Amable (French)
188 Rue St-Amable
Tel: 866-3471

Le Tour de Ville (French)
Le Grand Hôtel
777 Rue University
Tel: 879-1370

Les Chenets (French)
2075 Rue Bishop
Tel: 844-1842

Les Cuisiniers (French)
3834 Rue St-Denis
Tel: 844-0997

Les Halles (French)
1450 Rue Crescent
Tel: 844-2328

L'Habitant (French)
5010 Blvd Lalande
Pierrefonds
Tel: 684-4398

Restaurant Le Maritime (Seafood)
Hôtel Ritz-Carlton
1228 Rue Sherbrooke Ouest
Tel: 842-4212

Restaurant Saint-Honoré (French)
1616 Rue Ste-Catherine Ouest
Tel: 932-5550

Rib 'n' Beef (Steaks and Seafood)
8105 Blvd Decarie
Tel: 735-1601

Troika (Russian)
2171 Rue Crescent
Tel: 849-9333

Vent-Vert (French)
2105 Rue de la Montagne
Tel: 842-2482

MODERATELY EXPENSIVE

($20–$30 per person)

A la Catalogne (French)
311 Rue St-Paul Est
Tel: 866-6254

Abacus (Chinese)
2144 Rue Mackay
Tel: 933-8444

Alexandre (French)
438 Place Jacques Cartier
Tel: 866-9439

Alexandre (French)
1454 Rue Peel
Tel: 288-5105

Auberge de la Belle Poule (French)
406 Rue St-Sulpice
Tel: 288-7770

Au Vieux Carrafour (French)
440 Rue St-François Xavier
Tel: 845-7727

Au Vieux St-Paul (French)
262 Rue St-Paul Est
Tel: 874-7600

Baci Restaurant-Bar (Italian)
2095 Avenue McGill College
Tel: 288-7901

Bistro Saint-Joseph (French)
364 Blvd St-Joseph Ouest
Tel: 272-4211

Butch Bouchard (Steak and Seafood)
881 Blvd de Maissonneuve Est
Tel: 527-1221

Casa Napoli (Italian)
6728 Rue St-Laurent
Tel: 274-4351

Chez Antoine Grill (Steak House)
Le Grand Hôtel
777 Rue University
Tel: 879-1370

Chez Bernard (French)
275 Rue Notre-Dame Ouest
Tel: 288-4288

Chez Desjardins (Seafood)
1175 Rue Mackay
Tel: 866-9741

Chez Pierre (French)
1263 Rue Labelle
Tel: 843-5227

Chez Queux (French)
158 Rue St-Paul Est
Tel: 866-5194

Deli Peking (Kosher Chinese-Canadian)
6900 Blvd Decaire
Tel: 738-2844

François et Fils (French)
Basilaire 1

Complexe Desjardins
Tel: 843-4088

Gibbys (Steaks and Seafood)
298 Place Youville
Tel: 282-1837

Guillaume Tell (Swiss)
2055 Rue Stanley
Tel: 288-0139

Hélène de Champlain (French)
200 Tour de L'Isle
Ile Sainte-Hélène
Tel: 395-2424

Ile de France (French)
80 Blvd de Maissoneuve Ouest
Tel: 849-6331

Katsura (Japanese)
2170 Rue Montagne
Tel: 849-1172

L'Avventura (Italian)
99 Rue Laurier Ouest
Tel: 271-3095

La Bodega (Spanish)
345 Avenue du Parc
Tel: 849-2030

La Boucherie (Steak and Seafood)
343 St-Paul Est
Tel: 866-1515

La Diligence Restaurant (Continental)
7385 Blvd Decaire
Tel: 731-7771

La Lucarne d'Outemont (French)
1030 Rue Laurier Ouest
Tel: 279-7355

La Menara (Moroccan)
256 St-Paul Est
Tel: 861-1989

La Mer à Boire (French)
429 Rue St-Vincent
Tel: 397-9610

La Picholette (French)
1020 Rue St-Denis
Tel: 843-8502

La Rapière (French)
1490 Rue Stanley
Tel: 844-8920

La Sila (Italian)
2040 Rue St-Denis
Tel: 844-5083

Le Caveau (French)
2063 Rue Victoria
Tel: 844-1624

Le Centaure (French)
Hippodrome Blue Bonnets
7440 Blvd Decaire
Tel: 739-2741

Le Fripon (French)
436 Place Jacques-Cartier
Tel: 861-1386

Le Latini (Italian)
1130 Rue Jeanne-Mance
Tel: 861-3166

Le Mas des Oliviers (French)
1216 Rue Bishop
Tel: 861-6733

Le Paris (French)
1812 Rue Ste-Catherine Ouest
Tel: 937-4898

Le Pavillon De L'Atlantique
(Steak and Seafood)
1188 Rue Sherbrooke Ouest
Tel: 285-1636

Le Relais Terrapin (Continental)
295 Rue St-Charles Ouest
Longueil
Tel: 677-6378

Le Restaurant (French)
Hôtel Le Quatre Saisons, 1050
Rue Sherbrooke Ouest
Tel: 284-1110.

Les Quatre Canards (Continental)
Le Château Bromont
90 Rue Stanstead, Bromont
Tel: 534-3433.

Les Trios Arches (French)
11131 Rue Meighen
Pierrefonds
Tel: 683-8200.

Moishe's (Steak House)
3961 Blvd St-Laurent
Tel: 845-3509.

Papa Dan's (Steak and Seafood)
Place Bonaventure
Tel: 878-4569.

Piazetti (Italian)
351 Place Youville/350 St-Paul Ouest.
Tel: 843-6113.

Porto Fino (Italian)
2040 Rue de la Montagne
Tel: 849-2225.

Restaurant Manhattan (French)
1181 Avenue Union
Tel: 866-4275.

Restaurant Prego (Italian)
5142 Blvd St-Laurent
Tel: 271-3234.

Restaurant Rustic (Steak and Seafood)
47 Blvd St-Jean Baptiste
Tel: 691-2444.

Restaurant Szechuan (Chinese)
400 Rue Notre-Dame Ouest
Tel: 844-4456.

Vieux Kitzbuhel (Austrian)
505 Blvd Perrot
Ile Perrot
Tel: 453-5521

MODERATE

($10–$20 per person)

Alpenhaus (Swiss)
1279 Rue St-Marc
Tel: 935-2285

American Rock (Bistro)
2080 Rue Aylmer
Tel: 288-9272

Asha (Indian)
3490 Rue Park
Tel: 844-3178

Bistro Saint-Joseph (Bistro)
364 Blvd St-Joseph Ouest
Tel: 272-4211

Brisket (Deli)
1063 Côte du Beaver Hall
Tel: 878-3641

Brochetterie du Vieux-Port
(Steak and Seafood)
39 Rue St-Paul Est
Tel: 866-3175

Café Laurier (French)
394 Rue Laurier Ouest
Tel: 273-2484

Café-Restaurant le Bolvert (Continental)
12 Rue Notre-Dame Est
Tel: 397-0222

Chez la mère Tucker/Mother Tucker's
(Steak and Seafood)
1175 Place du Frère André
Tel: 866-5525

Curly Joe's Steak House (Steak House)
1453 Rue Metcalf
Tel: 845-5226

Darbar (Indian)
205 Price-Arthur Street Est
Tel: 844-9376

El Coyote Restaurant-Bar (Mexican)
1202 Rue Bishop
Tel: 875-7082

El Toro (French)
1647 Rue Fluery Est
Tel: 387-7367

Genghis Khan Mongol BBQ Restaurant
(Mongolian)
4961-B Chemin Queen Mary
Tel: 739-3838

La Boîte à Spaghetti (Italian)
Complexe Desjardins
1560 Rue Ste-Catherine
Tel: 842-8047

La Bourgade (French)
Hôtel Bonaventure Hilton International
1 Place Bonaventure
Tel: 878-2332

La Cage aux Sports (BBQ and Ribs)
2250 Rue Guy
Tel: 931-8588

La Campannina (Italian)
2022 Rue Stanley
Tel: 845-1852

La Casa Grècque (Steak and Seafood)
200 Prince-Arthur Street Est
Tel: 842-6098

La Forge (Continental)
1100 Rue Cremazie Est
Tel: 727-3729

La Marguerite (French)
1472 Rue Crescent
Tel: 284-0307

La Piazza (Italian)
1 Complexe Desjardins
Tel: 843-4088

Le Bifthèque (Steak House)
6705 Côte de Liesse
Tel: 739-6336

Le Bistro d'Autrefois (French)
1259 Rue St-Hubert
Tel: 842-2808

L'Etoile des Indes/Star of India (Indian)
1806 Ste-Catherine Ouest
Tel: 932-8330

Le H.P. Café-Crème (Bistro)
1025 Square Dorchester
Tel: 397-9723

L'Intercontinental (Continental)
Hôtel Ritz-Carlton
1228 Rue Sherbrooke Ouest
Tel: 842-4212

Le Keg (Canadian)
21–25 St-Paul Est
Tel: 871-9093.

Le Montréalais (Bistro)
Hôtel Reine-Elizabeth
900 Blvd René-Lévesque Ouest
Tel: 861-3511

Le Piemontais (Italian)
1145A Rue Buillion
Tel: 861-8122

Les Filles du Roy (Québécois)
415 Rue Bonsecours
Tel: 849-3535

Les Voyageurs (International)
Hôtel Reine-Elizabeth
900 Blvd René-Lévesque
Tel: 861-3511

Lily Bistro Bar (Bistro)
Complexe Desjardins
Tel: 842-8047

Maison Kam Fung (Chinese)
1008 Rue Clark
Tel: 866-4016

Matty's Restaurant and Bar (Armenian)
2075 Rue de la Montagne
Tel: 843-3591

Pizza Mella (Italian)
107 Prince-Arthur Street Est
Tel: 849-4680

Restaurant Berlin (German)
101 Rue Fairmont Ouest
Tel: 270-7398

Restaurant des Gouverneurs
(International)
458 Place Jacques-Cartier
Tel: 861-0188

Restaurant Trois Frères (Continental)
8625 Blvd St-Laurent
Tel: 381-5490

Solmar (Portuguese)
111 Rue St-Paul Est
Tel: 861-4562

Stash Café Bazaar (Polish)
461 Rue St-Sulpice
Tel: 861-2915

($5–$10 per person)

Aliments naturels, "Les jardins du soleil"
(Vegetarian)
201 Rue St-Viateur Ouest
Tel: 279-3828

Ben's Delicatessen
990 Blvd de Maissoneuve Ouest
Tel: 844-1000

Il était un de fois/Once Upon a Time
(Canadian)
600 Rue Youville
Tel: 842-6783

La Crêperie (Pancakes)
Complexe Desjardins
150 Rue Ste-Catherine
Tel: 842-8047

La Tulip Noire (Continental)
2100 Rue Stanley
Tel: 285-1225

Le Commensal (Vegetarian)
2115 Rue St-Denis
Tel: 845-0248

L'Oiseau du Paradis (Vegetarian)
3440 Rue Durocher
Tel: 845-0076

Le Tramway (Pub)
1122 Rue Ste-Catherine
Tel: 875-6300

Le Vieux Munich/Old Munich (German)
1170 Rue St-Denis
Tel: 288-8011

Schwartz's (Hebrew deli)
3895 Rue St-Laurent
Tel: 842-4813

DRINKING NOTES

The drinking age in Quebec is 18. Some establishments (especially on Prince-Arthur Street) do not have a liquor license, but allow customers to bring their own wine.

THINGS TO DO

CITY

Angrignon Park and Zoo: A large children's zoo with over 300 small animals is one of the main attractions of this park. In the winter an ice palace, skating rink, and cross-country skiing are featured. The Zoo is open: daily 10 a.m.–5 p.m. Admission: $2.50 adults, $1.25 children and seniors. For more details, tel: 872-2815.

Boulevard St-Laurent: International restaurants and specialty stores line this boulevard known as "The Main". Originally settled by Jewish merchants, this street now is home to Greeks, Slavs, Portuguese and Latin Americans. For smoked meat, both *The Main* restaurant and *Schwartz's* are well-known.

Chinatown: This section of Montreal bounded by Blvd René-Lévesque, Rue Viger, Blvd St-Laurent, and Rue Jeanne-Mance is at its most active on the weekends.

Dow Planetarium: 1000 Rue Saint Jacques Ouest, tel: 872-4530. Through a Zeiss projector and 100 auxiliary projectors, the sky is produced on a dome screen 20 meters in diameter. Shows are narrated in both French and English and change every few months. Open: 12.30–8.30 p.m. Special reservations are needed for handicapped. Admission: $3 for adults, 50¢ children ages 5–17 and $1.50 for seniors. Children under 4 get in free.

Ile-Sainte-Hélène: This park offers swimming pools, a year-round aquarium, a summer amusement park and is also the site for the International Festival of Fireworks each May. Admission to the island is free but there are separate fees for admission to the various activities offered. To check on specific events, tel: 872-6093.

Mont Royal Park: Reached from Camillien Houde Parkway or Remembrance Road, tel: 872-2644. This park of 495 acres (200 hectares), one of Montrealers' favorite places to relax, overlooks the city and the region. A variety of recreational activities, from cross-country skiing to birdwatching, are offered. To find out about special sporting or recreation events, tel: 872-2644.

Montreal Aquarium: This aquarium located on Ile Sainte-Hélène houses 250 species of fish, 20 invertebrates, 10 species of reptiles and eight species of birds. Six species of penguins are one of the main attractions. Open: September–May, daily 10 a.m.–5 p.m; June, July and August, daily 10 a.m.–8 p.m. Admission: $3 for adults, $1.50 for children and seniors. For more information, tel: 872-4656.

Montreal Botanical Garden: 4101 Rue Sherbrooke Est, tel: 872-1400. The third most important botanical garden in the world after London and Berlin, this unique botanical garden spans an area of 180 acres (73 hectares). Included in this area are 62 acres (25 hectares) of Japanese gardens which include 10 exhibition greenhouses and the largest bonsai and penjing collections outside of Asia. In 1988 construction began on an Insectarium to house more than 50,000 insect specimens from around the world. There are special exhibitions at Christmas, Easter and Halloween. The garden is open 8 a.m.–sundown. Greenhouses open: 9 a.m.–6 p.m and the boutique is open: 10 a.m.–5 p.m. Admission: free to outdoor gardens; Greenhouses: $3 for adults, $1.50 for seniors and children under 17.

Notre-Dame-de-Bonsecours Chapel: This Catholic chapel is known as the "Sailors' Church" and was built on the remains of the wooden chapel built for Marguerite Bourgeoys in 1657. The Marguerite Bourgeoys Museum is located in the basement of this chapel. Hours for the chapel are: November–April 9 a.m.–11.30 a.m. and 1 p.m.–5 p.m; May–October 9 a.m.–5 p.m. Open: May–October 10 a.m.–4.30 p.m; November–April 10 a.m.–11.30 a.m. and 1 p.m.–4.30 p.m. The museum is closed on Monday. Admission: $1 for adults, 25¢ for children. Included is a climb to the rooftop lookout for a fine panoramic view of the waterfront area.

Notre-Dame Basilica: Located in the Place d'Armes, tel: 849-1070. Montreal's oldest parish is well-known for works of art and its neo-Gothic architecture. Concerts are held here throughout the year. The church is open: Labor Day–June 24 7 a.m.–6 p.m; June 25–Labor Day 7 a.m.–8 p.m. Guided tours are available.

Old Montreal: This 100-acre section of Montreal contains some of the greatest concentrations of 17th, 18th and 19th-century buildings in North America. In the 1960s efforts began to restore both the interior and exterior of Old Montreal's buildings. The area is bustling with activity at any time of day or season.

Old Port: On the waterfront, this important part of Old Montreal offers many summer and winter activities. River cruises depart from these shores.

Olympic Park: This site of the 1976 Olympic Games includes the world's tallest Inclined Tower, a stadium which houses both the Expos baseball games and rock concerts, and a swimming center which is open to the public. For more information, tel: 252-4737.

Place Jacques Cartier: Once a marketplace, Place Jacques Cartier in Old Montreal is now a flower market and handicrafts center and is a favorite spot among artists and young people.

Prince-Arthur Street: This lively street is largely reserved for pedestrians. Greek, Vietnamese and Italian restaurants are found in abundance along this street. In the summer, stroll by street musicians and magicians.

Rue Crescent: A stroll down this lively street, the "older brother" of Rue St-Denis, will take you past renowned art galleries, antique dealers, jewelry and gift shops, and many exceptional restaurants.

Rue St-Denis (Latin Quarter): Victorian buildings abound on this street where the French elite lived at the turn of the century. The densest concentration of restaurants, boutiques and night spots in Montreal.

Square St-Louis: Located on Avenue Laval, this square offers some of the most attractive architecture in Montreal. Generations of poets and artists have been attracted to this square whose houses were restored in the 1960s.

St Joseph's Oratory: 3800 Rue Queen Mary, tel: 733-8211. Built in 1924, this mountainside basilica is the world's largest pilgrimage center devoted to St Joseph, the patron saint of Canada. Although the interior is rather uninteresting, the dome of the basilica, one of the largest in the world, is quite remarkable. Behind the basilica is the sanctuary, tomb and votive chapel of Brother André, the monk who constructed the first small chapel to St Joseph in 1904. The Oratory is open: daily 6.30 a.m.–9.30 p.m. Admission: free. The museum is open: daily 10 a.m.–5 p.m. and a donation is suggested.

Underground City: This weatherproof, climate-controlled underground city allows you to avoid either the cold of winter or the heat of summer by strolling through nearly 14 miles (22 miles) of passageways. Combined in the underground network are two railway stations, a bus terminal, six hotels, two department stores, 1,400 boutiques, 150 restaurants, 40 bank branches, 30 cinemas, two exhibition halls and 1,200 businesses.

TOURS & ATTRACTIONS

There are many sightseeing companies to choose from in Montreal. Some focus on the standard tourist attractions, others focus on architecture and urban restoration.

FLIGHTSEEING

Delco Aviation: These tours offer flights over Montreal in a sea plane. The views are spectacular. The company also offers other destinations outside of Montreal. The fee is $85 for the flight (one to five people), which is available daily. Tel: 663-4311.

CRUISES

Amphi Tour: An amphibious bus combines a tour of land and water of Old Montreal and the Old Port. Open: May 1–October 31, 10 a.m.–11 p.m. Tel: 386-1298.

Croisières Bellevue: Open: May to end-September, these cruises leave from Saint Anne Locks. Tel: 455-4036 or 457-5245.

Croisières Maritimes de l'Archipel Inc.: A variety of cruises are offered by this company, including regular tourist excursions, sunset cruises, brunch and supper cruises, etc. The prices vary according to the option chosen but range from $7.50–$24 for adults, and $3.50–$13 for children. Boats depart from Lachine off 6th Avenue. Tel: 367-2840 for reservations and more information.

Lachine Rapid Tours: A 90-minute jet boat trip down the Lachine rapids. Open: summer 10 a.m.–6 p.m. The cost is $30 per person. Tel: 284-9607 for reservations.

Montreal Harbor Cruises: Boats depart from Victoria Pier at Berri Street. Excursions from one to three hours are offered. Open: May 1–October 1. Reservations can be made by phoning 386-1298.

BUS TOURS

Several companies offer narrated tours in buses, vans or limousines. Many of the companies offer walking tours as well. The length of tours vary and many options are available from most of the operators. Check with the companies below for more information.

Gray Line
1001 Rue du Square Dorchester at
Infotouriste Office
Tel: 280-5347

Murray Hill
1001 Rue du Square Dorchester at
Infotouriste Office
Tel: 937-5311

Les Montréalistes
221 Rue de la Commune Ouest
Tel: 744-3009

Hertz Tourist Guides
Tel: 461-0664 or 937-6690

Save Montreal
Tours of Montreal architecture.
Tel: 484-0104

Visites de Montréal
Tel: 843-3308

Guidatour
Tel: 844-4021

Taxi Lasalle
Tel: 277-2552

CARRIAGE RIDES

Calèche A. Biosvert Inc.: Departures from Notre-Dame Street, Square Dorchester, Mont Royal Park, Place d'Armes, and Place Jacques Cartier. The fee is $40 an hour. Tel: 844-1313

WALKS

Step on Guides: Offering 3-hour-long city tours. Walking tours of Old Montreal and the underground city. Tel: 935-5131

CULTURE PLUS

MUSEUMS

In addition to the permanent collections, many of the museums listed below have changing exhibits. Telephone for special exhibits and events, or check the arts section in the newspapers.

Canadian Center for Architecture: 1920 Rue Baile, tel: 939-7000. The only collection of its kind, it includes 20,000 prints and drawings, 45,000 photographs and architectural archives. Open: Wednesday–Friday 11 a.m.–6 p.m., Thursday 11 a.m.–8 p.m., Saturday and Sunday 11 a.m.–6 p.m. Admission: $3 adults, $2 students, and free for children under 12.

Canadian Railway Museum: 122A Rue St-Pierre, St Constant, tel: 632-2410. The most significant collection of railway, tramway and steam locomotive equipment. Has daily tram rides and Sunday train rides. Open: April 30–October 15, daily 9 a.m.–5 p.m. Admission: $3.75 adults, $1.75 children.

Château Ramezay Museum: 280 Rue Notre-Dame Est, tel: 861-7182. Housed in an impressive residence built in 1705, this ethnographic museum has exhibitions of furniture, paintings and costumes. Open: Tuesday–Sunday 10 a.m.–4.30 p.m. Closed: Monday except from June to the end of August. Admission: $2 adults, 50¢ children and students, and $1 seniors.

David M. Stewart Museum: Located at the Old Fort on Ile-Ste-Hélène, tel: 861-66701. This museum of Canadian history has a unique collection of firearms, ancient maps, scientific and navigation instruments and articles from the daily lives of Canadian settlers. Open: daily 10 a.m.–5 p.m. Closed: Monday September–April. Admission: $3 adults, $2 for seniors, students and children.

Lachine Museum: 110 Chemin de Lasalle, Lachine, tel: 932-7724. Furniture and artifacts of the early colonial period. Also features story of early commerce and industrial history of Lachine in the 19th century. Open: Wednesday–Sunday 11.30 a.m.–4.30 p.m. Admission: free.

Marc-Aurèle Fortin Museum: 118 St-Pierre St, tel: (514) 845-6108. Devoted entirely to the world of Canadian artist Marc-Aurèle Fortin and offering exhibitions on other Quebec painters. Open: Tuesday–Sunday 11 a.m.–5 p.m. Admission: $2 adults, 75¢ children and seniors.

Marguerite d'Youville Museum: 1185 St-Mathieu St, tel: (514) 932-7724. Features the tomb, religious objects and death chamber of Mother d'Youville. Open: Wednesday–Sunday 1.30–4.30 p.m. Admission: free.

McCord Museum of Canadian History: 690 Rue Sherbrooke Ouest, tel: 398-7100. After a major expansion project, this museum will offer exhibitions at different sites throughout Montreal. One of the most important history museums in Canada, the McCord owns collections of paintings, prints, drawings, textiles, decorative arts, and photographic archives dating from the 18th century to the present.

Montreal History Center: 335 Place d'Youville, tel: 872-3207. Offers interpretations of Montreal's history.

Montreal Museum of Decorative Arts – Le Château Dufresne: 2929 Rue Jeanne-d'Arc, tel: 259-2575. Houses the Liliane and David M. Stewart collection of international design dating from 1940. Regular exhibitions on furniture, glassware, textiles and ceramics are offered. Open: Wednesday–Sunday 11 a.m.–5 p.m. Closed: Monday and Tuesday. Admission: $2 adults, $1 seniors, and 75¢ children under 12.

Montreal Museum of Fine Arts: 1379 Rue Sherbrooke Ouest, tel: 285-1600. Founded in 1860, this museum is the oldest in Canada. Canadian and Quebec art are featured and the museum owns important collections of engravings, sculptures, paintings, furniture and silverware. Traveling exhibitions of masterworks are featured regularly. Lectures, films, workshops and concerts are held in the auditorium. Special children's activities and guided tours are also offered. Open: Tuesday–Sunday 10 a.m.–5 p.m. Admission: $4 adults, $2 students, and free for children under 16. Traveling exhibitions may cost slightly more.

Musée d'Art Contemporain de Montréal: Located at Cité du Havre. This museum features works of art created after 1940. In addition to exhibits, a specialized reference center is available for consultation. Open: Tuesday–Sunday 10 a.m.–6 p.m. The reference center closes at 5 p.m. and is not open at the weekend. Admission is free but a donation is suggested. Tel: 873-2878 (museum); 873-4710 (reference center).

Musée Notre-Dame: Contains collection of sacred objects, church vestments and paintings. Open: Saturday and Sunday 9.30 a.m.–4 p.m. Admission: $1 adults, 50¢ children.

Redpath Museum: 859 Rue Sherbrooke Ouest, tel: 398-4087. This museum houses a fossil exhibition with dinosaur bones and an anthropological collection including two Egyptian mummies. Open: September–June,

Monday–Friday 9 a.m.–5 p.m; June–September, Monday–Thursday 9 a.m.–5 p.m. Admission: free.

Saint-Laurent Art Museum: 615 Blvd Ste-Croix, tel: 747-7367. Located in the former chapel of Collège Saint-Laurent, this museum features a permanent collection of Quebec art and handicrafts from wood sculpture to textiles and Amerindian art. Concerts are frequently held on Sundays. Open: Tuesday–Friday and Sunday 12 noon–5 p.m. Closed: Saturday and Monday. Admission: free.

ART GALLERIES

Canadian Guild of Crafts Quebec: 2025 Rue Peel, tel: 849-6091. Inuit art and Canadian crafts such as blown glass, porcelain and ceramics.

Galerie Dominion: 1438 Rue Sherbrooke Ouest, tel: 845-7471. Canadian and international paintings and sculptures from the 19th and 20th centuries.

Galerie Franklin Silverstone: 1618 Rue Sherbrooke Ouest, tel: 933-3770. Contemporary Canadian art and ceramics.

Galerie La Petite Cour: 206 Rue St-Paul Ouest, tel: 849-7715. New age art.

CONCERTS & OPERAS

Montreal offers a wide selection of music from classical to various ethnic music groups. For a listing of what is available on a particular day, consult the arts sections of the city's newspapers. The following listing includes the permanent companies in the city.

McGill Chamber Orchestra is one of Montreal's oldest chamber groups. Performances are held in both the Place des Arts and in Eglise Saint-Jean-Baptiste.

Metropolitan Orchestra of Montreal, a young group of musicians, holds concerts at the Theatre Maissonneuve. Tel: 598-0870.

Montreal Symphony Orchestra has an international reputation as a result of recordings and overseas tours. Concerts are held regularly at Place des Arts and in the city's parks during summertime. Tel: 842-3402.

Opéra de Montréal was founded in 1980 and presents four or five operas a year. Considered one of the 10 best companies in North America.

BALLET

The **Grand Ballets Canadiens** has been performing for more than 30 years. Includes a repertoire of both the classical and modern pieces as well as work by new Canadian choreographers and composers. Tel: 849-8681.

THEATERS

Montreal offers at least 10 major French theater companies and many smaller theaters. (see Yellow Pages of Telephone Book for full listing). English-speaking theatergoers should check:

Centaur Theater
453 Rue St-François Xavier
Tel: 288-3161

Aidye Bronfman Center
5170 Chemin de la Côte Ste-Catherine
Tel: 739-2301

Some of the French-speaking theaters are:

Théâtre Saint-Denis
1594 Rue St-Denis
Tel: 849-4211

Théâtre Populaire de Québec
500 Sauve Ouest
Tel: 387-6219

Théâtre D'Aujourd'hui
1297 Papineau
Tel: 523-1211

Théâtre de la Ligue d'Improvisation
4150 Rue St-Denis
Tel: 845-3848

Théâtre du Nouveau Monde
84 Rue Ste-Catherine Ouest
Tel: 861-0563

Théâtre du Rideau Vert
4664 Rue St-Denis
Tel: 845-0267

MOVIES

The site of many major film festivals, Montreal's selection of films is quite noteworthy. There are close to 100 theaters in the city so check the newspapers for showings and locations. Some of the specialized cinemas include:

Cinémathèque Québécoise
335 Blvd de Maissonneuve Est
Tel: 842-9763

Cinéma Ouimetoscope
1204 Rue Ste-Catherine Ouest
Tel: 525-8600

Anne Du Cinéma Canadien
1600 de Lorimier
Tel: 523-5787

Cinéma V
5560 Sherbrooke Ouest
Tel: 489-5559

PUBLIC LIBRARIES

There are a number of public libraries in Montreal. The Montreal Central Library is located at 1210 Rue Sherbrooke Est, tel: 872-5923. Other resource libraries include:

Biliothèque National du Québec
Housed in three locations:
Saint-Sulpice Building
1700 Rue St-Denis
Tel: 873-4553.

Marie Claire Daveluy Building
125 Rue Sherbrooke Ouest
Tel: 873-0270.

Aegidius Fauteux Building
4499 Avenue de L'Esplanade
Tel: 873-4404.

Centre d'Archives de Montréal
1945 Rue Mullins
Tel: 873-3064.

NIGHTLIFE

It is worth strolling around Montreal at night as the streets are a buzz of activity. Cabarets, dinner theaters, clubs and bars provide varied avenues for entertainment. Check out listings in the newspapers for up-to-date happenings. Cocktail lounges stay open until 2 a.m., bars and cabarets until 3 a.m. The major hotels house nightclubs which feature discos, comic shows and other entertainment. Most clubs and bars are in the downtown district.

CABARETS & DINNER THEATER

Arthur's Café Baroque
Hôtel Reine-Elizabeth
900 Blvd René-Lévesque Ouest
Tel: 861-3511
Performances range from jazz and musical comedy to theater.

La Maison Hantée
1037 Rue De Bleury
Tel: 878-3555
A four-hour haunted house adventure including meal. No alcohol is served.

Le Stage Dinner Théâtre
7385 Blvd Decarie
Tel: 731-7771
Shows run from Tuesdays to Sundays. Dinner is at 6.30 p.m. followed by the show at 8.30 p.m. Comedies and musicals make up the repertoire.

JAZZ

L'Air du Temps
191 Rue St-Paul Ouest
Tel: 842-2003
Both local and international talent. Opens at 5 p.m.

Biddle's
2060 Rue Aylmer
Tel: 842-8656

Club Jazz 2080
2080 Rue Clark
Tel: 285-0007

The Rising Sun
286 Rue Ste-Catherine Ouest
Tel: 861-0657
Blues, jazz and reggae.

The Grand Café
1720 Rue St-Denis
Tel: 849-6955
Live jazz at reasonable prices.

DANCING

Metropolis
59 Rue Ste-Catherine Est
Tel: 288-5559
Largest disco in Montreal.

Studebakers
1255 Rue Crescent
Tel: 866-1101
Music from the 1950s and 1960s.

Thunder Dome
1254 Rue Stanley
Tel: 397-1628

Vieux Munich
Rue St-Denis at the corner of Dorchester
Tel: 288-8011
Oktoberfest atmosphere.

The Limelight
Rue Stanley near Ste-Catherine
Tel: 871-0057
Sound and light extravaganza.

SHOPPING

Montrealers are such avid shoppers that they have coined a word of their own for it: *le magasinage*, a term which warrants a separate entry in the French Robert dictionary. Small wonder Montreal economists worry whenever the consumer spending rate drops a few points!

Shopping can take a variety of forms. There is everyday shopping on local commercial streets, some reflecting the bygone charm of small-town main street, others boasting renewed vigor through renovation and revitalization. Then there is busy weekend shopping in one of a string of trendy regional shopping malls around Montreal, teenagers' favorite haunts. These shopping centers showcase local clothing manufacturers turned retailer such as Le Château or San Francisco; these were originally small concerns which have made it into the big time by going public through a government-sponsored stock savings plan, just one example of the many business success stories that Montreal has churned out of late.

Of course, there is also window shopping, and Montrealers go for it with their characteristic verve, especially along downtown Rue Ste-Catherine, where musing and browsing extend way past store hours and into the wee hours of the night.

For the well-to-do, Montreal, with its weekly auctions, antique dealers and many fur salons, will prove a bargain when it comes to shopping for furs (furriers the world over flock to Montreal every year for the international fair), Inuit art, antiques and collectibles. Furriers are heavily concentrated in the rundown shops of the fur district along Boulevard de Maisonneuve, east of Rue Union.

Scores of art galleries may be found in the Victorian row houses of Rue Sherbrooke, in what used to be called the Golden Square Mile, an exclusive area on the south slope of Mont Royal where the business tycoons of the Victorian era built expansive villas (many of which still stand to this day).

Items handcrafted by Quebec artisans may be purchased in the boutiques of Rue St-Paul in Old Montreal, in Le Rouet stores or at the Canadian Guild of Crafts on Rue Peel. Rue Notre-Dame, east of Rue Atwater, boasts a number of antique dealers specializing in Victorian furniture and European imports fit for a king.

For the fashion-conscious, Montreal is a treasure-trove, textile and clothing representing some 60 percent of manufacturing jobs in the city. Montrealers follow fashion with passion and love to parade the latest European trends on downtown streets. Watch for the up-and-coming in the dramatic store windows of Rue Ste-Catherine, in the trendy boutiques of downtown Place Ville-Marie and Place Montreal Trust, and in the lavish designer stores of Ogilvy's on Rue Ste-Catherine, Holt Renfrew on Rue Sherbrooke, and in Westmount Square and Rockland Shopping Center, located in the posh anglophone districts of Westmount and Town of Mount Royal.

If it's bargains you're looking for, shop right off the factory rack, in the Chabanel Fashion District, on Rue Chabanel west of Rue St-Laurent. This may seem a bit overwhelming at first: Rue Chabanel sports a solid row of six and more story buildings just packed with everything you can imagine: jeans, bathing suits, lingerie, sweaters, name it! On Saturday mornings, regulars (often Italian, Portuguese and Indian women who work in these modern-day sweat shops) go through these floors like nobody's business; newcomers just gawk and zigzag through this cornucopia, making for a unique shopping experience.

Along the same lines is Sunday shopping in Old Montreal. While the rest of the city recovers from Saturday night, bargain hunters flock to the clothes discounters that have congregated along Rue Notre-Dame east of Rue McGill.

Shopping in Montreal can take you into some of the more colorful neighborhoods in the city. Take, for example, Rue Laurier in Outremont, a posh French district on the northern slope of Mont Royal. Over the years, the merchants of Rue Laurier have built a reputation for coming up with the very latest of European trends, be it in clothes, food (world renowned pâtissier Lenôtre of France opened its first North American store on Rue Laurier) or home fashions.

Then there is also Rue St-Denis with its cafés and restaurant terraces spilling on to the sidewalk. Known as the Quartier Latin for its student population, Rue St-Denis has gone through a series of changes, from late granola to early avant-garde, and is now venturing into design and decoration, offering shoppers all things beautiful for the home.

Not to be missed on Rue St-Denis is Arthur Quentin, and, for true coffee lovers, La Brûlerie, where they roast coffee from the four corners of the earth. Also of interest is Plaza St-Hubert, a favorite with neighboring Greek, Italian and Middle-Eastern families. It comes alive in the spring, when preparations for the famous weddings these communities celebrate are under way.

Last but not least is Rue St-Laurent, also known as the "Main". It is a kind of no-man's-land between the mostly French districts of Eastern Montreal and the anglophone sectors of the westend, where successive flows of immigrants have left distinctive traces of their passage. From Rue Viger northward, Chinese, Eastern European, Greek, Portuguese and Italians have carved themselves a niche.

The Chinese community, for example, has congregated around Rue de la Gauchetière and placarded bright red and yellow signs on the Victorian grey stones of the area. It is a real pleasure to see whole families shopping for their weekly groceries on Sunday after the traditional Cantonese Dim Sum buffet in one of the local eateries.

Past Rue Sherbrooke, Hungarians and Polish Jews are still very present with their aromatic deli and sausages. Not to be missed are institutions like the Montreal Pool Room with its steamies, and Schwartz's smoked meat sandwiches. Only a few Greek signs remain on Rue St-Laurent, the Greek community having since made its way to Avenue du Parc and Rue Jean-Talon. They have been replaced by Portuguese immigrants with their clothing and ceramics stores.

Further north around Rue Jean-Talon is Little Italy with its espresso cafés, *gelateria* (ice cream parlors) and *pasticeria* (pastry shops). Little Italy huddles around the Marché Jean-Talon, one of the lesser known attrac-

tions of Montreal, with saris, tchadors and Mao shirts coming together in a visually delightful tapestry. In fact, wherever you hail from, you are bound to find a compatriot in Montreal.

WHAT TO BUY

Montreal, Canada's fashion capital, offers an astounding number of boutiques and department stores. Gourmet food, handicraft objects and fashionable clothes can all be found in abundance.

SHOPPING AREAS

Faubourg Ste-Catherine: 1616 Rue Ste-Catherine Ouest, Tel: 939-3663. Reminiscent of New York's Fulton Market and Boston's Quincy Market, this shopping spot hosts fruit, vegetable and import stands and an array of restaurants and snack bars.

Atwater Market: 138 Rue Atwater, tel: 872-2491. Very lively on weekends, this market features specialty foods. Over 60 farm producers sell fresh fruit and vegetables.

Jean-Talon Market: 7075 Rue Casgrain, tel: 872-2491. In "Little Italy" and bordered by cheese counters, fish markers and butcher shops. Has 100-plus farm producers.

Maisonneuve Market: 4375 Rue Ontario Est, tel: 872-2491. Outdoor market open May to October.

St-Jacques Market: Amherst and Ontario, tel: 872-2491. Open year-round, this market offers fruit and vegetable stands in the spring and summer and flowers and plants in the fall and winter.

Complexe Desjardins: 2 Complexe Desjardins, tel: 281-1870. Offering a tremendous number of boutiques, bars, and cinemas, this underground shopping center is decorated with fountains, trees and waterfalls.

Place Bonaventure: Tel: 397-2205. Includes 135 shops with merchandise from all over the world. Restaurants, cinemas, banks, a post office and a supermarket are all located within this downtown shopping concourse.

Place Montreal Trust: McGill College/Ste-Catherine, tel: 843-8000. Five levels of boutiques and services. Direct access to the metro.

Other shopping areas include Rue St-Denis, Boulevard St-Laurent, Avenue du Laurier, Rue Ste-Catherine, Rue Crescent and Rue Sherbrooke.

DEPARTMENT STORES

Eaton's: 677 Rue Ste-Catherine Ouest, tel: 284-8484. Quality and value are the trademarks of this department store founded in 1869. The dining room in the downtown store has a unique art-deco decor.

Holt Renfrew: 1300 Rue Sherbrooke Ouest, tel: 842-5111. Offers fine fashions for men and women and carries designer clothes from Europe, Canada and the US.

Ogilvy: 1307 Rue Ste-Catherine Ouest, tel: 842-7711. Has elite merchandise ranging from home fashions to high fashion.

SPORTS

PARTICIPANT

Outside sports in every season are very popular. Information about what facilities are offered at any time can be obtained from the Sports and Leisure Department of the City of Montreal, tel: 872-6211.

BICYCLING

A network of cycling paths covers some 140 miles (225 km) of Montreal. Maps are available from sporting goods stores or by calling 280-6700. Favorite routes include: Lachine Canal, the Seaway, Christophe Colomb and Berri Streets, Rachel Street, Angrignon Park and Mont Royal Park. Vélo Québec, an organization devoted to cycling, provides brochures, guidebooks and information of paths. They are located at 4545 Avenue du Pierre de Coubertin, tel: 252-3000. Rentals are available from:

Maison St-Jacques
Old Port, Blvd St-Laurent at Rue de la Commune
Tel: 844-9139

Quadricycle International Inc.
Old Port at Place Jacques Cartier entrance
Tel: 398-0634

La Cordée
Rue 2159 Ste-Catherine Est
Tel: 524-1515

Cycle Peel
6665 Rue St-Jacques
Tel: 486-1148

BOATING

Sailing is possible from May through to September.

École de Voile de Lachine
2105 Blvd St-Joseph, Lachine
Tel: 634-4326
Gives private or group lessons and is approved by the Quebec Sailing Federation. They also rent light sail boats and windsurfers.

RAFTING

Rafting is another popular boating activity. Two companies run excursions:

Lachine Rapid Tours Inc.
105 Rue de la Commune Ouest
Tel: 284-9607

New World River Expeditions
5475 Pare, room 221
Tel: 733-7166

FISHING

There are numerous lakes and rivers around Montreal which provide great fishing spots. For specific suggestions, fishing enthusiasts should call the Ministry for Leisure, Hunting and Fishing (*Ministère du loisir, de la chasse et de la pêche* [MLCP]) for day-trip ideas. Tel: 24–48 hours ahead at 1-800-462-5349.

GOLF

There are many golf courses both within Montreal and in the surrounding region. The following courses are close by and are open to non-members:

Fresh Meadows Golf Club
505 Avenue du Golf, Beaconsfield
Tel: 697-4036
A nine-hole course located 15 minutes from downtown.

Golf Dorval
2000 Rue Reverchon, Dorval
Tel: 631-6624
Reservations needed on weekends for this 36-hole course.

Golf Municipal de Montréal
Entrance at Viau, north of Sherbrooke
Tel: 872-1143
Accessible by the metro.

Brossard Municipal Golf Course
4705 Rue Lapinière
Brossard, autoroute 10 Est, Exit 9
Tel: 676-0201.

HORSEBACK RIDING

For information about horseback riding contact Québec à Cheval, tel: 252-3005, or the Fédération Equèstre du Québec, tel: 252-3055.

JOGGING

Joggers can find places to run in any of Montreal's parks. One of the most popular spots is Mont Royal Park for a view of the city.

SKATING

Outdoor skating rinks are abundant in Montreal and there are at least 21 indoor rinks as well. Ile-Notre-Dame has one of the largest rinks which is one mile long. Other favorite sports include Lafontaine Park, Angrignon Park, and Mont Royal Park.

SKIING

Cross-country skiing is popular in many of the city's parks. The Botanical Garden has a winter trail that is very scenic. Downhill skiing is also available in Montreal and its environs. Beginners flock to Mont Royal, Hirondelles and Ignace-Bourget parks. Experts have unlimited opportunities less than an hour away at the Laurentians or in Estrie. More details about specific slopes or about conditions can be obtained from Sports and Leisure, tel: 872-6211.

SWIMMING

There are many indoor and outdoor pools open to the public. Listed below are a few of the possibilities:

Cégep du Vieux-Montréal (indoor)
255 Rue Ontario Est
Tel: 872-2644

Centre Claude Robillard (indoor)
1000 Rue Emile-Journault
Tel: 872-6900

Université de Montréal (indoor)
2900 Blvd Edouard-Montpetit
Tel: 343-6150

Macdonald College (indoor)
Route 20 Ouest, Ste-Anne de Bellevue exit
Tel: 398-7010

Olympic Park (indoors)
4545 Avenue du Pierre de Coubertin.
Tel: 252-4737

Ile-Sainte-Hélène (outdoors)
Tel: 872-6093

For more locations call City of Montreal Pools, tel: 872-6211.

TENNIS

Public courts are available in Somerled, Lafontaine, Jeanne-Mance and Kent parks. Montreal Sports and Recreation (tel: 872-6211) can provide more locations.

Check the Festivals and Events section of this guide's Travel Tips as well as the local newspaper to determine what events might be occurring.

AUTO RACING

The Grand Prix Molson du Canada is part of the world circuit of Formula One racing. The event is held in June at Gilles Villeneuve Track, Ile-Notre-Dame, tel: 392-0000.

BASEBALL

The Montreal Expos play at the Olympic Stadium at 4545 Avenue du Pierre de Coubertin. For information, tel: 252-3434; for tickets, tel: 253-0700. From other parts of Quebec or from Ottawa, tel: 1-800-361-0658 to reserve tickets. Admission for adults ranges from $1–$12 and is half-price for children under 15 and for seniors. Children under three are free.

CYCLING

The Grand Prix Cycliste des Amériques (World Cup) is held in August. Professional cyclists cover 124 miles (200 km) of streets in Montreal and in Mont Royal Park. Tel: 879-1027 for specific information.

FOOTBALL

The Alouettes play in the Olympic Park stadium from July to November. Tel: 252-1052 for more information.

HARNESS RACING

The Blue Bonnets Racetrack at 7440 Blvd Decarie hosts many major events in the trotting circuit. The Prix d'Été, the Prix de l'Avenir and the Blue Bonnets Amble are a few of the more important meets. The track is open Monday, Wednesday, Friday and Saturday at 7.30 p.m., Sunday from 1.30 p.m. Closed: Tuesday and Thursday. Admission for the clubhouse is $4 and is $3 for the stands. Tel: 739-2741 for more details.

HOCKEY

The Montreal Canadiens are 23-time winners of the Stanley Cup. Games are held at the Forum, 2313 Rue Ste-Catherine Ouest, tel: 932-2582.

MARATHON

The Montreal International Marathon is usually held in September. Runners depart from Jacques Cartier bridge and cover 26 miles (42 km) of Montreal's streets to finish at Lafontaine Park. Telephone 879-1027 for information.

SOCCER

A new professional soccer team was formed in 1988. The Supra de Montréal play at Claude Robillard Centre, 1000 Rue Emile-Journault. Open: May 28–September 18, Wednesdays and Sundays. Reserved seat admission $9, bleachers $5 and a season ticket costs $105. Tel: 739-6266.

TENNIS

The Players Ltd International Challenge held at Jarry Park draws the world's best players. Usually held in August. Tel: 272-1515 for tickets and information.

SPECIAL INFORMATION

CHILDREN

Montreal offers many entertaining possibilities for children from zoos to theater productions. Most of the major sightseeing spots have special programs for children. Check the listings elsewhere in Travel Tips or the local newspapers for more ideas. Some of the most popular child-pleasers are listed below.

African Safari Park: Tel: 454-3668. Drive-in wild animal park. Open during the summer and early fall. Located 43 miles (70 km) from the city in Hemmingford.

Angrignon Park and Zoo: Tel: 872-2815. Featuring a seal show.

Aqua Parc de la Ronde: Tel: 872-5638 or 872-8852. Biggest water slides in the region.

Cirque du Soleil: Tel: 522-1245. Inventive circus (no animals) that appeals to all ages.

Dow Planetarium: Tel: 872-4530. Many special season events.

Expotec: Tel: 397-6832. Offers workshops, demonstrations and shows of all kinds.

Granby Zoo: Tel: 372-9113. More than 1000 animals. In Granby.

Grands Ballets Canadiens: Tel: 849-8681. Performs *The Nutcracker Suite* every year around Christmas.

Images du Futur: Tel: 849-1612. New technologies applied to art and communications.

Kahnawake Indian Reservation: In Kahnawake, 11 miles (18 km) from Montreal, tel: 632-6030. Native Canadian dances in summer and ethnographic museum open all year round.

La Ronde: Tel: 878-6222. A 136-acre (55-hectare) amusement park on Ile-Sainte-Hélène with international shows and circus. Open: seasonally.

Maison Théâter: Tel: 288-7211. Theater devoted exclusively to children and youths. Closed in summer.

Montreal Aquarium: Tel: 872-4656. Offers special organized visits for children.

Montreal Museum of Fine Arts: Tel: 285-1600. Has several programs designed for children and includes family activities on the weekends.

Musée d'Art Contemporain de Montréal: Tel: 873-2878. Children and family activities of all kind involving current displays.

Saint Leonard Cave Exploration: Tel: 328-8580. Investigate 500-million-year-old rock formations.

Winter Fairyland – Angrignon Park: Tel: 872-6211. Landscaped and lit up for kids.

DISABLED

A brochure published by the Montreal Convention and Visitors Bureau (tel: 871-1595) gives complete information about facilities accessible to the disabled. Other associations which can provide information include:

Association régional pour le loisir des personnes handicapées de l'Ile de Montréal: Special information on recreational activities.
1800 Blvd René-Lévesque Ouest
Tel: 933-2739

Canadian National Institute for the Blind: Escorts supplied if desired.
1010 Rue Ste-Catherine Est
Tel: 284-2040

Raymond Dewar Institute: Library, viewing room and reference center for the deaf and mute.
3600 Rue Berri
Tel: 284-2581

Bell Canada: Offers a relay system for the deaf and mute. Special telephone may be obtained from the Raymond Dewar Institute. Tel: 1-800-363-6511 (with audio aid); 1-800-363-6600 (without aid).

Keroul: Provides assistance to disabled persons.
4545 Avenue du Pierre de Coubertin
Tel: 252-3104

SENIOR CITIZENS & STUDENTS

Discounts are available for seniors and students at most museums and interesting sites. For detailed information about special events or programs call the Tourist Office at 873-2015.

Further Reading

W.H. Atherton, *Montreal 1535–1914*
Miriam Chapin, *Quebec Now*
Marcel Chaput, *Why I Am a Separatist*
John Irwin Cooper, *Montreal: The Story of 300 Years*
Donald Creighton, *Canada – The Heroic Beginnings*
Aline Gubbay, *The Mountain and the River*
Hugh MacLennan, *The Two Solitudes*
Brian Moore, *Black Robe* (novel)
Francis Parkman, *The Jesuits in North America*
Mordecai Richler, *Home Sweet Home – My Canadian Album*

Useful Addresses

TOURIST INFORMATION

Infotouriste: The main office and smaller branch locations are designated by street signs with a '?'.
1001 Square Dorchester (main office)
Place Jacques Cartier, 174 Rue Notre-Dame Est (branch office) Montreal International Airport. Tel: 871-1595.

Convention and Tourist Bureau of Greater Montreal
1010 Rue Ste-Catherine Ouest, Suite 410.
Tel: 871-1595.

EMBASSIES & CONSULATES

Argentina
1010 Rue Ste-Catherine Ouest
Tel: 866-3819

Austria
1010 Rue Sherbrooke Ouest
Tel: 849-3709

Bahrain
1869 Blvd René-Lévesque
Tel: 931-7444

Belgium
1001 Blvd de Maissonneuve Ouest
Tel: 849-7394

Bolivia
18 Rue Severn
Tel: 989-5132

Brazil
2000 Rue Mansfield
Tel: 499-0968

Britain
1155 Rue University
Tel: 866-5863.

Chile
1010 Rue Ste-Catherine Ouest
Tel: 861-8006

Colombia
1010 Rue Sherbrooke Ouest
Tel: 849-4852

Cuba
1415 Rue Pine Ouest
Tel: 843-8897

Denmark
2020 Rue University
Tel: 849-5391

Eygpt
3754 Côte des Neiges
Tel: 937-7781

Ecuador
1010 Rue Ste-Catherine Ouest
Tel: 874-4071

France
Place Bonaventure
Tel: 878-4381

Germany
3455 Rue Mountain
Tel: 286-1820

Greece
2015 Rue Peel
Tel: 845-2105

Guatemala
1140 Blvd de Maissonneuve
Tel: 288-7327

Guinea Bissau
2075 Rue University
Tel: 848-0769

Haiti
Place Bonaventure
Tel: 871-8993

Honduras
1500 Rue Stanley
Tel: 849-4053

Iceland
6100 Rue Deacon
Tel: 342-6451

Iraq
3019 Blvd St-Sulpice
Tel. 937-9143

Italy
3489 Rue Drummond
Tel: 849-8351

Japan
600 Rue de la Gauchetière Ouest
Tel: 866-3429

Korea
1000 Rue Sherbrooke Ouest
Tel: 845-3243

Lebanon
20 Court Ste-Catherine
Tel: 276-2638

Liberia
1080 Beaver Hall Hill
Tel: 871-9121

Mexico
1000 Rue Sherbrooke Ouest
Tel: 288-2502

Monaco
1800 McGill College
Tel: 849-0589

Morocco
1010 Rue Sherbrooke Ouest
Tel: 288-8750

Netherlands
1245 Rue Sherbrooke Ouest
Tel: 849-4247

Norway
1 Place Ville-Marie
Tel: 849-4247

Pakistan
3421 Rue Peel
Tel: 845-2297

Peru
550 Rue Sherbrooke Ouest
Tel: 844-5123

Philippines
1839 Rue Ste-Catherine Ouest
Tel: 939-2809

Poland
1500 Rue Pine Ouest
Tel: 937-9481

Portugal
1010 Rue Ste-Catherine Ouest
Tel: 876-1604

Romania
1081 Rue St-Urbain
Tel: 876-1792

Rwanda
1600 de Lormier
Tel: 526-1392

South Africa
1 Place Ville-Marie
Tel: 878-9217

Spain
1 Square Westmount
Tel: 935-5235

Sweden
1155 Blvd René-Lévesque Ouest
Tel: 866-4019

Switzerland
1572 Docteur-Penfield
Tel: 932-7181

Thailand
3766 Côte des Neiges
Tel: 933-4607

Tunisia
511 Place d'Armes
Tel: 288-8633

USSR
3655 du Musée
Tel: 843-5901

USA
Place Desjardins
Tel: 281-1886

Uruguay
1889 Rue Worman
Tel: 931-2138

Venezuela
2055 Rue Peel
Tel: 842-3417

ART/PHOTO CREDITS

Photography by

Page 30/31, 34, 36, 37, 38, 39, 40, 43, 49, 50, 51, 52, 58/59, 60, 61, 64, 65, 66, 68/69, 72, 73, 104/105, 106, 107, 108, 109, 111	Archives Canada
23, 83, 98, 133, 144, 145	Nancy Hoyt Belcher
25, 70, 77, 90, 112, 113, 163, 206/207	Dirk Buwalde
20/21, 180/181	Lee Foster
213, 220, 221, 222, 223	Gouvernement de Québec
48, 53, 54, 55, 56, 57, 62/63	Illustrated London News Photo Library
179	Jean-François Leblanc
94, 134, 209, 212, 214, 217	Nancy Lyon
7, 14/15, 74, 114/115, 148/149, 177	Donald G. Murray
132	Anita Peltonen
33, 41, 44, 143, 146, 182, 185, 190, 193	Ann Purcell
Cover, 1, 12/13, 16/17, 18/19, 20/21, 22, 24, 26, 27, 28, 45, 46/47, 71, 75, 76, 78/79, 81, 82, 84/85, 86, 88, 89, 92/93, 95, 97, 99, 100, 120, 124, 125, 127, 129, 130, 135, 136, 137, 138L&R, 139, 140, 141, 142, 147, 150, 151, 153, 154, 155, 156, 157, 158, 159, 160, 162, 164L&R, 165, 166L&R, 167, 168, 169, 170/171, 172, 174, 175, 176, 178, 183, 184, 187, 188, 189, 191, 194/195, 198, 199, 200, 203, 204, 210, 218	Carl Purcell
29, 34, 80, 101, 128, 131, 161, 173, 186, 196/197, 201, 202, 205, 208, 211, 215, 219	Réflexion
96, 110, 216, 224	David Simson
102, 103	Topham Picture Source
116/117, 118/119, 192	Ville de Montréal

Maps	Berndtson & Berndtson
Illustrations	Klaus Geisler
Visual Consultant	V. Barl

INDEX

A

Abbaye St-Benoît-du-Lac 216
Abenaki tribe 225
Académie Querbes 189
Agouhanna 37
Algonquin tribe 36
American Revolution 51
Amerindians 129, 217
Amherst, Lord Jeffrey 50
apartment living 82
Aquarium de Montréal 205
architecture 71
　British legacy 25
　château-style 154
Avenue du Musée 155
Avenue McGill College 161

B

bagels 23
Bank of Commerce 140, 158
Bank of Montreal 139, 160
　founding of 161
Banque Royale Tower 160
Baxter Block 168
Beaver Club 54
beaver 37
Beebe Plain 217
beer garden 174
Bibliothèque Nationale du Québec 175
Bill 101 75, 98
Bill 178 99
Biodôme 202
Birk, Henry 71
birth rate 24, 25
Boer War monument 157–158
boîtes à chanson 135, 212
Botanical Gardens 202–204
Boulevard St-Laurent 167–168
　ethnic areas 72
Bourassa, Robert 33
Bourgeau, Victor 138, 158
Bourgeois, Marguerite 32, 133
　canonization 33, 41, 45
　founder of church 131
　origins of 44
British North America Act 65
British
　defeat of Montcalm 50
　ousting Americans 54
Brome County Historical Museum 214
Brother André 194–195

Brother Marie-Victorin 202
building boom (1950s) 151
Burns, Robert (statue) 157

C

calèches 136
Callières, Hector de 42
Calvet, Pierre de 129
Canadian Pacific Railway 33
Canadian Railway Museum (St-Constant) 218
Canadiens (hockey team)
　cultural pride 112
　fans 26
　founding of 109
　legendary players 111
　reputation 110
　rivalry with Maple Leafs 112
Cartier (shop) 154
Cartier, Jacques
　arrival of 36
　origins of 36
Caserne Centrale des Pompiers 144
Cassons, François Dollier de 42, 45
　views on fur trade 49
Catholicism
　first Mass 38
　influence of 44
　waning power 45, 76
Centaur Theater 145
Chambly, Jacques 219
Champlain, Samuel de 32, 38, 142
Charter of Rights and Freedoms 98
Château Apartments 154
Château Champlain Hotel 158
Château Ramezay 42, 128–129
Chateauguay, battle of 60
Chinatown 164–167
Chinese 28
　immigration 164
Chinese Catholic Church 166
cholera epidemics 62
Chrétien, Jean 101
Christ Church Cathedral 161–162
Christianity
　first baptism 40
　first religious order 41
　introduction 38
Church of St Andrew and St Paul 154–155
church, influence of 76
Cinéma Parallèle 168
Cinémathèque Québécois 173
Cirque du Soleil 149
Cohen, Leonard 81
Collège Ste-Marie 165
Colonial House 71
Company of One Hundred Associates 39
Concordia Salus 61
confederation 96
costume parades 205
Côte St-Antoine 183
Côte-Ste-Catherine-Locks 219
Crystal Palace 33
cultural life 29

D

Dali, Salvador 154, 155
David M. Stewart Museum of Discoveries 205
Dawson College 188
de Gaulle, Charles 128
de Ramezay, Claude 128
department stores
   Eatons 161
   Ogilvy's 155, 160
   Simpsons 160
Dickens, Charles 130
Dimakopoulos, Dimitri 173
Dollard, Adam 44
Dominion Square 155, 157
Dominion Square Building 159
Drapeau, Jean 33, 75, 151, 199
driving habits 29
Ducharme, Réjean 29, 81
Duplessis, Maurice 73, 76
Durham, Lord 64
d'Youville, Maria 144

E

Eatons store 161
Ecole Nationale de Cirque 147
Ecurie d'Youville 145
Edward VII statue 162
Eglise du Gésu 164
Eglise St-Germain 190
Eglise St-Viateur 189
Equality Party 100
Erskine and American United Church 154
Estrie 209, 214
Expo '67 33, 133

F

Fenians 60
Ferguson, Maynard 179
Festival International de Nouvelle Danse 177
festivals 147, 176
   range of 28
Fête des Neiges 126
Fête Nationale 176
filles du roi 45, 52
Fort-Chambly 219
Fort Lennox 220
Fortin, Marc-Aurèle 145
Fowke, Edith 57
francophone influence 26
Franklin, Benjamin 53, 128
French settlers 35
Front de Libération de Québec 33, 74
Fuller, Buckminster 133, 204
fur trade 37, 49

G

Gagnon, André-Philippe 147
Gazette du Commerce et Littéraire, La 53
Gendreau, Maurice 218
gentry 157

Gilles Villeneuve Race Track 205
Golden Square Mile 153
Granche, Pierre 164
Great Fire 32, 64
Greeks 28
Greene Avenue, Westmount 187
Griffintown 71
Gubbay, Arline 35

H

habitants 42, 49, 52, 56–57
Habitat 133
Harbor Commission Building 133
Haskell Free Library 216
hockey *see* ice hockey
Holocaust Memorial Center 91
Hôpital des Soeurs Grises 144
Hosmer, Charles 156
Hôtel de Ville 128
House of Wing 166
Hudson 210
Huron tribe 36

I

ice hockey 107–113
   invention of 108
   quality of play 110
   rules codified 109
Ile Notre-Dame 204
Ile-Ste-Hélène 38
immigrants 71, 168
Insectarium 204
International Film Festival 147
International Fireworks Festival 147, 205
International Jazz Festival 147, 176–177, 179
International Mime Festival 177
Inuit carvings 154
Iroquois tribe 36, 40, 219
   peace treaty with 42
   raid on Lachine 42
Italians 27

J

Jacques Cartier Bridge 33
Jardin Botanique 202–204
jazz 147, 176, 179
Jesuits 44
Jews 27
   first synagogue 87
   Hassidim 89
   influence of 27
   Jewish areas 87
   Sephardic Jews 90
Just For Laughs 132, 147
Juste pour rire 132, 147

K – L

Keeley, Patrick 165
Krieghoff, Cornelius 49–50

La Presse 142
La Ronde 205
Lac Brome 214
Lac des Sables 212
Lac Memphrémagog 215
Lac-des-Deux-Montagnes 210
Lachine (origins of name) 42
Lachine Canal 61
lacrosse 184
language 23, 26, 132
    and identity 99, 101
    Bill 101 effects 98
    disputes 75
    linguistics 132
    lurid signs 176
Laporte, Pierre, murder of 74
Laurendeau, André 77
Laval, Bishop 44
Le Devoir 142
Lévesque, René 25
    beliefs 101
    in government 97
    Parti Québécois 74

M

Macdonald John A. 65
Magog 215
Main, The 167, 168
Maison des Coopérants 162
Maison du Calvet 129
Maison Hurtubise 185
Maison Papineau 129
Maisonneuve, Sieur de
    fight with Iroquois 41
    Mount Royal cross 186
    origins of 39
    statue 136
Man and His World exhibit 204
Mance, Jeanne 41
Maple Leaf flag 77
maple syrup 49
Marché Bonsecours 130,131
Mary Queen of the World Cathedral 158
Mauricie National Park 223
McDonald's restaurant 135
McGee, Thomas d'Arcy 60
McGill University
    first classes 32
    founding of 54
    view of 161
McGill, James 54
McLennan, Hugh 26
Meech Lake Accord 33, 75, 98
Mesplet, Fleury de 53
Métro 153
Moishe's Steakhouse 168
Molson brewery 55
Molson Grand Prix 205
Molson's Bank 140
Molson, John 55
Mont Condor 212
Mont Orford 215
Mont St-Hilaire 220
Mont Tremblant 213
Montagnais tribe 36
Montcalm, Marquis of 50

Montreal Contemporary Arts Museum 163
Montreal Gazette 142
Montreal Jazz Festival 147
Montreal Symphony Orchestra 147, 163
Montreal
    city motto 61
    first hotel 55
    first theater 55
    geology of 35
    incorporation of 61
    origins 23
Monument National 167
Moroccans 28
Mount Royal
    cross 33, 40, 186
    geology of 35
    park 186
Mulroney, Brian 98, 101
Museum of Fine Arts 154

N

National Theater School 167
Nelson's Monument 127
newspaper industry 141
nightlife 26
North-West Company 54
Notre-Dame Cathedral 42
Notre-Dame-de-Bonsecours 41, 130, 131–132
Notre-Dame-des-Neiges 186
Nouveau Palais de Justice 128
numismatic display 140

O

O'Donnell, James 138
Ogilvy's Department Store 155, 160
Oka 210
Olier, Jean-Jacques 39
Olmstead, Frank Law 186
Olympic Games 33
Olympic Stadium 199–202
Ostell, John 138
Outremont 188–191
    cafés 191
    cinema 189
    City Hall 189
    origins 183
    population breakdown 26

P

Palais de Justice 127
Papineau, Louis Joseph 61, 129, 175
Parc Joyce 190
Parc Mont-Royal 186
Parc Paul-Sauvé 210
Parc Pratt 190
Parchemin, Le 162
Paris, comparisons with 23
parlor games 67
Parti Québécois
    defeat of 75
    gains power 74
Patriotes, Les 61–64

Pei, I.M. 159
Peterson, Oscar 179
Philips Square 161
Pilote (dog) 40
Place d'Armes 127, 134, 141
Place des Arts 163
Place Desjardins 164
Place Jacques Cartier 125–126
Place Montreal Trust 160–161
Place Royale 142, 144
Place Victoria 141
Place Ville-Marie 159, 161
Place Vouquelin 127
Pointe-à-Callière 142, 144
Pointe-du-Buisson Archaeological Park 217
political debate 95–101
population growth 71
Price, Bruce 158

Q

Quebec Act (1774) 51
Quebec
  independence, call for 97
  political structure 24
Quiet Revolution 25, 45, 74, 76–77, 97

R

racial groups 23
railways, coming of 65
Ramezay family 49
Rasco's Hotel 130
reading habits 29
Récollet Order 38
Relations 39
Richelieu Rapids 219
Richelieu, Cardinal 39
Richler, Mordecai 81
  and Ritz-Carlton 156
  on ice hockey 108
Rigaud 210
Ritz-Carlton Hotel 153, 156
Ritz, Charles 156
Rochon, Gilbert 147
Rock Island 216
Roman Catholicism 42
Ronde, La 205
Rouge River 210
Royal Bank 140
Rue Bonsecours 130
Rue de la Commune 133
Rue de la Gauchetière 158–167
Rue McGill 145
Rue Notre-Dame 126
Rue Prince-Arthur 177–178
Rue St-Denis 173
Rue St-Jacques 140
Rue St-Laurent 28
Rue St-Paul 130, 134
Rue St-Pierre 134
Rue St-Vincent 134
Rue Ste-Catherine 160
Rue Van Horne, Outremont 188

S

St George's Anglican Church 159
St James United Church 163
St Joseph's Oratory 194–195
St Lawrence River 151
St Lawrence Seaway
  opening of 33
  route 219
St Patrick's Basilica 165
St Patrick's Day 27
St-Faustin 212–213
St-Jean-sur-Richelieu 219–220
St-Timothée 218
Ste-Adèle 212
Ste-Agathe-des-Monts 212
Salle Wilfrid-Pelletier 163, 173
Santrapol 168
Schubert Baths 168
Schwartz's Delicatessen 168
Scottish merchants 25, 51, 54, 55, 183
seigneurs 42, 56
separatism 75
Seven Years' War 49
She Stoops to Conquer 55
Shopping 249–251
Simpsons department store 160
Sisters of Charity 144
skiing 213
slavery 51
slums 71
Sorel 221
Southam Building 165
Stanstead Plain 216
Stowe, Harriet Beecher 42
style 28
Sulpicians Order 42, 139, 183, 184
Summer Olympics (1976) 75
Sun Life Building 158
Sutton 214
Sutton Heritage Museum 215
Swinging in Paradise 179

T

Taillibert, Roger 199
theater 147
Théâtre du Rideau Vert 173
Théâtre La Butte 212
Théâtre St-Denis 173
Ticonderoga, battle of 50
Toronto Maple Leafs 109,112
tour buses 137
Trafalgar Girls' School 155
Tremblay, Maurice 67, 190
Trudeau, Margaret 102–103
Trudeau, Pierre 102–103
  and October Crisis 74
  beliefs 101
  on French Canadians 97,101
  vision of Canada 98
  where he lives 81
Twain, Mark 42
typhus epidemic 64

U

Underground City 151–153
Union Nationale 76
Unity Building 165
Université de Québec à Montréal 173, 176
Université Laval 175

V

Vélodrome 202
Vieux Beloeil 221
Vieux-Port 126, 131, 135
Vieux Seminaire 139–140
Viger, Denis-Benjamin 175
Viger, Jacques 61
Village d'Antan 222
Village de Séraphin 212
Village du Bûcheron 223
Ville-Marie, founding of 32
Voltaire 50

W – Y

Wells, John 139
Westmount 55, 183–188
    City Hall 185
    origins 183
    population breakdown 26
Westmount Lookout 187
Westmount Park 185
Wills, Frank 161
Windsor Hotel 158
Windsor Station 71, 158–159
Wolfe, (General) James 32, 50
women, role of 52
world wars, impact of 72

Young, John 144